ATLANTIC CHILDREN

Part 1

Juliet Dearlove

Dearlove Publishing Limited
Easton Green
Kettleburgh
Woodbridge
IP13 7LN

First published by AuthorHouse 6/22/2010

ISBN: 978-0-9568538-0-6

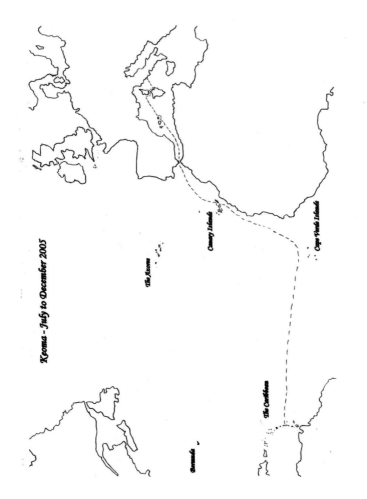

Keoma - July to December 2005

The Azores

Canary Islands

Cape Verde Islands

Bermuda

The Caribbean

CHAPTER 1

The roofs surrounding St Paul's fanned out below me in uneven lines. Wet slates stacked in steep ridges. Dawn was sweeping along the streets and alleyways, into the pores of the city, gradually overcoming grey as the sky lightened. A taxi whirred. I had moved my nose close to that cold, bombproof window, to see down as far as street level, and glimpsed my own reflection. A pallid face, a web of fine lines beneath dead eyes. The glass smelt of grime, old newspapers.

Someone moved behind me. I'd been here all night, working on the final touches of a deal that had taken nine months to construct, negotiate, finesse. Checking and scheduling documents. Searching for the missing links. Now, I was awaiting the last shareholder consents. My lips felt slightly numb and I pressed them together with my teeth.

"Juliet, has that fax come in from Jersey yet?" My General Counsel stood in the doorway of the meeting room. His New Zealand twang was tense, his pale pink shirt crumpled.

"Not yet. I'll give Ian another call." I dialled the number and shunted my brain to the right level of diplomacy. It was tedious to have to ask for this, but I couldn't let my touchiness show; we needed his co-operation. I'd phoned him at home at five in the morning, again, and, really, he must be annoyed.

The impetus now was a final push to achieve completion by 7.30, in order that the announcement would be released as planned to the London Stock Exchange, the news of the morning across the City.

I hurried along the worn grey carpet towards the fax room. A sign on the door read "Authorised Personnel Only". I didn't qualify on either count, but I couldn't wait until the right person reappeared. Looking around, the room was empty but my ears picked up a quiet whirr. The machine was churning out paper. Eagerly, I grabbed the pages, whispering, "Yes. Yes". I checked them, leafing though, as I hurried to the meeting room where I knew my new directors would be waiting. I hoped my stomach wouldn't rumble and heaved it tighter. I'd spent the previous evening in my office finalising my files of verification notes and documents for inspection. Around 9.30pm I'd come here, to the offices of the purchaser's lawyers, to a meeting room table holding the debris of a meal, a faint whiff of something stale. I hadn't been home for over 24 hours. I tapped, and, without waiting for an answer, pushed down on the cold metal handle and leant against the door.

In front of me stood a long polished table with ten sets of documents lined up in even stacks. Thick, shiny paper, the signature boxes flagged by yellow stickers embossed with a little hand holding a pen. Various people were sitting around the table; the representatives of the vendors, our team of lawyers, and opposite, the purchaser's directors and their lawyers. The atmosphere in the room was not friendly, but there was a unity of purpose. Worn faces lifted as I entered.

"I have the consents." I placed them on the table for scrutiny and took a seat.

One of the lawyers spoke. "OK. Looks like we may have a deal."

The documents slid around the table. It took a couple of minutes for the signatories to repeat the quick scribble and suddenly, with a joyless handshake, it was done, the transaction had completed. There was no transition phase. The Board I had served for the last four years had stepped down and the new directors were already appointed.

Chairs were pushed back and we filed from the room. The departing Finance Director waved me through the door ahead of him.

"So you've agreed to work for Delia, have you?" he asked quietly.

"I have."

"Good luck. I think she's utterly intolerable."

Wandering through Liverpool Street Station, I felt numb, distracted. I should have felt elated that the transaction had been a success, but something niggled. I told myself to give it a try. It might be the best career move of my life.

The morning rush had subsided to a few hurrying late starters, but I was going the other way, heading for home. I climbed onto the deserted train and sat down heavily, dropping my case and bag on the seat next to me. The train trundled along emptily, slowly, and I just sat there, vacant. No newspaper. I couldn't read anything. I found my car, with a parking ticket slapped on the windscreen. I drove the short distance home, forcing my eyes to focus on the road. Pushing open the heavy front door, I collected the post from the doormat and closed the door behind me, throwing my bags and coat on a chair.

In the bedroom I drew the curtains and undressed, pulled on my pyjamas, and fell into bed. I lay wishing for the deep comfort, the dreamless sleep that I had been craving. But my limbs and stomach felt as though they were threaded with fibre-optic cables. The pulsing electricity was worst in my stomach and chest, at the junction boxes. My mind wouldn't switch off. My eyes felt dry and prickly. At last I started to doze, but then the window cleaner's ladder clanged against the wall outside, his cloth wiping squeaky squares. I charged and buzzed with energy again. I gave up trying to sleep and pushed back the covers, left leg flopping from the side of the bed. Slightly nauseous, I telephoned Lauren to tell her there was no need for her to collect the girls from school.

Standing in the school playground, I waited amidst a hum and chatter. A few minutes later a small boy with sandy hair came out of a classroom ringing an oversize handbell, closely followed by a jumble of other children carrying bags and coats, smiling and talking. "Mummy!" Alice, 7 years old, thudded into me. "I wasn't expecting to see you!" She smiled proudly. "My Mummy is here!" she told her friends, looking around. Something inside my stomach squeezed into a tight ball. Pip wandered out, looking pale, eyes scanning for Lauren. She spotted me and her face lit up. Then she started to run, clumsily, hampered by her bag, coat dragging along the ground, arms wide, hug-shaped. I crouched down. Her cheek felt warm and sticky against mine.

We walked home, down the tree-lined school drive. Crisp, golden leaves floated side to side on the air. The children kicked through the layer on the ground. It was warm and sunny, the sky blue. A stream of cars passed as we walked through the village. We waved back.

Around six, Charlie's car pulled into the drive. Opening a bottle of wine he broke his news.

"I've booked a holiday for half term."

I was peeved. It was my realm to organise things like holidays, and I wouldn't do it without consulting him first. I told him this, adding, "Anyhow, I have a new boss who I haven't agreed this with and I don't want to get off on the wrong foot with her."

"No! You've worked yourself to the limit on this deal. I've had enough. It isn't fair on the children. Tell them to take it or leave it." I knew he was right and I didn't have the energy to argue, especially as I was just starting to feel normal, with some help from the wine.

"OK, OK, I'll clear it with her."

The departing directors had their secretaries pack up the contents of their desks and someone organised a leaving party at a nearby Michelin-starred restaurant. They were relaxed and happy with their bonuses and golden goodbye payments. None of them needed to work again. I was awarded a bonus for my work on the deal. There were two problems with this. First, I knew what everyone else had received, which made mine look pathetic. I received less than 2% of what my boss was paid. Second, it took nearly a week for anyone to mention that I would be paid a bonus, or to thank me.

At the party I was buoyed up by compliments but left feeling flat, oppressed by the mass of drudgery I knew I had to work through. Over 1000 forms to complete and file at Companies House, including notifications of changes of Registered Office and Accounting Reference Dates and the production and filing of last year's accounts, for each of the old group's 64 UK companies. The work was supposed to have reverted to normal levels when the deal completed. It seemed that for everyone else, it had.

My new boss emailed to ask whether I would like to go out for lunch. She chose a French restaurant just off Charterhouse Square. My ankles wobbled on the glossy cobbles, struggling to cope with the heels on my shoes, as we hurried out of the rain. She spoke about her houses in France and Austria. They were going on holiday to one of these the following week and her husband had been tasked with loading some antique furniture into their car to drive out there. She told me she was pleased to have me as her assistant, since she worked part time and took long holidays. Feeling slightly uneasy about the arrangement, but determined not to be influenced by what others had said, I reminded myself of my resolution to give the arrangement a try. But it was hard to trust her after what I had heard. She agreed to sign my holiday form. Then she broke the news that I was no longer to work from home, consoling me that the new offices were next to Liverpool Street Station, and a very easy commute from where I lived.

Delia gave me her views on the Head of Legal. "We hate each other. Jumped up little empire-builder. What did he think he was doing, interviewing you for *his* department, anyhow?" I had already, unwittingly, been the subject of considerable office politics and was wondering whether things would settle down. I took a sip of wine, carefully, avoiding a particular tooth. The previous day, I had finally found the time to visit the dentist. It was absurd that it had taken so long. The dentist had told me that I needed a root canal treatment, telling me to make an appointment for the treatment at reception. At the front desk a buxom girl wearing black underwear beneath her semi-transparent white dental assistant's uniform had informed me they had no available appointments for six weeks.

Delia and I talked about my previous role, and the one before that. She knew the Chairman from my first in-house role. "Oh, yes, I know him. He is a complete bastard. My husband worked for him for a year and he didn't even pay him his bonus!" To me, this Chairman was a friend, he had even come to my wedding, but there seemed little point in mentioning that now.

CHAPTER 2

The sound of the 4.00am alarm pierced the pitch blackness of our bedroom. Charlie's hand floundered around, groping for the clock on the table next to him. Blearily we dressed and zipped up bags. No-one talked. We pulled clothes onto the children, urgently, ungently, as they moaned and tried to fall back into bed. It didn't seem worth the suffering. But we struggled into the car and soon dropped back to sleep, heads lolling and snapping, except for Charlie, who drove for an hour and a half.

The freezing, dusty, wind circled as we unloaded the car in the multi-storey car park. The whole place, the whole day, was filthy, polluted, grey. I couldn't believe that we had brought the right clothes with us. We queued to check-in, under bright white lights. I tried to ignore the faint nausea that came from getting up unnaturally early, closed my eyes against the glare and briefly imagined sun and sea. The children curled up on our bags on the floor.

Four hours later, in Greece, Preveza airport was a considerable improvement on Gatwick, but we were still queuing, now hot and sweaty. The children were annoying each other with pinches, little kicks and face-pulling when they thought I wouldn't notice. The rep, cheerful, suntanned, hungover, herded us onto a coach which displayed a sign; "Sunsail". Icily air conditioned, we passed through sunbaked villages. I stared out at the piles of rocks along the side of the road and the arid landscape. Local people with piercing eyes and cracked leather faces watched us pass by. It looked like the land that time forgot and that we were in a separate, parallel universe. They must have thought the same of us with our pasty faces and holiday clothes.

At the end of the first day we waited to collect our children from the kids' club. "We sailed on a Hoby-cat and capsized! This is my friend Annie." Alice pointed to a cheeky-faced little girl. She smiled and confidently said, "Hello". Annie's parents were there to collect her, too, and we introduced ourselves.

Later that evening we were in the bar before dinner, children in bed, and we found ourselves standing next to Mike and Jane again. Charlie soon discovered that they had spent a year living on their sailing boat, an Oyster 46, including crossing the Atlantic when their children were two and five years old. He was intrigued by the idea of such a trip and the conversation flowed fast. I was caught off balance by a question from out of the blue; later I asked myself how I didn't see it coming.

"What do you think, Juliet, about us doing a similar trip?" There was a pause in the conversation, all four of us waiting to hear my answer. The question hung in the air. I'd answered the question before, but there was something different this time. Something I hadn't considered, that had been lost in the whirl of our lives. In the past I had always refused, slamming the door on the idea. I had thought it would be too boring; what would we do on long passages? I was not the kind of person who sat around. The thought of days on end in a small space was not welcome. I liked the challenge of working, the security and the routine, and I had spent years building a career. But now I realised that the door was ajar.

We were all still waiting for an answer, everyone looking at me. Jane saw the indecision and broke the ice. She was keen for me to make the right choice. "It would be easier for you because I couldn't even sail when we decided to do it! Before we started the trip I had to have sailing lessons." I saw an exchange of glances between Charlie and Mike. From that moment, whenever we met there was one dominant topic of conversation. I started to think; if Jane survived, no, more than that, if Jane had the time of her life, then, surely, I would, too. No-one tried to persuade me, and as the conversation rolled, I realised that it had been an unbelievably good experience for Mike and Jane and their children.

I asked Jane, when we were standing apart from the others, what my conditions should be, if I were to agree. She answered, "The only thing I can think of, really, is that you should insist on being named as joint skipper. That means that when you arrive somewhere *you* can check in with customs while Charlie goes off to get whatever parts he needs to fix the boat." My heart sank as I considered the work involved in maintaining a yacht, although I consoled myself with the thought that Charlie was an engineer and brilliant with any kind of mechanical breakdown. I had often been amazed how innovative he was at mending things, even without tools and parts. He actually enjoyed it, which I found peculiar, but pleasing. Jane warned me of the perils of home education. "The biggest rows we had on board were with Emily, about school, and she says now that it was the worst thing about the trip. She was always stamping her feet and shouting at us." Finally, Jane said, "Don't let anyone talk you out of taking the children with you. I had offers from both our children's godmothers to fly across with them and was so glad that I didn't take them up."

Every day we strolled though the shady gardens to breakfast. We sat together in the sunshine and enjoyed Greek yoghurt and honey, cereal, toast, bacon and eggs, and talked about the day to come. Then we would drop Alice and Pip off at the kids' club. Down at the beach there was usually a light breeze and we would take a small boat out, together or separately. Then we would play tennis to the point of desperate dehydration, have a leisurely lunch, swim in the pool, soak up the sun, and talk. When the kids' club ended for the day we would collect them and take them for a sail or a swim, or waterski; spend a few hours with them having fun. The skies were a solid azure, there were orange and lemon trees all around and we felt healed in mind and body. Many of our conversations returned to the theme of spending a year sailing, but it all felt slightly dreamlike and I knew reality would kick in once we arrived home.

One afternoon we watched the skies, as a drama began to unfold. Dark thuggish clouds cruised in and gathered over the sea. A loud thunder clap heralded the start of a magnificent storm. We moved beneath the shelter of a marquee as the first big drops fell. The children were dressed in their homemade costumes, as witches, vampires and wolves, for Halloween, the weather the perfect backdrop for their performance. Afterwards they ran outside in the pelting rain. Paper witches' hats wilted and face paints smudged, but they were ecstatic wild things, dancing, whirling around, growling, faces scowling and fingers bent into claws. We headed back to our room, soaked to the skin, and got the children ready for bed.

That night at dinner Charlie asked me again about going sailing for a year. "I can't give you an answer yet but I may be coming around to the idea." We laughed at the possibility of me being bored, with the children around. The conversation turned to the practical issue of how we would afford such a trip and we talked about ways to raise the money. "We could sell the house," suggested Charlie, tentatively. It had already occurred to me that this would enable us to buy a boat, and would provide cash for our living expenses. I had been twinging at the thought that neither of us would be earning a regular salary for over a year.

"I think we ought to get home and see what happens. We might think it is a crazy idea when we are back to reality." Preoccupied in my thoughts, I took a drink of iced water. It flooded over my painful tooth and penetrated like a knife.

"When are you going to get that sorted out? You've been having trouble with it for weeks." I couldn't answer for a minute. I sat, left palm pressing on the side of my jaw, rocking slightly, eyes closed, until the pain dulled.

Still holding my face, words slightly muffled by the pressure, "I told you, the dentist can't fit me in until after Christmas."

"Bloody NHS. I think you should go private. You can't carry on like this. I know it's been waking you up in the middle of the night and it's not good to be popping so many painkillers."

CHAPTER 3

England was just as grey when we arrived home. We slotted back into school and jobs. The concept of a year sailing in sunnier places bobbed in the back of my mind and when it came to the foreground, as it did daily, it didn't seem crazy. For so many reasons it seemed the obvious thing to do. Work. The weather. The war in Iraq. Yob culture. One weekend I was in the supermarket car park with the children, walking back to the car pushing the loaded trolley, when Pip ran ahead across a zebra crossing. A car, driven too fast, only just stopped in time. I looked at the driver as Alice and I passed in front, shocked. He was a middle aged man with a boy of around eight sitting in the passenger seat. The driver wound down the window.

"You should keep your kids under control, you fucking old cow!" I knew it wouldn't help to get into a conversation. Alice and Pip had never witnessed aggression like this. I hurried the children away, Pip quizzing me sweetly, "What did he say, Mummy?"

"You don't want to know," said Alice, her face grim.

Back at home, I unpacked plastic bags in the kitchen. "The kind of boat I want," started Charlie, "is a big old pirate ship, you know, with all the toys. Windsurfers, dinghies, barbecues, davits, a Jolly Roger flag and a bowsprit with a net underneath to lie in."

"Well, I'm not so sure. We've only ever sailed on reasonably modern boats and I am keen on the idea of comfort and having things that work. On older boats there will always be something going wrong and no spare parts available. Anyhow, you'll want speed."

"Hmm, I suppose you're right. I'm going to have a look on the internet to see what's for sale."

We continued to keep our idea a secret from the children, in case things didn't work out and we ultimately decided we were not going. Our conversations felt snatched and illicit. It was strange having this deep secret that could impact on everything we did, which no-one else knew about. It lurked in our minds. I worried that I would let slip at the wrong moment. Not only would the secret be out, but I would be committed.

A colleague at work recommended a dentist to me, whose surgery was just around the corner from the office. He was Greek, handsome, and very expensive. For some reason I found all this reassuring. He looked in my mouth and advised me to have an extraction because of the state of the tooth and its position, right at the back. I was relieved to hear this, since this was what I'd wanted in the first place. It was a slow business taking the tooth out. The roots were twisted around the jawbone and I could feel liquid spraying as he drilled away at the bone. I imagined it was blood. But surely blood wouldn't feel so cold. My jaw ached from holding it open for so long. I wondered whether my mouth would ever close again or if it would be stuck open, and I would be permanently sucking in the wind like a whale eating plankton. My tongue felt as if it were the size of a king-sized bed, in a room too small and right in the way. I'd tried to move it to the side, but now it ached. At last the ordeal was over and he stitched the gum up, gently wiping the blood from my face and then he prescribed me antibiotics. I was not to drink alcohol and must take it easy. He told me that the top part of the tooth crumbled as he tried to get it out, and then it was all rotten beneath; a real mess. It was the right decision not to try to rescue it.

It was Friday afternoon and I took the train home and lay down on the sofa. It felt weird, as I rarely had the time to lie on my own sofa. The children came in from school, with Lauren. "What's the matter Mummy?" asked Alice, concerned.

CHAPTER 4

A few weeks later I was still very busy at work. Delia was wearing earrings made of diamonds the size of peas. She saw me looking at them. "These are my Christmas present. I've just been to Hatton Garden to collect them." The combination of the earrings and the hefty diamond rings that she always wore made her look very sparkly. I was working on a reorganisation of our group corporate structure; a complex set of sales and purchases of different companies within the group, involving UK, US and Dutch companies. I had been asked by our tax department to get the series of transactions completed by year end, which I had agreed to do because I liked a challenge, and they were charming men, but I regretted having agreed to do it. I spent hours on conference calls with our US lawyers and our tax advisers and flew to Amsterdam for a completion meeting a couple of days before Christmas, meaning I missed the office party, and adding further stress to an already overfull week. My life seemed as fraught as ever. At least the children were now on holiday so there was no more sorting out of homework, Christmas cards, presents for the teachers, uniform, costumes for the school play and games kit, as my extra-curricular evening activities. The Christmas hat that they'd needed for their turkey lunch had nearly been the straw that broke the nativity camel's back.

Days later we were eating Christmas lunch. There was no more trouble with the tooth and I was relishing being able to take big gulps of liquid without pain. Seated around our table, full of Christmas booze and wearing party hats, were both sets of grandparents and my brother Sam. The night before, while I was stuffing the turkey, and Charlie was lining up bottles of red wine, we had decided that we ought to say something to them about the possibility that we may be going away for a year. We had agreed that it was better to tell them at the "might be" stage than shocking them with a full-blown decision to go, and in truth we were still at the "might be" stage. I was conscious that the "might be" was more on my side and that Charlie was secretly determined to go. He knew he just needed to approach me in a certain way and rushing the decision or trying to push me could backfire. There were a lot of other factors that needed to fall into place. For example, we needed to resign our jobs and sell the house. We still had to investigate whether we would be locked up for our children's truancy as soon as we set foot on British soil again. One other small thing; we needed a boat.

The cooking of the lunch had gone to plan, without bullet sprouts or soggy potatoes, although it all tasted of nothing to me. All food tasted of nothing when I'd cooked it. Perhaps I was a terrible cook and no-one had been blunt enough to break this news to me, or else I was sick of the food by the time I got to eat it, having already prepared it, watched it, smelt it, tasted it. Charlie was demonstrating his idea of the correct preparation of a mince pie. The top had to be removed and as much cream, brandy butter, crème fraiche, custard and anything else that was available, crammed in, before replacing the top and opening the mouth wide to eat.

The children finished their meal and were itching to leave the table and play with their presents. The adults remained seated and were all in a relaxed frame of mind, giving us the perfect opportunity to broach the subject, letting them in on our big secret. They asked lots of questions but seemed neither positive nor negative about the idea. Perhaps they were thinking we were just dreamers and wouldn't actually get ourselves organised to go, or that it was our life so we should go if we wanted to. They all appeared to be in good health, so from that respect it seemed like a good time to go. The next year would be a landmark year for us; Charlie's 40th birthday, 10th wedding anniversary... mid-life crisis...

CHAPTER 5

Charlie had been surfing the internet for all sorts of information that may prove useful, including investigating the ARC; the "Atlantic Rally for Cruisers". We decided to take a day off work and look around the London Boat Show, with the ulterior motive of attending the presentation given by the ARC organisers. Every year the ARC left Las Palmas in the Canary Islands in late November, bound for St Lucia in the Caribbean. Entries were limited to around 200 boats in the Cruising Division, and around 35 in the Racing Division.

The distinction between the two divisions was that the cruisers were permitted to use their engines for propulsion whereas the racers were not. In reality, the cruisers limited their engine use because they wouldn't have nearly enough fuel to motor even a quarter of the 2,800 miles to St Lucia. They liked to preserve their fuel, in case it was needed (for example, in the event of a dismasting). Plus, they would be required to declare all distances travelled under motor, which would be factored into their adjusted finish time (which also took into account the handicap allotted to each yacht before leaving Las Palmas), in order to determine the finishing placings. In short, the racing division raced, but so did the cruisers.

The ARC was organised and sponsored by Yachting World magazine, and the presentation began with Andrew Bray, the Editor. He chaired a panel of six further individuals, each of whom contributed, and the session concluded with questions and answers. We found the morning to be a real insight into what it was like to do an Atlantic Crossing, and began to appreciate the highs and lows of life at sea.

Some boats were fitted with water makers (a miniature desalination plant), which was said to take much of the stress out of preserving water on a 22 day crossing, although a generator was needed to produce enough battery power for the reverse osmosis process, and water makers were expensive to buy and install. For those that had water makers, they made a big difference, to crew morale as well as hygiene, when the weather started to get sticky in the less northern latitudes.

We were told that the boats received a daily email from the ARC organisers, of all the participants' positions, and those in the cruising class that did well usually decided they were definitely racing, whereas those that finished further down the pecking order would often declare they were "just cruising".

Jimmy Cornell was a member of the panel and my ear took a few moments to tune into his thick Romanian accent. He was recognised as the founder of the ARC, 20 years before, and had written many books on cruising the world. Sitting next to him was a woman who had done the ARC the previous year, with her husband on their small cruising boat. Jimmy was asked a question about a certain kind of spinnaker, which had a pressure release valve in the sail. He said he was delighted with it (particularly as the makers sent him one for free) and said that the great benefit was that when he was cruising with his wife he didn't need to get her up on deck to help him deal with wind squalls. He looked at the woman sitting next to him and said, "She is only about your height," as if that said it all. The comment was taken in such good heart that the room was filled with laughter. Andrew Bray told us of a two handed

Atlantic crossing that he did with a good friend. There had been a cloth in the heads that Andrew used as his face flannel. After they had arrived in St Lucia he discovered that his friend had been using it to clean the toilet.

Charlie and I felt encouraged that we could do it. They seemed ordinary people, although weather-worn and high on beard-count. As we left the room, Charlie's mobile phone rang. I could hear a loud voice on the other end of the line.

"Hello mate, it's Nick. Manda and I are at the boat show and we heard you two might be around here somewhere."

"That's wonderful news! Shall we meet at the Guinness stand?" Five minutes later we were dumping bags and coats in the corner. Nick had already been to the bar. He passed us our drinks with a suspicious sideways look.

"What have you two been up to, then?"

We blurted the whole thing out. The façade we had kept up for months crumbled and it was a huge relief to be telling someone. Amanda listened intently. She looked me in the eye, deadly serious. "Can we come with you?"

That morning, we had been warned about trips that had been disasters because of "people problems". One of the overwhelming messages from the ARC seminar was to choose crew members with great care. 22 days was a long time to spend in a small space with anyone. The other consideration was that we were keen to make it a "family" experience, so we answered them guardedly. But it wasn't ruled out.

There were still so many factors that needed to fall into place. We hadn't yet told our children. I took a day off work and three sets of estate agents came to look at our house. They gave us wildly varying valuations, and we quickly dismissed the highest one as a joke. We were warned that we were looking for a particular type of buyer and the house wouldn't appeal to everyone. In truth, the house needed some work. When we had bought it we'd intended to improve and update the kitchen, but never got around to doing it, and this room was a big detraction. We had never found the energy for such a major project. I'd always loved the house, but now I felt relieved that we hadn't done the work. If we had put our hearts and souls into an improvement programme we would have been more tightly bound to the property.

Charlie didn't like the lack of view (we were right in the middle of the village) and would have liked to look out over fields, or ideally, a river. He felt very hemmed in. He felt Harlow encroaching on our village. They were building new houses for the town only one field away. Harlow had a legendary road system, with a roundabout every 100 metres and a traffic jam in between, which made it extremely frustrating to drive anywhere (unless you only drove before dawn and after dark, like me). How would the town cope with even more people?

I believed his feeling of enclosure also came from his job as manager of the family engineering company. The major shareholder was his great aunt, who had been married to the founder, Great Uncle Herbert. She controlled the board of directors, who were all family members. But she didn't have any real understanding of the business. She couldn't read a balance sheet. She was risk averse. I suspected it was also the kind of family who were capable of bearing a serious grudge if things didn't work out in their favour, and I worried how they might take it if Charlie resigned.

Back at work, I was given a pay rise, which was totally unexpected. Although I felt the quality of my work was good, and I was now one of the "survivors", therefore in a unique position to know the background information to any scenario, my new employers were notoriously stingy. I wondered what was going on behind the scenes. I was slightly surprised that the possibility of giving up my job to do the trip had not been the catalyst for a slow erosion of my level of diligence. In fact, it seemed the opposite was true.

Charlie downloaded the form to reserve a place on the ARC for November that year. We didn't want to enter too late and the Boat Show seminar had indicated that the entry list was filling up. It was now February and November seemed like an unachievable date. Sending in our form didn't mean we were committed to taking part, and we hadn't paid any fee yet. We didn't even have a boat, meaning large sections of the form had to be marked "TBA". No doubt the organisers saw this all the time. I wondered how many dreamers filled out the form and never actually took up their place? But the boat part of the equation was being worked on by Charlie, who was spending hours scouring the internet for a suitable craft.

CHAPTER 6

I was sitting in my office looking out at the glass ants' nest that was Deutsche Bank, thinking about my task list. On reflection, my workload had started to come under control, but the other side of the coin was that I had lost many of the interesting aspects of the job, as the senior work now went to Delia (when she was around) and I did the remainder. Our relationship was frequently put under pressure by her approach to work. That morning Delia had called me from home to say they needed to hold a meeting of the Pension Fund Trustees to resolve to close one of the Pension Schemes to new members. She said, "Just ring up two of them and get them to have a telephone meeting to agree it." I looked at the Scheme Rules, just to check, as I would always do. I knew that if we did it wrong, there would, at some stage, be all hell to pay, especially as the scheme was already under investigation by the regulator. There was no provision in the rules for telephone meetings, nor for two trustees to meet without the rest having been given notice of the meeting and electing not to attend. It was tedious but I couldn't risk it, and so I consulted our pensions lawyer, who confirmed my interpretation. I telephoned Delia to explain the problem. She was not pleased.

I set up the meeting. I collated all the documents required and spoke to our in-house pensions consultant. I telephoned all seven Trustees, beginning each call with a tedious explanation of who I was and my role. They, at least, were grateful for my assistance.

The telephone rang. Charlie asked, "Can you go to Rome for a long weekend on Thursday week and come back on the Sunday? Obviously this means you'll have to take two days off."

"I will ask, but I have been told that Delia and I aren't allowed to take holidays at the same time and she has booked half term off," I replied.

"Please try to organise it, because I want us to look at a boat there."

"OK, I'll do my best. Presumably we will take the girls. Alice will be very excited because they've been doing the Romans at school."

My holiday form was signed, and we booked Easyjet flights. It was time to tell our children about the planned trip. We impressed on them that they *must* keep it a secret, because we needed to tell their headmaster before all the parents found out. It would not be right if the headmaster and his teaching staff were the last to know. Alice asked us who knew about the trip. I told her about the Christmas day conversation.

"What!" She said, her small face livid, "You told the grandparents *at Christmas* and you've only *just* told us?"

"Yes. But think about it – would you and Pip have been able to keep it quiet? We thought it was fairer to tell you later, when you wouldn't have to bottle it up for so long." She stomped off up the stairs and along the landing to her bedroom.

A few days later Charlie and I attended a weekend course in First Aid. The idea of having to treat a major injury was terrifying. We had to imagine that we were ten days from land and consequently unable to call an ambulance. We were taught about CPR, illnesses, seasickness, bleeding, breakages, and anaphylactic shock. I felt overwhelmed with information. How would I cope in the panic of a real emergency? The course was run by medical professionals; a GP and a nurse. They presented the course well and made it amusing and memorable but there was a lot of fooling around with bandages, which gave me a feeling of lingering foreboding. I wondered if the whole idea of crossing the Atlantic was too much for us to take on. Perhaps it should have stayed just an idea, but it hadn't. It had started to take on a momentum of its own. I felt out of control.

The idea continued to roll, like a wave, growing and expanding all the time. The following weekend we flew to Italy.

Alice was looking out of the window of the plane. "I can see the Coliseum!" Because of the sheer scale of so many of Rome's buildings, it was easy to spot them and the city looked like a Blue Peter model beneath us. The buildings were even a brown cardboard box colour. We landed and caught a taxi to the hotel, where we dropped our bags off. It was February, and chilly, but we enjoyed walking beneath bright blue skies, bundled up in layers of clothing. Perhaps it was a trick of the light, but everything seemed somehow super-three-dimensional, with an ultra-crisp line drawn around the edge. We walked for miles, absorbing the history, the presence of the city and the Italian spirit. Pip grew tired and Charlie lifted her onto his shoulders to give her a rest. Late in the evening we found the Trevi fountain. It was disappointingly mobbed with people and Pip was shivering with cold, but Alice persuaded us that she must have a Euro to throw in. "I'm going to be coming back to Rome."

The following day we caught a train from Terminus. The station was stylish, clean and efficient. We were struggling with the Italian language, but somehow managed to buy tickets and find the right train. It was a 40 minute journey to Civitaveccia, the coastal town where we had arranged to look at a boat.

After hours of internet research Charlie had identified what he thought would be the perfect boat for our trip, and one of these was for sale here. It was a Grand Soleil 46.3.

Around mid-morning we emerged from Civitaveccia station into a parking lot full of dusty, tired-looking Fiats. We still couldn't even say the name of the town properly. "Chivvy da vechia" we muttered over and over again, hoping the repetition would make it memorable and familiar. A taxi driver took us to the marina. He could speak a little English, which was lucky, because we now fully understood how pathetic our language skills were. The driver elaborately waved his way past the security barrier into the marina complex and dropped us off in the car park.

The marina was semi-circular with a line of small shops and restaurants around the edge. A bitter, sandy wind whistled along the arcade and we huddled the children to our sides as we walked along, following the curve. Somewhere along here was the office of Alessandro Aquilani. To our left was a wide concourse and beyond that, a thousand yachts were tied to pontoons. The wind screeched through their rigging and caused the rhythmic tap of rope on metal as halyards knocked against masts. We passed a coffee bar with enticing smell and steamy windows. The children wanted to stop for hot chocolate but we pushed them on. They moaned and slowed their steps but just then we saw the broker's sign ahead. "Come on, we're here now. We'll get you a hot chocolate later. Don't you want to see the boat?"

Charlie pushed the heavy glass door open. As it closed behind us the noise of the wind and frapping halyards shut off. The broker stood up slowly and came to greet us. He looked around 40, with dark curly hair, tanned skin and hazel eyes. A few flecks of grey, a few lines. He introduced himself with a warm handshake "Alessandro". The jeans and shirt were casual but his manner was serious. Charlie had already spoken to him on the telephone. He pointed us to seats and showed us the particulars. Pip sat on my lap and I helped her blow her nose. She felt a little feverish. Alice wandered around his office and picked up things she shouldn't touch. I reminded her to look just with her eyes, and tried to concentrate on the particulars, which were in Italian, but there were photos and it was possible to pick up some meaning from the text. Alessandro apologised that his English was not very good. Then he said, "Would you like to come and see Keoma?"

Charlie was having difficulty disguising his impatience to see the boat. We walked along the concourse towards the yard. There were some incredible yachts here. I had never seen so many large cruising boats, with so much gear on them. These Mediterranean boats were very different from the boats I knew. They were all over 40 foot long, very wide and high off the water. They looked so comfortable and manageable. Despite those cold, windy conditions, it was easy to picture sunny, outdoor living, and I felt a sudden pang that I *wanted* that life. Every boat had a sprayhood and a bimini, self-furling headsails, "lazy jack" systems for stowing the mainsail, and, most surprising of all, television ariels.

Keoma was in the boatyard, out of the water, surrounded by around a hundred large yachts and motorboats. She seemed to have an incredibly long keel, making her stand high above the ground. She looked unreachable, even by ladder. But we all managed to get up there, eventually. Alessandro unlocked the hatch and we climbed down the companionway, relieved to gain shelter from the wind. The cabin had an atmosphere of space and luxury. The boat was immaculate. Cherry wood panelling and gleaming taps. Charlie's eyes were on stalks, looking at everything, trying to be sensible, filling in ticks on his mental checklist. I could see he had made up his mind.

The children soon wanted to get off the boat. I helped them carefully down the ladder, slowly, one step at a time, and we walked to the coffee shop, while Charlie stayed on board the boat. We sat down on plastic chairs in the corner and waited for our hot chocolate and cappuccino. I asked them how they felt about the idea of going sailing for a year. Alice was impulsive and enthusiastic; "I can't wait to go." "Will I have my own bedroom?" asked Pip. I explained that one of the good things about this boat was the layout down below. The aft twin cabins, beneath the cockpit, meant that they could each have their own cabin, although when friends or family came to stay, they would have to move in together for a week or two. Pip nodded unenthusiastically. She was feeling ill and depressed, full of cold, and I felt guilty about taking her from the warmth of the hotel room. Eventually Charlie appeared at the door, glowing and happy. I hadn't seen him so excited for years.

We ate at a restaurant nearby, recommended by Alessandro. We were not quite sure what we had ordered but when it arrived it was a white fish baked whole with chopped tomato, onion, garlic and parsley, served with spaghetti which had been salted and doused in olive oil. We were overwhelmed by how different and good it was, and everyone tucked in with vigour. I couldn't believe that I had never eaten (let alone cooked) something so good. An Italian man, eating alone at the next table, struck up a conversation, but we couldn't speak Italian so we switched to French. He complimented us on our choice of food. He told me that the yacht brokers here were very highly regarded. He told me how to ask for the bill in Italian. "Il conto."

Back in Rome we visited some more sights. The following day we headed to the airport. We were early for the flight, so we checked our bags in and then went to the airport café for something to eat. We sat on school chairs at plastic tables but the pizzas were crisp disks of steaming bread, topped with a rich tomato sauce, stringy mozzarella, flavoursome palma ham and glossy black olives. It was a long way from the usual airport food.

CHAPTER 7

On Monday I was back in the office. I was organising the redemption of loan notes with a total value of £22m, which had been issued to 650 individuals five years before. These were the shareholders of a company that had been taken over by my previous employer. At that time the shareholders had agreed to sell their shares in exchange for the loan notes. The loan notes now had to be converted to cash, as a condition of the recent take over. I started by working out a timetable. I wrote to all the loan note holders and explained the process, so that they knew when they would receive the funds. I asked them to respond so that I would know that I was sending the cheques to the correct addresses. Many of them had moved over the preceding 5 years, and I guessed that not all had updated me with their new address, in which case the letter I was now sending would not reach them. But this was the only information I had that might help me find them. Many were employees or ex-employees of the company, so I started to make efforts to trace those for whom I suspected we no longer had a correct address, by asking their colleagues and former workmates to try to contact them to let them know that there would be a payment. In some cases it amounted to a significant sum, even running to six figures, which would certainly make a big difference to their lives.

Delia thought my efforts a waste of time, and told me to stop trying to trace them. She was open about her gameplan; if recipients were not traced the company would hold onto the funds and after ten years, any remaining unclaimed money would revert to the company.

I no longer attended the parent company Board meetings, nor had any hand in preparing the Board papers. I did handle Stock Exchange announcements when Delia was not in the office, but these were all of an unexceptional nature; routine director's share dealing notifications and the like. It felt strange to be so divorced from the workings of the Board and consequently the strategic direction of the company, and daily life was becoming less interesting as time went on. I explained this to Delia. I suggested to Delia that I should be made redundant, but she smiled and said she did not feel inclined to do this right now. It seemed unfair that so many of my former colleagues had received redundancy payments. My job had changed dramatically but in ways that were difficult to define and so although I felt my original job was technically redundant, I was not confident that an Industrial Tribunal would appreciate the subtle differences. I gave up trying to argue the point with Delia.

CHAPTER 8

Charlie and I attended a course entitled "Survival at Sea." It involved learning strategies for staying alive in the event that your yacht sank mid-ocean. We heard about people who had survived in life rafts for extended periods. One case study described a couple who spent 117 days in a liferaft and small rubber dinghy, during which time they were beset by sharks and each lost around 40lbs in weight, and were eventually rescued by a Costa Rican fishing boat. I found myself standing on the side of an indoor swimming pool, wearing my foul weather gear. There was an inflated life raft in the pool, which looked like an orange paddling pool with a plastic tent stretched over the top. I jumped into the water, feeling quite buoyant with the amount of air trapped in my coat and trousers. But any movement quickly displaced that air. It bubbled out of my sleeves and trouser hems and then the clothing felt as cumbersome and unmanageable as a huge tarpaulin. We were told to get ourselves into the liferaft. I swam heavily towards it. The entrance was triangular and the raft had a high inflated lip that had to be breached in order to get in. I flopped inside like a beached whale, my face landing in the lap of a man I had met for the first time only a few hours previously. Inside, it smelt strongly of rubber and there was a depth of several centimetres of water over the floor.

I tried to envisage the trauma of losing the boat and then having to do this. How would we get the children inside? What about food and water? What about going to the toilet? There was a small vent at the side for anyone who was being seasick. Obviously it would be necessary to be sufficiently disciplined to throw up one at a time. I was not normally seasick but the smell of rubber was so strong that the back of my throat had started to arch upwards, even in those waveless, fearless, conditions.

Later, back in the classroom, the discussion turned to emergency grab bags. This was the bag that one of us would take to the liferaft. What would you put in it then? A solar still, to make fresh water from sea water. It would taste awful but might keep us alive. Flares for attracting the attention of a passing vessel (if there were any passing vessels). The First Aid Kit. It must be kept dry, so the grab bag had to be totally waterproof. A fishing line. Fish couldn't be cooked so it would be sushi only. No, not sushi, not delicately prepared mouthfuls of art but the roughest hewn lumps of bony flesh. A sharp knife. Liferaft repair kit. I had another pang of "I can't do this". Passports. Credit card. I had a vision of a hovering helicopter, and a helmet framed face shouting down through the gale. "How would you like to pay? Mastercard or Visa?"

It was a dark February night when we left the seminar. I stood shivering next to the passenger door waiting for Charlie to unlock the car. We got in and sat in the quiet. "Why are we doing this?" I asked.

"It'll be ok," he said. "How many people do it and *don't* end up in a life raft. You know it will be the trip of a lifetime."

"But it's not falling into place like I thought it would. The house hasn't sold, we don't have a boat and there's such a pile of crap to deal with. Other people don't do this kind of thing."

"It will be fine. We can't let a few setbacks stop us going. And no-one ever said it was going to be easy."

I wasn't happy at work, either. The culture of the company had changed, with so many redundancies. The business had lost its gloss. My job was dull and I was frequently required to compromise my ways of working and personal ethics. I felt overqualified for it. Perhaps if I waited long enough they would do the right thing and offer me redundancy, but they were probably too mean to bite that bullet.

CHAPTER 9

We made an appointment to see the Headmaster. He showed us into his office which had exactly the same smell of school dinners and Pledge that I remembered from my own schooldays. We explained our plans. He was surprisingly enthusiastic, telling us that he had travelled with his children when they were the same age, and had found it extremely beneficial. They had gone to Bahrain, where he had held a teaching post at the British School. We asked him about truancy. He told us that there was no official record of our children attending his school. It was not the case that all the children in the area were logged by the local authority as being at one school or another. I asked him whether he could advise us on any particular course of home education and he suggested that the best thing would be simply to follow the National Curriculum, with teaching materials that we could buy at WHSmith. We gave him notice that we would be withdrawing the children from the school at the end of the summer term, asking him to inform relevant teaching staff, but to request that they kept this information confidential for the time being.

Walking back from the school, we felt truly elated. I felt uncertainty subsiding and confidence blossoming. I had put the horrors of survival at sea to the back of my mind; after all, that was only the experience of a minute proportion of sailors and who knew what might happen to us if we stayed at home? We talked and planned as we walked. I had to give notice at work soon, as my contract required me to give three months' notice of termination. It was important not to leave the country too late, otherwise it would be autumn and a rush to get to the Canaries for the start of the ARC in November. If the UK were to be our starting point, we would need to have plenty of time so that we could pick the right weather conditions for the passage across the Bay of Biscay. It was not something that should be tackled in October, or probably even September.

Soon afterwards, an estate agent's board was placed outside our house, prompting a whirl of questions from local friends and parents at school.

"Will Charlie steer?"

"Well, we'll both have to steer. He can't be on the helm 24 hours a day."

"Won't you stop at night?"

"No, we won't be able to. We'll have to sleep in shifts so that either Charlie or I is always on watch."

"Can't you anchor?"

"Not in the middle of the Atlantic. We won't have a long enough anchor chain - the water is 4000 metres deep!"

"Can I have your dining room table?"

One friend said, "Don't tell my husband – it's just the kind of thing he wants to do!"

I insisted that we had to have schools arranged for the children for when we returned. We had decided that we wanted to return to our roots and live in Suffolk, to live near the coast, and we visited three schools in the area. The children sat various interviews and assessments, and a week later we received letters offering places at all three. September 2006 sounded such a long time away.

CHAPTER 10

I tendered my resignation at work. Delia was stunned. I found it surprising that she hadn't seen it coming. She went out for a walk and missed a conference call. I could see that she thought me unbelievably ungrateful, and was secretly asking herself, "What am I supposed to do now?" Many of my other colleagues were very kind, and expressed admiration for the decision. I suspected that they thought it very risky to ditch my career and embark on such a voyage. There were many comments about Delia. I didn't need to complain about her because everyone felt the same.

The following weekend, Charlie and I flew to Italy for one day. The children went to stay with Granny. The 5.30 am flight from Stansted to Rome got us to Civitaveccia around 10.00 am. It was very easy without the children and with only one holdall as hand luggage. I didn't even take a handbag. Alessandro greeted us with warm handshakes, his left hand placed over the top of our joined hands, steady eye contact. Keoma was in the water and looked magnificent as we walked along the pontoon towards her. Her shiny blue hull sparkled in the sunshine. She seemed very large. Our bag of sailing clothes contained thick waterproof trousers to wear over our jeans, jackets, sea boots, extra socks, fleeces, gloves and hats. After all, it was only March. Only the very hardy would sail in March at home. But it was very bright and sunny and I reached in my pocket for my sunglasses.

We untied her mooring lines and motored out of the marina, with Alessandro's colleague, Richie, and Sergio (described by Alessandro as "Keoma's boat boy" but actually a handsome Italian in his early twenties) on board to demonstrate the yacht to us. The weather conditions were sublime. I had never felt happier on a boat. The bag of warm clothes lay below on a berth, never unzipped, and soon we peeled off a layer. I revelled in the feel of the strong spring sunshine on my face, hitting us from above and below, reflecting off the glinting water. I pulled up the mainsail, hand over hand on the halyard, to be sure I could do it alone. We knew there may be times when I had to manage on my own. It was reassuringly easy; with a special Harken system on the mast, the cars attaching the sail to the mast track slid up easily. It felt as though they were defying gravity. The slight effort involved caused me to remove another layer and then I was down to just a T-shirt and jeans. Keoma cut through the water without any fuss and she was so fast, skimming over the flat calm sea.

Sergio brought up the spinnaker. It took an age to clip it on correctly, as none of us were familiar with the set up. Perhaps it had never been used before; the fabric was certainly in pristine condition. It was asymmetric in cut, meaning that it was fuller on one side, making it more of a traditional foresail shape, although the tapes along the edges of the sail measured the same distance. One of the bottom corners attached to a glinting metal pole that protruded from the bow – a modern day, retractable version of a traditional bowsprit. I pulled hard on the halyard, for a long time. Suddenly the sail was up, and with a snap of fabric, the stitching took the strain and ropes tensioned. We felt the boat surge forward and hold the speed; a speed that we were not used to on a boat, and the motion was addictive. So smooth and fast, like a ride on Santa's sleigh. "To Sardinia?" Charlie asked, pointing. Richie and Sergio laughed; Sardinia was 120 miles away and they had other things to do that day. We dropped the spinnaker and turned back. The wind was ebbing away and we had to motor the last couple of miles, but we were entranced by our sail and itching for more. We flew back to Stansted that evening with bronzed faces.

CHAPTER 11

The next morning was my birthday and we were enjoying a rare leisurely Sunday lie-in. Charlie handed me a present. I slowly tore the paper, enjoying the suspense. It was a digital camera.

We researched essential gear for the boat. Charlie worked on a spreadsheet of chandlery items. It was an extraordinary list, including a life raft for six people. It sounded appealing to have a larger one, but we were told that it would collapse in a rough sea, when such rafts relied on the bodies within to form a frame. We listed new waterproof jackets and trousers, in breathable fabric, which were expensive, but we would be wearing them every day on some parts of the trip, and so we wanted to buy the most comfortable. We also listed lightweight jackets for those tropical rains, when it was hot but torrential. We added an inflatable dinghy with small outboard engine. The dinghy could be rolled away and put in a bag the size of a large holdall. This was important because on long passages we would not want to tow it behind the boat. They tended to be a nuisance when towed; if the rope broke then we would have lost it for good; in some conditions the dinghy would be bumping into the back of the boat or flipping over in the wind (not good for the outboard engine). It would be preferable not to have to keep an eye on it while we were sailing. The other consideration was that it would slow us down, and on a crossing of 3000 miles, a small reduction of speed would make a big difference. The model that Charlie wanted had an inflatable floor, called an "air deck", which became almost rigid when pumped full of air, so the dinghy would behave like a rib. Charlie was adamant that the dinghy had to be a Zodiac. There were cheaper brands around, but he was definite. We opted for a 5 horse power engine, which was suitable for this dinghy, but not over-powered, so that it would be safe for the children to drive the dinghy themselves.

Many small items were listed; distress flares, sea anchors (a big fabric funnel that you could deploy from the boat in very bad weather), torches, a waterproof grab bag, light sticks for emergency lighting, and life jackets for adults and children. The life jackets were the type that inflated automatically when you hit the water, and we also ordered re-inflation canisters so that they could be re-armed. On our sea survival course, everyone had brought a life jacket of this type with them. Three of these life jackets, out of our group of eight, had gas canisters that had come slightly unscrewed, so would not have inflated in an emergency. The life jackets we had chosen for our list had harnesses included, so that whenever we wanted to clip ourselves to the boat, we wouldn't need to wear a separate harness. Additionally, they had lights and clear plastic hoods which covered the face, which we were told were invaluable if you happened to be in the water for an extended period. I tried not to picture this scenario. Charlie emailed the list to three chandleries, who quoted for the business. It was over £4,000 worth of kit.

One evening we talked about the situation where one of us fell overboard at night and had to be searched for. There was a gadget which had a base station on the boat and each person would keep, in their pocket, a tag which communicated with the base. If a tag moved away from the base by more than a certain distance then the base would sound an alarm. It could be linked into the GPS so that the precise location where the alarm sounded was logged. But it couldn't take account of drift; a person in the water would drift with wind, waves and current, and in a very different manner to the drift of the boat. Also, it was expensive. On balance, we decided against it.

Charlie telephoned Alessandro, and they started to outline a deal. When we were in Italy, Alessandro had described the process for buying a boat there, which was more complex than buying a house in the UK. There were various stages of the transaction, involving a contract, payment of a deposit, two surveys, staged payments and a complex registration process. We wanted to have the boat re-registered, as a British vessel, rather than keeping her Italian flag, which meant further bureaucracy. We added a large British ensign to the chandlery list, with a pole to hold it up. I was keen to have a big flag, like the Dutch sailors, who visited the UK with flags so large they dipped in the water on a still day at anchor. Charlie told Alessandro his requirements; he wanted to buy Keoma but would like the boat to be equipped with a spinnaker pole, which we felt would be a better arrangement than the current bowsprit, since it was more suitable for trade wind sailing, when the wind would be directly behind the boat. Additionally, we asked that the boat be fitted with the associated gear, like a downhaul (to keep the pole stable by attaching it to the deck) and an uphaul to attach the pole by rope to the top of the mast. I was initially unconvinced that we needed Alessandro to organise all this as part of the deal, but Charlie assured me that for us to buy, and have delivered, a pole of the size that Keoma would need, would be difficult.

Charlie also wanted Keoma to be equipped with new electronic instruments. We would need a GPS with chart plotter (a screen that showed navigation data, including our past course and projected track). We also needed an autohelm, so that the boat could be set up to steer herself, and instruments that would measure windspeed, boatspeed, water depth and many other types of data. The boat currently had all of these, but they were a brand that we had not heard of and there were certain issues with the functionality and set up. One big factor was that the chart plotter was set up with two screens, one attached to the binnacle which would restrict my view when I was helming (and would it be too bright at night?) plus a second screen in the cabin. We would rather have one chart plotter screen only, next to the chart table, in the cabin. Another issue was that the instruction manuals were in Italian. Alessandro was receptive to all this and he agreed to work on a deal. The next stage was that we must make a financial offer.

CHAPTER 12

Our house was still on the market. After an initial flurry of interest, including quite a few people who were just snooping around, things went very quiet. We dropped the price, but to no effect. We were surprised that the house was not more popular, since there had been a lot of interest when we bought it, and we thought it had a lot going for it. We wondered whether we had chosen the right agent. We were using an agent who we had dealt with before, who was streetwise and who had been very helpful to us in the past, but who was not known for the marketing panache that another local agent had. The agent was working hard for us, efficiently pursuing all lines of enquiry and advertising in the local newspapers, but viewings had tailed off and we were starting to become concerned. We would soon reach the stage when we needed cash to buy the boat, and the house had not sold. Our agent suggested an advertisement in one of the Sunday newspapers, and we agreed to meet half the cost. In the meantime we visited a financial adviser to explore the possibility of borrowing money to fund the boat, using our house equity.

At work Delia was avoiding contact with me. I was not concerned, in fact it was a relief not to be involved with her.

We had such different approaches. The Tax Department asked me to take on another group restructuring project. I explained to the Head of Tax that I was happy to do the work, but that I was leaving in two months' time. He smiled. "We'll all have to get on with it then, so that it's done before you go!" I offered to help Delia with the recruitment of my replacement, and suggested that it would be a good idea to start with a job description, which I offered to draft. I also gave her the details of a recruitment consultant I'd used before.

CHAPTER 13

It was a beautiful spring day and the doctor's surgery window was open, birds singing nearby. He seemed quite fascinated by the journey I was describing.

"So, you're taking the children with you?"

"Yes." I answered hesitantly, wondering for a moment whether we were going to be reported to the social services or NSPCC.

"OK, sounds great! What a family adventure! I will write out a list of medicines for you to take with you for emergency use, including dosages suitable for the children. Are you qualified in first aid?"

I told him about the course. I didn't tell him how useless we were.

"Oh, and you may need inoculations. You'd better make an appointment for the whole family to come in for those. The nurse will be able to talk to you about whether you need malaria tablets."

One Saturday afternoon I spent several hours reading a website called FirstAid4Sport, working out what supplies were needed for the first aid kit. Finger supports and bandages for sprains and breaks, burn treatments for accidents while cooking at sea, thermal blankets, self-activating ice packs because we wouldn't have ice on board and all sorts of other bit and pieces. Each time I clicked the mouse I hoped none of it would ever be needed.

I collected the prescription from the doctors and spent a small fortune in the pharmacy. Along with the antibiotics (in powder form) I bought ten boxes of sea-sickness pills, neurofen, paracetamol, plasters, gaviscon, piriton (in case of an allergic reaction), savlon cream, dettol, tweezers, calpol, sinex and night nurse. I also slipped some hydrocortisone cream into the kit, left over from a time when Pip had impetigo. A pink mark around the size of a fifty pence piece had appeared in the centre of her back. The cream had soon cleared it up. Charlie and I talked about whether to take needles and decided not to, because we didn't know how to sew up a human. We did take butterfly stitches and we had been told that superglue could be very useful for sealing a wound. That was already in the toolkit.

Every day we tried to achieve something towards our ultimate aim. I often reflected on how far we had come, without having left home yet. We were busy with jobs and home life, but somehow found time to achieve these extra things. I began to long for the end of my notice period, to be able to relax and concentrate on the final things we needed to do. To put that final tick on the list. To lie down on the sofa.

Charlie was speaking to Alessandro almost every day, trying to reach a deal. One evening as I stepped onto our doormat, he broke the news, "Alessandro has said, if we offer 5,000 Euros more, Keoma is ours." I put down my bag and took off my coat. We looked at each other. This was the big decision, that would hurl us from the life we knew into something completely new and different, that would challenge us beyond anything we could imagine and change our lives forever.

Our mortgage company had agreed to lend us the additional funds, which meant we had enough money available to purchase the boat, although the monthly payments were way more than we could afford. Charlie was waiting for an answer. He looked at me expectantly. He placed both hands on my shoulders and squeezed his fingers together gently.

"We've got to do it."

"I know we have." He pulled me towards him.

CHAPTER 14

We told the children we had bought the boat. They were high with excitement, dancing around, hands in the air, singing. From the spare bedroom, where all the items for the trip had started to accumulate, we brought out a big chart and opened it out on the dining room table. It showed the whole of the North Atlantic. It looked a huge place, but now the decision had been made, I felt galvanised, unafraid, ready for the challenge. Having sailed on Keoma I felt great confidence in her, but most of all I was looking forward to feeling that sensation of her cutting through the water again.

When Alice and Pip were in bed, the conversation turned to more practical things. We talked about renting the house out to tenants while we were away. But this would give us cash flow problems – the rent would not cover the mortgage and the boat financing costs. My feeling was that I wanted freedom from everything "back home", and we didn't want to be tied to phoning the managing agents to sort out tenant issues and other problems. We didn't even want to *think* about domestic things. The conclusion we reached was that we would instruct another estate agent, to act in a dual agency capacity, in the hope of selling the house before we left the country.

We started to think about communications on the boat. When we were away from land, and sometimes when we *were* on land, we would be in areas where there was no mobile phone signal. A condition of the ARC was that we had to have a means by which we could communicate with the organisers. They would record our position every day and send us weather forecasts. Further, if we or another boat near us, found ourselves in trouble, we would need to be able to let them know or to help out, as the case may be. Many boats did this via a SSB (single side band) radio. However, these were expensive to buy and install, and atmospheric conditions could mean that reception was not always reliable. We considered a satellite phone which we could use for expensive conversations, and would send and receive email into a laptop computer. This method of communication would also enable us to maintain a website, which was something we were both interested to learn how to do.

A box arrived by courier. Charlie opened it excitedly. "You won't want to be seen in public with this thing," he said. It looked like one of the original "brick" mobile phones. It cost £550 and we were yet to buy the laptop, still a matter of research.

At work, CVs for my replacement began to arrive. I looked through them and emailed Delia my views. It was clear the applicants were all less qualified than me and it looked as though they would be paid half what I was paid, but I didn't bother making this point.

It was the first day of May. Under my employment contract I was entitled to receive a bonus, which had always been paid and at the rate of around 25% of my annual salary. But there had been no mention of the subject and I had received neither payment nor letter. I began to get nervous that they might not pay it, but told myself that surely after everything that I had been through for the company, they wouldn't stoop so low. As usual, Delia was not in the office, so I emailed her asking what was happening. I received an email back which read, "Am a bit confused by this email. What bonus were you expecting? I spoke to Siobhan in HR about your contract when you handed in your notice and she said that you are not entitled to a bonus when working out notice. (And as you know from what happened to Helen, as a group we have a policy of not paying bonuses to people in such circumstances)".

I felt angry and abused. I wrote back; "I believe I am still entitled to my annual bonus – I have just pulled out my contract and checked – I'm not sure what Siobhan is saying, as it does not say that I am not entitled to payment in the event that I have given notice, and I have not subsequently agreed to such a term. You did say that Helen was not receiving one, but I did not appreciate that that would apply to me also. I don't believe a group policy can be imposed on me unilaterally, in any event."

Delia's response was, "This is a new one on me – I will contact Siobhan."

Thirteen days later Delia ventured into my office. She looked harassed and unkempt. She verbally repeated what she had said in the email. I was determined to stand my corner.

"Well I'm not going to get into an argument with you about it," she said as she flounced from the room.

I decided to consult an employment lawyer, who was the husband of a friend. He advised me that I had a strong case, and drafted a letter that he sent to my employer. The letter requested that all future correspondence on the subject be sent via him.

A few days later I left the office for a few minutes. I went to the sandwich bar on the corner and returned with my lunch. There was a letter on my desk. It was one of the most spurious, unpleasant, bullying items of correspondence that I had ever read. I was tempted to walk out and not come back but it wouldn't achieve payment of my bonus and it would be deeply unprofessional, as well as causing many of my valued colleagues difficulties. So I stayed, and tried to be diligent, but from now on I was definitely counting down the hours. And, I made a vow to myself. Never again.

I asked one of the major shareholders, who had made millions from the sale of the company the previous October, whether he would intervene on my behalf, by talking to the current management, as he knew how hard I had worked and my personal cost, over the previous year. But he didn't want get involved and I felt very let down. He didn't even reply to me directly – I received an email from his legal advisor.

CHAPTER 15

At home we discussed computers. In the end we chose a Dell, because we had been advised that if it went wrong, the after sales support was superb, wherever we might be. We hoped it would be able to cope with heat and humid, salty conditions. We would be depending on it.

The family travelled to Civitaveccia for a weekend, to discuss the details of the deal with Alessandro. We signed the document of sale and paid a deposit by credit card. Although the deal was not yet complete, the owner had agreed to let us stay on board Keoma. After lengthy discussions in Alessandro's office, we returned to the boat to try to work out what equipment we needed on board. Sitting in the cockpit, enjoying the warm sun, we talked it through. Charlie was interested in installing a water maker. He started opening lockers, looking for a suitable space to house what would be a fairly large unit. The boat had air conditioning and we wondered whether we needed it. It took up the space of four large lockers, and we were conscious that we would need to stow a lot of food and water for the Atlantic crossing. In the end, we decided to take out the air conditioning, believing that our bodies would adjust to the heat and we could swim or shower to cool off. I pictured Caribbean days in the baking sun. Aquamarine water, white sand, hot sun and us on our boat. It sounded perfect. "Anyhow," Charlie was saying, "it would use up too much fuel to keep running the air conditioning." He had calculated the amount of power that the generator would need to produce to feed the air conditioning system, and explained the figures while I glazed over.

Alessandro lent us his car and we drove to the local co-operative store. The fruit and vegetables seemed so brightly coloured, they almost jumped off the shelves at me. They were displayed in boxes that looked as though they had just been delivered from the farm. I saw mamas filling up bags with all sorts of things. The herbs were in big bunches, not struggling to grow in flimsy plastic containers. One cantaloupe melon was never enough – they were buying six or seven at a time. It was cooking on a grand scale and I wished I could be sitting at their dinner tables. There was a whole aisle devoted to parmesan cheese, and it was cheap. We bought a big rough chunk. After dinner we ate the cheese while finishing off the bottle of red wine. It crumbled with a sweet, warm, salty crunch, granular between my teeth.

Keoma's forecabin had the largest, highest bed that I had ever slept in and we felt as though we were in sheer luxury, with soft cream leather on the ceiling and cherry wood on the walls. The panelling formed a shelf on either side of the bed, making two little bedside tables. Previously, we had only slept on boats which were utilitarian and uncomfortable.

When we woke on the Sunday morning Pip was covered in vivid spots. It looked like chicken pox. She was miserable and spent most of the day sleeping in her bunk. Fortunately, I had packed some Calpol, which seemed to help a little. We had flights booked for that evening to go home, and we decided we *should* return home, which would be the best place for her, although we worried that she might not be allowed on the plane home. Standing at the check-in desk she stood behind us, well covered up, and the flight staff did not notice.

CHAPTER 16

We received delivery of the chandlery order, and began to consider how we would transport these items to Italy. Now, we realised it would have been so much easier to buy a boat closer to home. Charlie researched the alternatives and chose to have the items freighted by road.

The ARC organisers sent a letter asking for payment. I wrote out a cheque for £650. It felt like money was just flowing down the drain. I was feeling uncomfortable about how much this was all costing, in fact I was deeply concerned, especially with our house still unsold.

Funds arrived from the re-mortgage. Charlie shopped around for a foreign exchange deal and had most of the money paid into the Euro account he had opened. A few days later we set up the transfer to Alessandro and suddenly the boat was ours. We phoned Admiral for insurance cover and opened a bottle of champagne to celebrate.

We ordered a (conventional-shaped) spinnaker for the boat. In trade winds we would gain a lot of speed (and the boat would be more stable and comfortable) with a full, regular-shaped spinnaker up.

The boat had now been re-registered as a British vessel, arranged by Alessandro via his cousin in Rome. He explained to us that we were lucky he had these "contacts", otherwise it could have been a very long-drawn out process. We needed to apply for a sail number. I filled out the form and posted it off, with the fee.

Charlie would be celebrating his 40th birthday in a couple of weeks' time and I decided that we had to see all our friends before we left, so the obvious solution seemed to be to organise a party. More expense! A friend's band agreed to play. We shipped in wine and beer. Lots of old friends came. The dominant topic of conversation was our forthcoming trip. Everyone seemed to think it was a great idea, and many of our friends said they would miss us and wished us luck. "You've really made us think about our own lives, too," one friend said.

On Monday morning I was back on the train to London, standing room only. I wondered where we would be this time next year. Perhaps it would be a disaster and we'd be back in England. At least the first part of the trip would be in the Mediterranean, which should be warm, easy sailing. I pictured us leaving Civitaveccia, sunny sailing on a flat blue sea.

At work someone asked me whether we would take a gun with us. I was horrified. "No, definitely not. I hate guns."

"I would, if I were you," he said.

That evening, I told Charlie about the conversation. "I think it invites a very different response if you point a gun at someone. Also, it doesn't seem a great idea to be blasting holes in the boat," he said.

We packed up two crates to freight. We were worried about including the liferaft and flares, because they were banned cargo, having explosive components. But how else were we to get these things to Italy? In the free space I put in tinned food, as I was not sure what I would be able to buy there. Soup and tinned fruit, which I thought could be useful emergency rations. Beach towels and summer-weight duvets. Alessandro agreed to take delivery of the crate and arrange storage until we arrived there.

CHAPTER 17

Charlie was invited to sail in the Isle of Wight "Round the Island" race. It was a "boys only" boat and I was jealous. I was stuck at work with all the home chores to deal with. I arrived home in the evening and straight away started organising homework, baths (essential in this hot sticky weather), bedtime, my dinner, telephone calls. Alice had accidentally worn Pip's spare school dress and so I had to wash both dresses and dry them overnight, running a quick iron over them before I went to work in the morning. It was my mother's birthday in two days' time, so I wrapped a present and wrote a card, putting them in a big envelope to post. I hurried to the post office on my way to work, cursed the queue, grabbed the stamps at the counter. Mid-lick I paused. What had my life come to that I resented the time taken to post a gift for my mother. The person who had given me more than anyone else ever could.

I was working on the release of bank security linked to pre-take-over borrowings. These had now been paid off and all the companies with charges registered needed to have these released, requiring a Deed for each. I negotiated with Clifford Chance, the lawyers representing the bank, on the wording of the Deeds, and then arranged execution of each one. There were around 30 companies affected, including US, Bermudian, Polish, Singaporean and Hong Kong registered companies.

At the weekend the children and I were having lunch before going to the school fete. There was a knock at the front door. Jo, who worked in the shop next door was standing outside. "I've got some bad news. The bus just hit your car and looks quite badly damaged. But I've written down the name on the side of the bus, and registration number." I thanked her and stepped out onto the pavement to look. The whole of one side was caved in.

Charlie arrived home the following evening, very sunburnt but elated about the race. They came 3rd out of 70 boats in their class. I felt green with envy but relieved he was home to give me a hand.

I discovered that my replacement had been recruited, but that she would not start until the Tuesday of my final week. What a tough call, for both of us, to handover a job with so much history, so much detail, in four days. Also, it was a busy week at home and school. Charlie had gone to Italy to work on Keoma. I had two sports days to attend on separate afternoons and a ballet performance, which meant I *had* to leave work on the dot of 5.30 on Thursday evening. The sports days were, as usual, classic displays of English eccentricity. All the parents lined up along the side of the running track and gestured and shouted at the little darlings standing at the start line. Most of the children were looking around them, waving nonchalantly at their parents and smiling. One or two were waiting seriously for the whistle, one skinny leg and arm poised in front, ready to push off with the back foot. You could identify the winners before they started. The weather was reminiscent of sports days from my childhood; hot and sunny. But the children no longer won Curly-Wurlys and packets of Lovehearts, which would have been far too unhealthy.

On Thursday night I attended the children's ballet performance. The school theatre was swelteringly hot and it lasted for over two hours. It didn't come naturally to Alice, and she thumped around on the stage, her hair determined to escape from the hasty bun. I sensed it would be the last time she put on ballet shoes. Pip was fine-boned and graceful, and enjoyed the performance. She stood with hands held high, the lights shining in her auburn hair, a perfect little ballerina.

CHAPTER 18

At last it was Friday, my final day at work. I sat down at my desk and started up the computer. In my email in-box there was an email from Delia, written the evening before. It read, "You didn't say goodbye when you left today and as you know, I'm not in the office tomorrow." Several responses sprang to mind but I hadn't got time to write them. I reflected that it added to the body of evidence that the decision to leave was the right one. I had ten sets of accounts that I wanted to get signed that day, since if it was not done there would need to be additional work in explaining the reports and changing the signature boxes to reflect the change of Company Secretary. Each set of accounts required the holding of a board meeting to approve the accounts and authorise signature, and it would be easier for me to deal with these than for my successor, who did not know the individuals and issues concerned. I wanted to get these signed before I left, but the auditors had still not confirmed that they were happy with the accounts. At last I got the call, mid morning. Then I received an email from the company Treasurer, asking whether I would like to go out for lunch. It was decent of him to offer, and because of his thoughtfulness I felt I had to go, even though it was already a busy day. I rushed back from lunch and immersed myself in meetings. I managed to get all ten sets of accounts approved and signed. People dropped in to my office to say goodbye. Then I tackled my letters of resignation – slowly, the printer churned out one for each of the 64 companies. I *had* to be home by 6.00pm because Alice and Pip were in a play that evening and Charlie was still in Italy. What a sweat.

I grabbed my bag and ran for the train. I didn't know what I would do if the train was delayed, especially as I had handed my (company) mobile phone back, so I couldn't call Lauren. The feeling of relief that I had expected was marred by the stress of the day and of getting home on time. But I did feel relief as I walked through the door. "Come on, children, we've got to get going straight away." Thanks to Lauren, they were ready to go and we got into the car. It was their last day with her and we were all sad to say goodbye. Earlier in the week we'd given her presents. Alice had known exactly what to buy; a big serving plate and bowl to match the rest of the set that she had. We wrapped it up together, carefully, me with anxious hands suspended, worried that the children would have an accident.

In the car, Pip said slowly, "I don't think I am going to be able to talk in front of all those people." I gently asked her why. "I'm worried about getting it wrong," she replied. I worked hard to convince her that she knew her lines and, anyhow, it didn't matter if she made a mistake. Everyone in the audience was on her side. She walked onto the stage with confidence, and her performance, in fact, the whole show, was faultless.

We arrived home around 9pm, tired and hungry. The children were emotional, so I made them hot chocolate and toast while they washed off the greasepaint. By the time they were in bed it was 9.30 and I was ready for bed too, emotionally frazzled.

CHAPTER 19

At last there was some interest in the house, generated by the new estate agent, and their superior mailing list. Two couples would like to view the house on Saturday and two on Sunday. I was up early, cleaning and tidying. The weather was fantastic; hot and sunny, and I opened all the doors and windows. Pink roses climbed up around the walled garden, and I imagined them puffing tiny drops of scent into the warm air. Even the weeds looked beautiful, with king sized dandelion heads standing proud above the flower beds.

The following week was a whirl of viewings, for which I had to tidy the house in advance, and a general sorting out of our affairs. The peaceful time I had envisaged was obliterated. There was now quite a clamour for the house with four families seriously interested. We had sold a house before and knew that it was a teeth-grinding experience; as my father put it, "buyers are liars". So, we suggested to the agents that we should invite bids on a "best and final offer" basis, which they agreed was a good idea. We gave the interested parties ten days to submit their offers.

I started to think about removal companies, to pack up and store our belongings while we were away, and representatives of two came to see me to quote for the business.

One evening we drove to The Crown, a pub in Stoke-by-Nayland, to have dinner with the grandparents. Even the meal seemed too busy, too rushed. There was too much to say, too much to think. David, Charlie's father, was about to go on holiday and we would not see him again before we went away. Suddenly our departure seemed imminent. We all enjoyed the evening, but the parting was emotional. I had never seen David so choked up. He hugged and kissed his son, gripping his arms. Perhaps he thought we wouldn't be coming back.

It was almost the end of term and I took the children to Speech Day. Charlie stayed at home and cleared out the loft. I would have liked him to come with me but there was so much to do. Pip danced around the maypole with her classmates; boys and girls twirling around laughing, skipping, weaving in and out of each other. They got the sequence wrong and the streamers tangled, so it wouldn't unwind. The teacher intervened, although the children were unwilling to stop, and tried to sort out the knot but it took embarrassingly long, her face turning pinker and pinker, until she declared the dance abandoned.

When we arrived home there were boxes and bags everywhere. Piles of baby clothes. I wondered how we would tidy up before the next viewing. The following day Victoria, my sister, and her husband Juan, came for lunch. They filled up their car with baby clothes and other boxes and bags. I felt purged to be rid of it all.

I headed to the bookshop and bought travel guides for the Med, thinking it would be useful to have these in English. I had to guess where we would go because we had no planned route. We expected it to evolve as we started to travel, influenced by advice we received along the way. I also bought schoolbooks, following the Headmaster's guidance.

The following week was the children's last week of school before they broke up for the summer holidays. On the Tuesday we held Pip's birthday party. Her sixth birthday was actually the following week, the first week of the holidays, but school would have finished by then and many of her friends would be away. At a quarter to four, twenty-five six year olds arrived. They came roaring through the front door and raced around the house. Outside, the heavens opened. For the first time in three weeks, we had rain. It hosed down.

We held the party games inside and the children screamed with excitement. The house felt charged with energy. They crammed together around our table with another table wedged on the end, and tucked into the kind of tea we had at parties when I was small. Sandwiches, sausages, crisps, orange squash. Then I brought out the biscuits and cakes. Arms reached to pile the food on a paper plate. I had made the birthday cake and secretly decorated it with a picture of a dolphin jumping in the sunset. A week or so ago Megan's mum had asked Pip what she most wanted to see on the trip and she had described a colourful sunset and a dolphin leaping, so I had depicted this (in an amateur, home-made kind of way) on the cake in different colours of icing.

After the food, they needed to jump around. I put the music on and started a game of musical bumps. Charlie went to answer the phone in the other room. He returned and cupped a hand over my ear to be heard above the music. The results of the "best and final" offers; the sealed bids for our house, had arrived. He told me the offers that had been made; two at the asking price and one marginally above. The fourth couple had decided they didn't want to get into a competitive situation. We agreed to accept the highest offer, and Charlie phoned the agent to let them know.

The party came to an end and the children departed with parents in ones and twos. Pip was left with a pile of presents to unwrap, which made her less unhappy about the end of the party. She unwrapped sarongs, bikinis, hats, beach bags, books and diaries.

CHAPTER 20

I was printing off letters to send to all our contacts, letting them know of our change of address. We gave them Charlie's parents address, as David had agreed to look after our affairs while we were away. He was retired and fastidious. The telephone rang; it was one of the women who had viewed the house. "I'm sorry to ring you but we just wanted to let you know that we are terribly upset not to have got the house. I really had my heart set on it. I could see us living there and not to get it is devastating."

I took a breath and said, "Well, I'm really sorry, too, but we had to take the highest bid."

"The thing is," she continued, "the agents gave us the impression that we had put in the highest bid. They said we didn't need to increase our bid. Is there any way you could reconsider? We'll pay more than the highest offer."

I sighed. "The house has been on the market for several months and it has been a very trying time for us. We have accepted the highest bid and it wouldn't be fair on that bidder, or on us, to go through it all again. We really need to move on, especially as we will be flying to Italy in less than two weeks' time. I'm sorry." She accepted what I said but asked me to get in touch if there were any problems with the sale, to which I agreed. Later that day a letter was put through our door by the other unsuccessful bidder, with a similar content to the phone call. I was utterly amazed that the estate agent had done such a poor job. Why hadn't they pushed the buyers to give their best bids? Surely that was the opportunity for them to earn their fee by emphasising to the buyers that they needed to put in a strong bid. But we had agreed and couldn't go back. I booked the removal company to move us out in ten days' time.

I couldn't wait to leave the country. I felt let down by so many people; my employers, the estate agent, even the bus driver who drove off without confessing to wrecking my car. Then I reminded myself that I was so fortunate to be going, and it was time to move on. There was no point in carrying bitterness around like a stone in my pocket.

I turned on the radio "…four bombs have exploded in central London, thought to have been set off by terrorists…" and slowly exhaled. The date was 7th July.

We were invited to a party on HMS Grafton by a naval friend. We somehow *had* to find time to attend, as neither of us had been on a warship before and we were very excited at the prospect. As we approached the gangplank a line of male and female officers in uniform saluted us. I trotted up the ramp in high heels. I had been expecting the heat of recent days, but instead I shivered in my summer dress. We were given a tour of the ship, including the bridge and the navigation and communications equipment. I imagined how small Keoma would look to these sailors, looking out from the deck of Grafton. Afterwards we went to a restaurant for dinner with a group of friends; the last time we would see them for a year. In the boot of the car we had the children's bikes, to give away. Alice and Pip would be too big for them by the time we arrived home.

The next morning was the last day of term. I packed up boxes while I could do it in peace. The spare room was getting fuller; piles of clothes and other items to take to Italy. I walked down to school at midday to collect the children. They were having their photos taken with groups of friends. I watched, holding an armful of cards which read "sorry you're leaving", "good luck" and "bon voyage". I hoped we were doing the right thing for them. It would have been so much easier to say "we'll be back in a year," but we couldn't. I had written to the schools in Suffolk and accepted places at one, starting in September 2006.

CHAPTER 21

I picked up the cat and cuddled her, stroking her soft black coat. A purr started up. Then, to her surprise, she was bundled into a cage, which was carried joltingly to Charlie's car and plonked unceremoniously on the back seat. She had only been in the car a few times before and had hated it. This would be the longest journey of her life and she mewed pathetically for an hour and a quarter. Alice sat in the front next to me and Pip sat in the back of the car and tried to soothe the cat. We drove to David and Bridget's house. David was away on his sailing holiday but Bridget gave us lunch. She was delighted to look after our cat, although the relationship between her dog and the cat had yet to be defined. We said our goodbyes. Next stop was the sail loft to collect the spinnaker. It was bagged but still looked enormous, and it weighed 24kg. Charlie's brief had been for them to make us a "bullet proof" spinnaker that we wouldn't have to take down for wind squalls in the Atlantic. At the time I had thought this quite a tall order, but the sailmaker had agreed to it. I wrote out a cheque for the sail and he put it in the boot of the car, next to the empty cat basket.

We spent the afternoon at my parents' house. Mum, very emotional, red veins in her eyes, was trying desperately to appear normal. They had been picking cherries from the tree in their garden and we hung the doubles over our ears.

The following day the packers started on our house. They arrived at 7.30am and worked solidly until 6.30 in the evening. I was on tea making duty. Every hour, on the hour, they each had a cup of tea with two sugars. We started packing our holdalls, to take to Italy. We weighed each bag to try to avoid being fined by EasyJet for having overweight bags. By the end of the day half the rooms of our house were empty. I picked up the strange collection of small things that had accumulated under seldom-moved furniture, depositing most of it in the bin, and hoovered the carpets.

Charlie had now finished work. He phoned up some dealers and arranged to sell my car. The bus company had, after repeated attempts to deny responsibility, at last agreed to reimburse me for the damage. I hadn't had time to have it repaired, so it was still badly dented and scratched. I accepted the quote for "Yachtsman's Gold" insurance. This was a travel and medical policy which lasted one year, and was designed for long-distance sailors. The children harvested their small area of the garden. It was much too early and they were disappointed with the fairy-sized carrots, but enjoyed eating the small broad beans raw. Pip leant a bony shoulder against me as she said sadly, "I really wanted to see our sunflowers open up."

CHAPTER 22

The final day of packing dawned. Tonight we would stay with friends nearby, and tomorrow we would fly to Italy. We were physically and emotionally drained. We started at 7.30am and by 5.30pm almost everything was packed. Charlie went off to the optician's mid-afternoon. The packers and I tackled the kitchen last and by the time the final few drawers came around, we just tipped the whole lot into a box and taped it up. I'd given up thinking about how I didn't want to pay to store rubbish for a year. I'd given up trying to sort stuff out. I'd given up wrapping things up. Finally the hoover went in and the lorry was sealed up. I wondered when we would see all our things again, and whether we needed them at all. I had forgotten about the fridge, which the buyers had asked to keep, and I kneeled down to clean it out. It was becoming a massive effort to force myself to finish the clearance off. There were dishes in the fridge that I was now left with. I put them in a box. Now we had a final box that we would have to leave somewhere. Charlie returned and we put our bags and the last box in his car. We would drop the car off at Charlie's former workplace the following morning, and get a lift from there to the airport. It was a squeeze to fit the spinnaker in, and I worried that EasyJet would refuse to carry it.

We stayed the night with our friends who lived nearby, Kate and Simon, who witnessed the signing of our wills and the paperwork for our house sale. I put the documents in envelopes to send to David and our solicitor. After dinner we watched the news. Iraq was still headlining.

Kate said, "Do you realise this is the last television you'll watch for a year?"

"Yes. I'm not going to miss seeing this."

We went to bed but it took what seemed like hours to find sleep. When I did, they were wild chaotic dreams, and I woke up at 5 o'clock with scratchy eyelids and a dry mouth.

CHAPTER 23

At last, we were standing in the queue at Stansted. We had all our personal items for a year in one bag each. I thought of all the things I had failed to get done. I hadn't achieved that final tick on the list. My tax return. I would just have to pay a late-filing fine when we returned. The cancellation of the home contents insurance. We'd just have to live without the reimbursement of premium. The airline staff looked at us through thick make-up, eying the spinnaker suspiciously. We were told to take it to the check-in for "unusual and oversized items". It cost an extra £100 to get it into the hold.

In Rome we waited in sweltering heat to collect our bags. I imagined the spinnaker blocking the exit from air-side, causing a mountain of bags to build up behind. But, piece by piece all the bags arrived and then the spinnaker. There were no trolleys so we tried to carry everything, which was impossible. The children couldn't lift any of the bags. To move our luggage we had to carry some bags forward a short way and then go back for the others, like some sort of crazy relay race. Little by little we got there.

Charlie always liked to find the smallest hire car possible and this time we had a Renault Twingo. With extreme tessellation and discomfort we managed to cram everything and ourselves into the hire car and headed for the Rome orbital road. It took around an hour and half to drive to Civitaveccia.

We parked in the outer car park at the marina and stepped out into the warm sunshine. Finally, it felt as though the appalling web of stress, from the lives we had created for ourselves, was beginning to lift away. We were in Italy!

Charlie found a large trolley to transport our gear to the boat, and trundled the bags and the spinnaker down to the marina. The place looked dusty and dull, but the water sparkled in the sunshine. We walked along the concrete waterfront and down onto our pontoon. Keoma looked so enticing, we couldn't wait to get aboard. Charlie unlocked the cabin hatch and slid the door out, stowing it in one of the cockpit lockers. I passed bags over the manrails to him, and he placed them on the cockpit seats. Then I pushed the trolley back to the trolley park, and ambled along the dock, breathing in, enjoying the scene. Alice and Pip ran along the pontoon towards me and grasped my hot, dusty hands.

We filled Keoma's tanks with fresh water, using the hose on the dock next to us. Charlie led a long cable from one of the cockpit lockers and plugged it into the electricity. I flicked the switch to heat water and, ten minutes later, tried out the shower. Hot water on a boat!

CHAPTER 24

We spent several days arranging everything and doing final fitting out jobs. The Twingo was used for a trip to the supermarket. Stopping at the meat counter, I was trying to decide what to buy. The assistant looked like Andre Agassi in a white polyester trilby and coat. He showed me his palms, smiling. "Mi dica?" "What would you like?" He laughed at my attempt to explain, using gestures as much as words. I pushed the trolley around the end of an aisle to find Charlie and the girls trying on flippers, snorkels and masks, and the children had chosen body boards and buckets and spades, which they begged us for. We took it all back to Keoma and stowed it. The body boards and snorkelling gear went in a large locker under the helming seat. Charlie took the Twingo back to the car hire depot, and we were, for the first time in years, carless.

The marina was strangely quiet. Boats bobbed on the water, shiny and empty, and a few elegant Italians, dressed in black, white and red, would promenade up and down the pontoons. Long, healthy, dark hair swung as they sauntered along.

The new British ensign was bright red with a stitched Union Jack in one corner, and made of thick cotton fabric. To my mind, it wasn't quite big enough. It didn't come close to touching the water, but it did look in proportion with the boat, and it did look very smart. We rigged an Italian courtesy flag on the starboard crosstrees. I still couldn't quite believe she was ours. I couldn't bring myself to throw away the plastic flower arrangement, just in case I woke up and we were packing our bags to go home again. The weather was warm with a very light breeze. We untied the mooring lines and motored out of the marina, just the four of us, then hoisted the sails and sailed a loop of around three miles.

We anchored off a small beach and swam from the back of the boat. Keoma's swimming platform had a lid which lifted up and a useful swimming ladder could be deployed. The children giggled as they rose and fell on the waves, clutching their body boards. We winched up the anchor and headed back to the marina before sundown. It had been a very careful first excursion. Charlie reversed the boat back into the space and I leant overboard and picked up the mooring line with the boat hook, pulling it tight and tying it onto one of the cleats at the bow. The line was full of sharp barnacles which cut into my hands, and it smelt of sewage. We finished tying up the boat and I went below to wash my hands thoroughly, then sat in the cockpit to enjoy a glass of chilled Italian wine as the sun set over the sea.

CHAPTER 25

The following morning we set sail for Isola di Giannutri, a small island northwest of Civitaveccia. It was around 30 miles away and we unrolled the big genoa foresail, and pulled up the mainsail. Before leaving we had sat side by side at the chart table and plotted a course on the GPS. Now our instruments on the binnacle were telling us the direction to head in for the next waypoint. The wind was on the beam and the boat, slightly healed over, cut through the water at a steady seven knots. We had found the motion, the momentum that we'd been dreaming of since our first sail on Keoma. The sea sparkled in the sunshine and we were in our swimsuits, Alice and Pip wearing their life jackets over theirs. They looked pale in the bright sun and I coated their skin in sun cream and insisted they wore sunglasses. Their hair was sleek and tidy. We put out a fishing line, behind the boat, but there was no interest from the fish. Pip enjoyed helming. She stood on the bench seat that spanned the back of the boat, arms outstretched holding the big wheel. Above her head flew a fish kite that we had tied to the backstay. I had not imagined she would have such a feel for the helm, such a natural instinct for it. It was easy sailing and took less than 5 hours to reach our first destination.

Giannutri was tiny, just above sea level, "C" shaped, rocky, and uninhabited. Attached to the wall of Keoma's saloon there was a decorative framed chart with knots attached to it. The chart on the wall showed Giannutri. It was as though it was pre-ordained that it should be our first landfall. We prepared to anchor, me on the foredeck and Charlie on the helm. The water was around 25 metres deep; it was really too deep to anchor, but there was no other option, since it didn't get shallower until we would be too close to the island and its surrounding rocks. We put down the anchor and let out almost all the chain. In home waters it was accepted practice to put out three times the depth in chain. This meant that if the water was deep and wind changed direction, the boat would swing to a very different place than where it was when the anchor first went down. We now had 75 metres of chain out and we hoped the wind wouldn't shift and blow us onto other boats anchored around us. Charlie put the boat into reverse to test the hold. The chain jolted up and down, telling me the anchor was bouncing along the sea bed. It hadn't held at all. I wound in the anchor and we tried again. It was the third attempt before we got a hold.

We swam from the swimming platform on the stern, enjoying the crystal clear water and abundant fish. About to jump into the water, Charlie suddenly remembered something. "Oh no, the fishing line!" He jumped in and ducked beneath the surface to inspect of the boat's propeller. "Shit, it's wrapped around. Pass me the knife, would you?" I was already out of the water, drying off with a towel, so I reached into the cockpit for the knife that we had taped to the binnacle. The knife was for emergencies such as ropes pulled tight around limbs, and it was very sharp. Charlie wiped his mask with his fingers, put it back on his face and swam beneath the boat. He spent around half an hour cutting line from the prop, coming up for a gasp of air every minute or so.

With the onset of evening, we sat in the cockpit enjoying the peace as the light faded. The anchor chain was slack, the water lapping gently on Keoma's hull. I went down to the galley and cooked some pasta and tomato sauce for our evening meal, which we ate in the open air. A few other boats were anchored in the same bay and their masthead lights reflected on the water. Although the conditions were tranquil, I felt a deep, stubborn, murmuring anxiety. We had only had good weather so far and I was not sure how we would cope with difficult conditions. What would happen if we wrecked the boat tomorrow?

During the night I woke a couple of times. I couldn't resist climbing down from the high bed and wandering through the saloon in the moonlight. I sleepily climbed the companionway steps and into the cockpit, happy to see we were still in the same place. Back to bed, to the sound of water caressing the hull, and then I was sleeping soundly again.

Bright sunshine filled the cabin as my eyes slowly opened. I looked across at Charlie, already awake. He was smiling to himself, completely at home and relaxed. He didn't know of my anxiety and would tell me not to be so paranoid. It was uplifting to have the big hatch wide open directly above our faces, so that fresh air and blue sky flooded in with the sunshine. We ate breakfast in the cockpit; bread bought yesterday and slightly hard, and no grill to make toast.

Charlie pumped up the dinghy, using a foot pump, standing on the foredeck. It took around twenty minutes and I washed up the breakfast things while he did it. I was missing the dishwasher. We grabbed our masks and fins and dinghied ashore, driven by Alice. When we got close, Alice switched off the motor and Charlie threw a small anchor over the front of the boat. We dived into the water and swam ashore, where we scrambled through the scratchy bushes, trying to reach the spine of the island to see over to the other side. Having swum ashore, we were not wearing any sunblock and the sun was merciless on our salty, pale, skin. I saw a discarded snake skin beneath a held back branch. Soon we gave up the battle with the bushes and made our way down towards the dinghy. Charlie wanted to swim back to the boat, so I started the outboard with a pull on the rip cord and Pip steered us back to Keoma. The tiller of the outboard had a handgrip which twisted to increase the engine revs. It was quite difficult for the children to master the twist while at the same time pulling the tiller from side to side for direction, all with one hand.

After another night in the bay, we were ready to set sail again. I wound in the anchor chain, as Charlie motored the boat slowly forward until the bow was vertically above the anchor. A jolt of the chain told me it had broken free of the rocky sea bed and it rose vertically to the bow of the boat.

I took the helm and pointed the boat into the wind while Charlie hoisted the mainsail, then swung the wheel to bear away as he unfurled the genoa. We were headed to Isola di Giglio, a larger, populated island another 8 miles away. The boat rose and fell in the small waves, again making effortless speed. As we sailed along, we discussed the concept of "Captain's orders" with the children. It was very important that they understood that when the Captain asked them to do something or not to do it, they had to do exactly as asked, otherwise it could be dangerous. They nodded seriously.

We anchored in a pretty bay called Cala Canelle and motored ashore in the dinghy for a swim off the white sand beach. The children dug and played happily with their buckets and spades in the sand for a couple of hours.

CHAPTER 26

Reaching across to the side table, for the torch and my watch, there was a noise of water gushing past the outside of the hull, centimetres from our heads. It was 1.00am and the wind whistled through the rigging, causing a fast tap, tap, tap of halyards against metal. I stood up on the bed and put my head out of the hatch. Charlie stirred in his sleep, next to my feet. I realised I needed to see the anchor chain, so pulled myself up through the hatch and stepped forward to the bow. The anchor chain was taught, holding the boat steady, with water streaming either side of the hull. I shone the torch around, on the rocks in front and the rocks behind, and felt unnerved. When we anchored earlier, the boat had been lying at 90 degrees to her current position and the conditions were calm. The rocks now looked very close and the wind and current had picked up.

I looked back several times, clicking the torch on and then off, and wondered whether we were getting closer. After ten minutes or so, I decided the anchor was holding and I headed back to bed. Lying in bed I tried to sleep, but deep maternal instincts were on red alert. They would not allow me to rest. If the anchor dragged, the stern would hit the rocks first. I imagined the sound of fibre glass crunching. Would we be able to get Alice and Pip out of their cabins, at the back of the boat? Was the noise getting louder? I went up onto the foredeck again. No, we hadn't moved, but the conditions were definitely worsening. I went below again and woke Charlie, who muttered grumpily, "For goodness' sake, Juliet, it's fine. Just calm down and go to sleep." But I couldn't sleep. I just lay there, disturbed by the images in my head, trying to persuade myself I was being paranoid. At around 3.30am I went up on deck again. The boat was bucking in the waves and I was seriously worried about the anchor.

I woke Charlie and forced him to come up on deck. He agreed that we had to move the boat, and I ran down to the chart table to turn on the electrics for the anchor winch. He fired up the engine and motored forward as I wound up the anchor. It was raining by now, and windy. I was not wearing a life jacket and my pyjamas stuck to me in the cold driving rain. Charlie motored away from the bay and I went down below and got out the pilot book to see where we could go. The options were limited; all the other bays looked exposed to the wind and waves. In any case we were unwilling to anchor in an unfamiliar place in the dark. However there was a walled harbour a few miles away, which looked as though it was more for local fishing boats and small motor boats. I put some waterproofs on and took over the helm from Charlie so that he could go down below to get more clothing on and consult the book. We decided to give it a try, as otherwise it looked as though we would be heading off to the weather-lashed exposure of the sea for the rest of the night.

Slowly we closed on the harbour, the lights like a beacon in the darkness. As soon as we rounded the protective wall, it was like flicking a switch on the elements and everything went still and quiet. The port was crammed with a hundred small boats, half the size of Keoma and smaller, and an enormous high-sided ferry. It looked as though this was going to be hopeless; the place was ram-jammed. We carried on motoring slowly in, between lines of tethered boats, relishing the peace of the haven. Suddenly we spotted a space, a big space, large enough for our boat. I blinked as though it couldn't be true. But it was, and we reversed in next to the one other yacht in the harbour. This boat was much smaller than us and we jostled it sideways slightly as we shoved our way in. An Italian man came up on deck, surprisingly cheerful given that it was 4.00am, and he helped with our ropes. His English was good and he told us we could stay where we were until around 5.00pm. Apparently a fishing boat had just gone out, but it would return in the late afternoon. We fell into bed and slept soundly.

The children woke us at 7.30.

"We're in a marina!"

"Well, it's a fishing port, rather than a marina. Didn't you know Daddy and I moved the boat in the night?"

"No. Can we go ashore?" Charlie got up and took them for a walk around the town. They returned in half an hour with milk, croissants and bread. I climbed out of bed and pulled on a T-shirt and shorts. We set up the table in the cockpit and put out plates and knives, jam and butter. The kettle boiled and I switched off the gas, pouring water on top of instant coffee in plastic mugs. Sitting in the cockpit we admired the small port. Square buildings lined the waterfront, painted in sunworn dusty pinks, yellows and browns. Each one had dark green shutters, closed against the hot sun. There was a small beach in one corner of the harbour, where some rowing boats were resting on the sand. I could just make out people on the waterfront, opening café umbrellas and walking to work.

CHAPTER 27

Charlie wanted to do a few jobs on the boat, so I took the girls ashore to see whether we could find a bus to take us to the local castello. I had been reading about it in the pilot book. We wandered through the two rows of houses and found the tourist office, where we learnt that we had just missed the bus, but there would be another in an hour, and I bought tickets. While waiting we found some shops selling postcards and an ice cream shop. The ice cream melted fast in the sun; I had some tissues in my bag and we managed to wipe the worst off our hands and faces.

It was a modern-looking coach and the three of us shared a double seat. The bus set off with a jolt and pursued the narrow ancient streets, twisting and turning, snakelike. I was soon grasping the side of the seat in front, trying not to fall off the edge of our seat with the violent cornering. The views started to become impressive. Although the landscape was brown and rocky, far beneath us was the azure sea. There were patches of turquoise near the island, where the water became shallow. We reached the highest point of the island, at 400 metres, in around 20 minutes.

As we entered this crenulated high walled village, we rounded a tight bend and the driver slammed on the brakes. The other bus that served this route was centimetres away. I wondered how many times a day this happened. We reversed a few metres and the oncoming bus slowly advanced until it had passed, the windows of one bus passing close to the windows of the other. Forward again, and then we climbed down into a square of market stalls beside the entrance to the castle. It had protected the islanders from the frequent visits of marauding pirates in the 13th and 14th centuries. Built of rock from the surrounding hillside, it looked as though it had grown there, like some kind of enormous mushroom. We wandered through the castle; it was actually a fortified village, holding houses and shops. Many of the dwellings were still inhabited and strings of faded washing were suspended across the shady narrow streets. Flowers grew in pots, but the places where the sharp triangles of sunlight could penetrate were limited. We stopped to admire the vertiginous view. "Can we see Keoma from here?"

"No, we've been around too many corners," said Alice. Retracing our steps back to the entrance, we were keen to feel the sun again, and hurried over the worn dusty flagstones. We browsed around the market while waiting for the bus. There was a stall selling olives, which look glossily enticing, but the thought of a lurching bus journey with a leaking plastic pot in my bag prevented me from reaching for my purse. We looked at the fossils for sale. Incredibly expensive but fascinating. There was a stall selling beautiful stones set into jewellery. The bus arrived and we hurried to join the crowd thronging to climb on.

Back at sea level we wandered back to the boat, with a sense of relief to be off the bus. I was conscious of the combination of salt, ice cream, sun cream, sweat and dust stuck to my skin, and took a shower. It was not the kind of shower we were accustomed to. Our watermaker was still not up and running. We had already finished one of our two tanks of water, each of which held 500 litres. The message was slowly getting through to us that we had to conserve it carefully, since we didn't know when we would next be able to fill up. So, I couldn't abandon myself to the gushing flow. I used just enough to get most of me wet, then stopped the water. I soaped up and then started the water again. I ran just enough to rinse off and then I turned off the tap. It felt very disciplined. I had already washed the children in the same way. I shouted through to Charlie, "Can you turn on the shower pump?" He flicked the switch on the control panel next to the chart table and I started to pump the shower water from the footwell.

A man wearing a faded blue short-sleeved shirt with epaulets stood on the quay behind us. He seemed to be some kind of official and he appeared to be suggesting something in Italian. We called upon our neighbour to help with translation. "He is saying you can park your boat on the end over there if you want to stay the night." We were very grateful and managed to stammer, "Grazie, grazie". Clearly some other boats had moved around and there was a space. He obviously wanted us to get out of the way before the fishing boat returned. We untied all our ropes and motored over. There was no buoy to pick up for our bow, so we had to motor well forward, drop anchor and let the chain out slowly as we reversed towards the quay. The first time we did not get a hold, so we motored forward and tried again. We crept back towards the quay and this time it held fast. A few people were standing on the quay and watching. When I had finished with the anchor, I ran back and climbed down onto the stern, with ropes threaded through the fairleads, ready to leap ashore and tie us on. I felt like some kind of manic rabbit, but it had to be done. We took a long time tweaking the ropes, getting the boat just so, and then we put the kettle on for a cup of tea. While we sat drinking, the ferry departed. We were so glad we'd taken care in our mooring! It seemed as though half the water of the harbour was sucked out of the port, then surged back in. The boats pulled one way and then the other, banging against each other and the walls.

That evening we ate at one of the restaurants on the waterfront. It was a structure built on stilts, and we could see water through the gaps in the floorboards. The children found this very exciting, and kept dropping to their knees to look through at the gentle waves beneath. My anxiety had ebbed slightly, which I attributed to the fact we had coped the previous night. I felt we had passed the first test, but I knew there were far greater challenges to come.

CHAPTER 28

The sun was a little too bright as I wound up the anchor chain. Charlie loosened the warps on the stern. The windlass was straining; running slowly with a harsh noise. I stopped it, and leant over the bow. Through the clear water I saw that the anchor had picked up a large stone. I decided to wind it up further. "Is the anchor up?" Charlie shouted, not wanting to steam off with the anchor dangling, knocking against the hull. "No!" I shouted as I lay on my stomach trying to dislodge the stone with my hands. "We've picked up a rock!" I grunted. It was at a difficult angle and I couldn't shift it. I slid myself back onto the deck and jumped up. I ran back to the cockpit, explaining the size of it to Charlie, who opened the locker near him and got a hammer out of his toolbox. I took the helm and he ran forward to the bow. The children ran to watch. The boat drifted slowly sideways. In a minute he freed the stone and it splashed heavily into the water. He wound up the last of the anchor chain and I pointed the boat between the green and red pillars of the harbour entrance and pushed the throttle forward, heading for the open sea.

It was a different sight from the sea we had left two days before. Calm and welcoming, a glistening blue, we hoisted the sails. I put the throttle into neutral. The boat slowed until we were stationery in the water. Keoma's sails flapped, and the creases wouldn't pull smooth; there wasn't enough wind. So, instead of switching the engine off, we put the sails away and motored ahead, steering Keoma towards Elba, around 30 miles away. The sun was relentless. Suncream, hats, sunglasses and swimming costumes. We had bottles of water in the fridge but the second tank was almost dry and we would need to fill up soon.

After three hours of motoring we noticed a slight change in the texture of the water. Charlie put the engine into neutral and we felt a light breeze on our faces. It was enough to sail, and we hoisted the sails again. The wind came from dead ahead and we winched the sails in tight. Keoma healed over and picked up speed. I checked the genoa and grasped the winch handle for one more turn, to catch a tiny bit more speed. Charlie switched off the engine. Alice, Pip and I sat on the high side, Charlie in the steering position behind the binnacle. After half an hour we consulted the GPS and determined that if we tacked, we'd be on course for Scoglietto Rock, outside Portoferraio. Charlie started to turn the boat. I took the genoa sheet and released it from the self-tailer, a moulded plastic gripper on the top of the winch, easing it and then letting it fly. The boat went flat. I had already set up the sheet on the other side and now I pulled it in, hand over hand. I fastened it in the self tailer, and reached for the winch handle. The handle had a red switch on the top and I pushed this across with my thumb as I inserted the handle into the top of the winch. I released my thumb and the handle locked into place. Leaning my body over, above the winch, feet and knees braced, I used both hands to push the handle around and the sail wound in. I turned my head to see the sail pulling back towards me, flattening, and winched until the sail looked exactly right, now I rotated the handle the other way for fine tuning. The boat healed as I wound, and soon my head was pointing downhill, leaning over the leeward side of the boat. I climbed back into the cockpit, and, flicking the red switch across, lifted the handle out of the winch, replacing the handle in its plastic holder near the floor of the cockpit.

As we sailed into the bay outside Portoferraio, we started to think about dropping the sails. Charlie pointed the boat into the wind and I pulled in the narrow chord that turned a drum on the forestay. The genoa wound away. He sparked up the engine and put the throttle forward a few degrees. I released the halyard that was holding the mainsail and it dropped cleanly down. Charlie turned the boat and headed towards the entrance of Portoferraio. As we motored in, we saw an elegant town. The colours were the same as in Giglio, but the houses were larger, squarer, more imposing. The centre of the town was a large harbour, cut into a rectangular shape. We found a space and again it was a case of deploying the anchor and motoring backwards to the quay, which we got right first time.

We stepped ashore for a walk. There were only a few shops but they were old style glamour. I thought of my parents here, on honeymoon in the 1960s, and imagined that the shops hadn't changed. There was a shop selling leather goods, including an exquisite chess set made from brown and black leather. Somehow it all looked so *Italian*. I would have loved to buy something, but forced myself to remember that we didn't have cash to spare. We went into the supermarket, which was a huge, high-ceilinged building. The roof had a dome of dusty glass and pigeons flew around inside. It looked as though it had once been a school or church. I wandered the dusty aisles pushing a small, rickety, trolley.

On our return Charlie went to find the harbourmaster to ask about water and to pay for our berth. It cost 34 Euros for one night and we were told we could fill up from the nearby tap, for free. We didn't have a hose so Charlie asked the skipper of the boat next to us if we could borrow theirs. Alice and Pip had noticed the ice cream shop, which was just across the road from where Keoma was moored. I took them across and they fantasised over the different flavours, at last making their choices. Charlie said, "You can't come on here with those. I've just washed the decks." Taking advantage of the hose, he had used a brush to remove sand and salt from the teak. The children happily stood on the swimming platform, licking and dripping ice cream. Alice already had a golden tan. Pip was paler, but looked healthy and her face was freckled. My skin was prickling slightly from a day in the sun, but not only that, it felt as though the warmth had penetrated right to my core.

CHAPTER 29

The next morning we woke late and went ashore to find a Vodafone shop. We wanted to get a local SIM card so that we could use my mobile phone to access the internet, which would be cheaper (and hopefully easier) than using the satellite phone. It took us hours to find the shop. We had to walk a long way and by the time we got there it had closed for siesta. We returned to the boat, frustrated, and I sorted out clothing to take to the launderette. In the afternoon Charlie went to the Vodafone shop, alone, and I went to the launderette, which again took a while to locate. There was another boat called Keoma in the harbour, and I walked past. Sergio waved; this was the boat bought by the man who used to own our boat. But there was no sign of the rich owner. I walked back towards our boat and suddenly saw an enormous motor boat, also called Keoma. She was dropping anchor in the middle of the harbour, reversing towards the far side, to moor up next to his sailing boat. I counted ten immaculately uniformed crew on board, holding fenders and warps. Someone was talking on a hand-held radio, giving instructions to the bridge.

In the evening we sat on board and watched the residents of Portoferraio take their evening promenade. Beautiful Latin faces, glossy hair and long slim legs, they were dressed to impress. Occasionally they would stop to chat with friends. Alice and Pip weren't interested in the beautiful people. They were watching an old lady dressed all in black, sitting on a canvas stool on the quay, fishing. Using a hand line with balls of putty pressed onto it, she sat with the line wrapped once around her index finger. As soon as the line tightened a tiny degree, she gave a practised flick and lifted the line, with a fish attached, which she deposited in a bucket next to her. It was filling up fast. Alice looked seriously at Charlie, "We *have* to get some of that stuff." They resolved to visit the fishing shop in the morning.

After a restful night, Charlie and the children went shopping. Then we walked to the ruin of an ancient Roman villa. It was strategically placed at the seaward entrance to the harbour, affording it a breathtaking view across the glittering water. The walls had unrestored mosaics, quite damaged and dusty. In the afternoon we motored out of the harbour. We anchored just off a beach a few miles from Portoferraio. We could still see the town but it was the other side of the bay. It was wonderful to be free to swim off the back of the boat again. Charlie pumped up an inflatable dinosaur and the children spent hours in the water with it. Later, we watched the sun setting behind the town; the exotic silhouettes of the towers black against the vivid pinks, oranges and purples of the sky. I turned on the mobile phone to call my parents, to let them know we were in Elba.

There was a message on the phone from our house buyers. It sounded problematic. I called them back. We had been expecting to exchange contracts on the house sale any day now and we were keen to get the transaction completed so we could stop thinking about it, and pay back the money we'd borrowed.

"We've been looking into the timber guarantee and it turns out that the company that gave it has gone to the wall.

So, we've had another specialist company do a survey and they have said there may be woodworm and death watch beetle." Apparently there were all sorts of other problems with the house and the bottom line was that they wanted £30,000 off the asking price. I relayed what she'd said to Charlie.

He was furious. "Of course a competitor timber treatment company would say anything to get the business. Let me talk to her." He grabbed the telephone. "Well, that's fine, we'll just put the house back on the market. There are other people who are keen to have it. We thought you'd got it at a bargain price anyhow." At this she backed down and the conversation was concluded. It had ruined the peace of our evening; the stress flooded back.

CHAPTER 30

Another perfect day as we lifted the anchor and hoisted the sails, bound for a cove called Golfo della Biodola. Throughout the short journey, sudden gusts of wind appeared from nowhere and Keoma's heel would increase with a jolt. It was very unpredictable. But we were soon there and we anchored close to the shore. Alice was suddenly gripped by a fear of deep water and didn't want to swim from the boat. Charlie and I were bewildered by this unprecedented irrational fear. Had she been reading a book about sharks? Charlie tried to persuade her to put on her mask so that she could see there was nothing down there, but she was stubborn and in the end we dinghied ashore. The wind died and we clambered over rocks at the shoreline. We couldn't stay out of the water for long because the heat was like an oven. Back on the boat we ate lunch. I had made the day-old bread into crostini, by slicing it and piling a slice of tomato and mozzarella on each, followed by a drizzle of olive oil. This had become a favourite lunch (better than stale bread!) and I often added an anchovy, an olive or a basil leaf, before giving it a blast in the oven for ten minutes. We drank copious amounts of water in an effort to chase away the thirst that was always lingering in the background.

Still fresh in our memory was our disturbed night on Giglio and we decided to return to the anchorage across the bay from Portoferraio, so up came the anchor again and we motored back. It was so still that the sea looked more like oil than water. I felt as though the salt on my skin was drawing water out of my body, actively dehydrating me. I took a shower but still felt sweaty. The heat was overwhelming and there was no escape from it. Back in the anchorage, Charlie and the children opened their new tin of putty and dangled lines in the water for hours, trying to imitate the old lady we saw, but without success.

Charlie was hunting around for his credit card, searching the obvious places on the boat. We mentally retraced our steps, to work out where he might have left it. He concluded that it must be in the restaurant in Giglio. By some stroke of luck we had taken the card of the restaurant, and Charlie switched on the mobile to phone them. They had it, and we arranged to collect it the following night.

We set sail in the morning, not sure where we would end up. Maybe Giglio, maybe further, we'd see how we got on. The wind was blowing from behind us, giving Charlie an idea. "Let's put the new spinnaker up." I was not sure about this. It was a very powerful sail and I would have preferred there to be more than just the two of us on board to handle it. "Come on Juliet, the conditions are perfect. Tell you what, if you don't like it, we'll take it straight down again." I reluctantly agreed, and he was kept occupied for the next 20 minutes, sorting out the ropes. I clicked the boat onto autopilot and went forward in the cockpit to pull the halyard up. I winched the guy in and the pole swung slowly back towards the cockpit, as Charlie released the giant sock that had held the sail in a sausage shape. I yanked on the sheet. We tweaked the ropes for a few seconds; a little bit in on this one, another gently eased, and then looked around and enjoyed the scene. I was so glad we'd done it. The boat immediately accelerated to a steady 8½ knots.

For a while I kept a watchful eye on the wind instrument, because I didn't want the spinnaker up if it started to get too windy. But we had the opposite problem and after a couple of hours the big blue sail was hanging loose. Charlie stood on the foredeck and tugged on the line dangling from the giant sock, pulling it down from above, having the effect of snuffing the spinnaker out swiftly. I was delighted with the way this system worked. It made the sail easily controllable for two people. We checked that none of the ropes were trailing in the water and started the engine.

It was dusk by the time we reached Giglio and we had already decided we would keep going, to Giannutri. But we had to stop to pick up the credit card. It was agreed that I would go ashore and run up to the restaurant, while Charlie slowly circled the boat around the small harbour. There was barely enough room to circle, but he had to keep her moving otherwise he would lose steerage. The next question was; how would I get ashore. We were unwilling to pump up the dinghy, if we could avoid it, because of the time it would take. I was not too keen on the idea of turning up in the restaurant soaking wet in my swimming costume. In the fading light there was suddenly a small light coming towards us, and it was a small boat, being driven by a familiar face; the epauletted Harbour Master. "So sorry..." he was saying.

"It's OK," Charlie said, and we somehow conveyed that we weren't after a berth for the night; we just needed to collect something from the restaurant. He agreed to take me ashore. I explained that I would need to be brought back also. He seemed to understand and I jumped into his boat. He dropped me off at the end of one of the pontoons. "I wait," he assured me. Yet again, I felt pathetic not to speak the language. All I managed to say was "grazie". I ran up the road to the restaurant.

The waiters were amused that not only had we left our credit card, but also Pip's track suit top, so I picked up both, with more "grazie" and hurried back to the dock. When I got onto the pontoon I saw that there were now four people standing near the Harbour Master's boat. They looked a bit shifty. One handed over a fat brown envelope to the Harbour Master, which I guessed contained money, and a plastic bag was passed back to him by the Harbour Master. Then they all turned to look at me. I stopped in my tracks. A man the size of a nightclub bouncer stood in front of me to block my view, although it was too late. I had already seen the exchange. My instinct was to get away but I needed a lift back to Keoma, so I hovered there. I imagined a glare of lights as the Police arrived, being handcuffed and put in a van with these four men. What would it be like to be questioned in an Italian jail? Charlie was on the boat around 100 metres away but not able to see anything and he couldn't have an inkling what was going on. I didn't have a mobile phone on me and the boat one was switched off. I didn't have any money or identification. The only thing in the pocket of my shorts was Charlie's credit card. I turned my back on the men, trying to look nonchalant. I waited. I had thought that when they saw me they would disperse. Presumably they knew I couldn't understand what they were saying.

At last the other men got into a speed boat and motored slowly away. The Harbour Master turned towards me, and I wondered whether he was embarrassed, but he was difficult to read. His head hung down slightly. The messages he gave off were very subtle and I could have got it wrong. It could have been an innocent situation. It was very dark now and he motored out to Keoma. I couldn't wait to get back onto our boat. Charlie leant over and passed him a bottle of wine as I climbed up, and then turned to me, a little annoyed, "Why did it take so long?" I told him the story as we motored out into the flat calm sea, heading for Giannutri, and I felt safe, at home.

Although it was dark, we were familiar with the bay at Giannutri and we anchored without hitch. It was around midnight by the time we got to bed.

CHAPTER 31

Another bright blue sky hung above our heads. I took the children ashore, as Pip was keen to try to find the ruins of the villa that had once stood on the island. Our pilot book told us that Nero's mother once lived here. But, just as before, the scrub proved impenetrable, and we made it only half way up the slope before turning back with seared and scratched legs and arms. I kept thinking about snakes too; I had read that the nearby island of Montecristo was rumoured to be infested with adders. We swam from the beach and I felt a brushing sting on my leg, like nettle rash; a jellyfish.

In the afternoon the sun was intense and the children watched a DVD in the saloon. Charlie opened up the sunshade over the cockpit and we talked about my Industrial Tribunal claim. It was difficult to know what to do, because I had three months from leaving the job in which to bring a claim, meaning that a decision was needed quite soon. I didn't want our year away to be dogged by me having to grumpily wade through documents and fly back to England to attend hearings. There *was* a second option, which had a longer shelf-life. Three years to be exact. This was to bring a case in the High Court, but if I lost I might end up having to pay not only my costs but those of my ex-employer also. I was fairly confident of success, however the thought that they might notch up £1m in costs made me hesitant. If I lost on a technicality, I would be bankrupt. In the end, my conclusion was that I wasn't prepared to tolerate these poisonous thoughts. The best course would be to put them behind me, as I had managed to do before we left England. Charlie agreed with me and we decided to just try to forget about the whole thing. I felt a weight lifted from my mind.

Charlie unpacked the laptop and satellite phone and spent an hour or so trying to get the two to communicate. We were keen to be able to send and receive emails, as we felt very cut off from family and friends. It was lovely being just the four of us, but after the intensely sociable period immediately before our departure, it had been a shock to the system. Charlie was very frustrated with the phone and the computer. I knew he would succeed, but not today, and he packed away the laptop and other equipment. The following night my sister and brother-in-law would arrive in Civitaveccia.

CHAPTER 32

At 7.30am we motored out of the bay. I wondered when we would come back here, if ever. It was a feeling I would have to get used to. Pip was sitting up on deck writing her diary. She asked me to write down the spellings of a few words, and I took a pencil out of her pencil case and wrote the words on a piece of paper, which I gave to her. She put the piece of paper down next to her. It flipped away into the water.

We enjoyed a close reach, with the wind just forward of the beam. Charlie pressed the autohelm button and tweaked the sails. He worked on one sail at a time, letting sheets in and out, loosened the halyards then tightened them again, winding the backstay on and off, adjusting the lines which ran down the leech of the sails by tightening them until the fabric curved upwards at the edge, then releasing them. He pulled out the clew outhaul, which tightened the foot of the mainsail, stretching it out towards the aft end of the boom, and then let it off. He adjusted the cunningham, the line which altered the halyard tension by pulling down the tack of the mainsail, towards the boom. He set up the autohelm to sail to a course and then re-set it to maintain a constant angle to the wind.

This went on incessantly for a couple of hours, and helped us get to know the boat and her controls.

We arrived at Civitaveccia around lunchtime. The marina looked very different. It was buzzing with people. Today was the first day of August and this was the month when the Italians holidayed. The sound of passionate debate and laughter came from cockpits. People were unloading boxes of food and wine. If we'd wanted to eat in the restaurants we would have to book.

We spent the afternoon cleaning the boat and borrowed Alessandro's car to go to the co-op. I went to the laundry to wash the sheets for Pip's cabin. They were sand and salt encrusted, despite our best efforts to shower the children off when they returned from the beach. The laundry was officially closed today, but I met the owner walking along the waterfront. He was very amused by my interpretation of the Italian phrase-book and trustingly lent me the key and tokens for the machines.

At 11pm Victoria and Juan arrived. I gave them some pasta and we stayed up late talking about our adventures. Victoria was pregnant and starting to expand around the stomach.

CHAPTER 33

The following morning was not what we had expected. Heavy grey skies and a strong southerly wind made us decide to delay our departure to Sardinia, after much discussion. Charlie and Juan visited the chandlery, where they bought lots of essential items. Fenders, mooring lines, courtesy flags. They tried to buy charts but the chandlery had very few of these. In the evening we ate some fish which I baked in the oven "Italian style". Juan, who was from Argentina, picked out a fish eye and casually popped it into his mouth. Pip, watching, picked out the other one and did the same.

We were still in Civitaveccia the next day, with the same southerly wind. There was red-brown dust everywhere. "Sahara sand," shrugged Alessandro. Apparently it blew across the Med. The boat was being blown forwards, away from the pontoon, by the force of the wind, and she was held in place by the stern lines. We sat at the saloon table, playing cards. Suddenly we felt the boat shunt backwards. The bow lines took the strain but there was some stretch in the ropes. We heard a crunch as the stern rammed the concrete support beneath the pontoon behind us. The wind had veered through 180 degrees in the space of ten seconds, and was now a mistral northerly. There was a hole in the fibreglass at the back of the boat, on the stern where it formed a sharp edge, fortunately well above the waterline, where water would not ingress.

Alessandro walked along the pontoon. "I think you need to wait three days before departing to Sardinia," he said.

I was amazed at Victoria's reaction. "But we're only here for a week."

I pointed out to her that it could be very rough if we left that day. I was not concerned for myself, because I knew I had a strong stomach, but she did not.

She said, "Don't worry about me. I'll just go to bed." So we decided to leave. I was not in favour of it but everyone else wanted to go, so I agreed. The waves were fairly large and the wind was now westerly, so we were heading into it. The barometer dropped 2.5 millibars in the first hour, and I worried that the wind could get very strong. But I didn't voice my concerns because the decision had been made. It was 120 miles to Sardinia.

Charlie and I stayed up all night. We put away the genoa and brought up on deck a small foresail which we rigged to the inner forestay, called the staysail. We dropped the main halyard by a metre or so, and attached an eye on the luff of the mainsail to a hook on the boom, then pulled in a line named "Reef 1" on the cam cleats. This line ran out to the end of the boom and pulled down the leech of the sail, having the effect of folding a slab into the mainsail, reducing the size of it. The boat sailed very manageably in the strong wind with this sail configuration. I was worried about Victoria, who was being sick into a bucket, and Juan, who felt ill. Both had taken to their bunk. The boat was slamming in the big waves in a very awkward motion. Worse was to come. I went below to record our progress in the log book, an hourly ritual, and discovered water lapping over the floorboards on the leeward side of the saloon. Were we sinking?

Charlie went below to investigate. With the boat being thrown around he had to remove floorboards and feel around in the water, while holding a torch to try to get a clear view. The cabin did have lighting but it did not penetrate those tucked away places. He tasted the water. It was fresh, not salt. He concluded that a water pipe must have ruptured.

We sailed endlessly on, wave after wave, and it felt like time was standing still. But at least we knew we weren't sinking and the night sky was stunning; the backdrop very black and the stars looked so clear that the universe felt ultra 3-dimensional, almost throbbing.

At 4.00am I clung to the cold metal bar in front of the gimballed stove, watching the flickering blue flame. It wasn't easy to walk back to the cockpit with cups of boiling coffee. I took one step at a time, carefully putting my feet where they would not slide and holding on with my free hand. I delivered the drinks to Charlie, then headed back to the galley again and opened the locker for the plastic box where the chocolate bars were kept, which I took up to the cockpit. We were feeling quite jaded from lack of sleep and from the physical activity of the sail changes, done in cumbersome foul weather gear. Wet sails of this size were very heavy to handle, and it was hard work to move around the boat, even to make coffee.

I made a tear in the top of a chocolate wrapper and a small head appeared at the top of the steps. It was Alice, closely followed by Pip. They were not in the least frightened, instead they were excited to be out of bed, eating chocolate, in the middle of the night, so we allowed them to stay up for a while, and they witnessed their first shooting star. But Alice started to feel seasick and so shortly afterwards, they, and Charlie, made for their bunks.

At 7.30am Charlie came up on deck again. "I can see Sardinia," I pointed. He turned around. It was still rough, but it had calmed down a little, and I decided to try to get some sleep. I woke at around 11.30am as we were motoring past rocky islands, the boat flat and weirdly calm. The others were sitting in the sunshine and Victoria was considering whether to eat something. I stood on the foredeck as we came through the shallows, looking through the clear water for rocks that we might hit, but there was nothing to concern me. We anchored the boat and I passed up bread, cheese, ham and salad for lunch. Looking around, the scenery was beautiful. The water was aquamarine blue and there were green mountains in the distance. Charlie had found out why there was water in the bilges; the motion of the boat had caused the watermaker to move and that movement had ruptured some of the pipes in the locker. We would need to find a way to keep it in place.

Charlie and Juan swam to a nearby island and I rowed across with Pip in the dinghy. We examined the rock pools, which were full of interesting things. Shells and stones, miniature prawn-like creatures, seaweed. I rowed back to the boat, while the other three swam. Pip seemed very confident in the water.

CHAPTER 34

Later in the afternoon we decided we should move the boat to a less exposed spot, in a sheltered bay close by. I raised the anchor and the boat motored forward slowly. We'd consulted our chart and the pilot book, as well as the GPS. I was standing on the companionway steps, looking down at the screen of the chartplotter, and talking to the others in the cockpit. There was a loud bang. At the same time the back of my head hit the edge of the open hatch. It was painful and I pressed against it with my hands. We had stopped dead in the water. Keoma's keel must have hit something. I checked the GPS again, in disbelief. There was no sign of any rocks on the screen. Charlie put the throttle into reverse and the boat motored slowly backwards. No-one said a word.

We returned to the same place as before and anchored. Charlie swam under the boat to take a look. The bulb had a scratch on the leading edge, which was not a concern, but there was a tab at the top of the trailing edge of the keel which had a small crack running down vertically from the hull. He suspected the crack lined up with one of the keel bolts, which attached the keel to the hull. These bolts were incredibly strong and to replace one was a major job. We might need a new keel, which could take weeks to build. I knew Charlie was devastated; this might be the end of our dream. Our beautiful boat might be irreparably damaged. I couldn't talk to him about it, beyond short factual conversations, because I was on the verge of tears. There were long gaps of silence between sentences. We decided to have an early night.

The next day Charlie turned on the mobile phone and spoke to our insurance broker, and Alessandro. Both recommended that we went to Olbia for the boat to be lifted out. There was a good boatyard there, which would be able to effect the repairs. The phone had a message from our solicitor, saying that we had exchanged contracts on the sale of the house. In the evening we rowed over to a nearby island and made a fire for a barbecue. We collected wood from all over the island and made a pile on the flat stones of the beach. There was no wind at all and the evening light gave the earth a rich golden glow as the sun dropped behind the distant hills. In the foreground Keoma lay at anchor, the only boat for miles.

Charlie and I woke at dawn. Neither of us spoke as we dressed and lifted anchor. The noise of the engine broke the stillness of the morning, but soon faded to a background hum as we motored towards Olbia, around 10 miles away. We didn't want to go fast because we were anxious about the keel. Charlie had tried to test it manually, underwater, and had thought it felt solid but we couldn't appreciate what stresses it was under as we moved through the water. If it were to fall off, Keoma would capsize instantly. It was flat calm as we passed the high wedge-shaped island of Tavolara. A solitary fishing boat combed the water. A lighthouse marked the entrance to the river, white and square, starkly functional, an appropriate introduction to the industrial town of Olbia. We passed huge mussel beds with miles of snagging nets suspended on poles. There were many buildings along the banks of the river; factories and other commercial concerns, and it was hard to see the boatyard we were heading for. We motored on up river, taking the right fork in the river, past four enormous ferries lined up in the centre of a fork, facing towards the sea. Eventually we saw the buoy where we had to turn. We were following the advice of a stranger in taking the boat up here, and I hoped we had interpreted his instructions correctly. It looked shallow and narrow, but we persevered.

In the distance we spotted three men standing around the edge of a concrete dock, waving us forward. Soon there were tough canvas slings beneath the boat and the hoist began to raise her. The sound of water draining off as she lifted. We stepped off onto the dock, shaking hands with Mr Guidot. He was around 50 with shoulder-length wavy hair streaked with silver. He looked strong and fit, as though he enjoyed an active life. Charlie led him down the companionway steps and they lifted the floorboards to examine the keel bolts from above. Mr Guidot emerged into the sunlight again. "All fixed?" asked Victoria.

Mr Guidot shrugged, palms held upwards, eyebrows raised, "But of course."

"You're *good*," said Victoria.

Mr Guidot's advice was that we should spend the weekend on the boat and bring her back on Monday morning. There was apparently no danger to us in doing this. His yard would then lift Keoma out and carry out the necessary work. They would repair the existing keel and there was no need to remove it, which could weaken the bond between the keel and the hull unnecessarily. It would take ten days, and we would need to find alternative accommodation in Olbia for that time. We could not stay on the boat while it was in the boatyard.

The hoist slowly lowered Keoma back into the water and the men removed the slings. As we motored away, Mr Guidot warned us, "Take care. There is a mistral coming. Find yourselves a mooring." We tied up at Olbia's old commercial dock, and, leaving Charlie on the boat, headed to the

supermarket for provisions. I couldn't believe there would be
another mistral so soon.

CHAPTER 35

Later we sailed for the Golfo di Maranello, anchoring a couple of hours later in a large picturesque bay with a white sandy beach at the end. I repeated Mr Guido's advice but there didn't seem to be any buoys, so the anchor would have to do. The chain of the anchor ground in the fairlead, making teeth-clenching noises when the gusts hit. Charlie ran a rope through the chain and tied one end to one cleat and the other end to the other cleat on the foredeck. He then let out some chain, so that the top part of the chain hung slack and the boat was being held on the rope, which silenced the metallic grind.

Helicopters were collecting huge bags of water and flying them over the hills, inland, presumably to drop on a forest fire somewhere, a spark in an arid landscape fanned by the steady wind. That night it started to get really windy. The boat had an alarm which would sound if the wind gusted above a certain strength. Charlie set it for 30 knots. There was also an alarm to let us know if the boat moved more than a certain distance from its location at the point when the alarm was set, and he put that one on, too. Like setting an alarm clock for an early morning start, these helped us to sleep, until the alarm went off. The wind was gusting at more than 30 knots. So we took it in turns to sit anchor watch, up on deck in the howling wind.

Charlie took over the watch and I slipped into sleep, but I was dreaming of a cleated rope that unwound itself like a serpent, and I woke up, sweating, feeling adrift.

The blasting wind continued all night and was still building the following morning. Twice, the dinghy, tied to the back of the boat, flipped over. The outboard engine was submerged. We turned it upright again straight away, but the damage was done. We moved the outboard from the back of the dinghy onto its bracket on Keoma's stern. The wind gusted up to 37 knots several times. I sat in the cockpit and watched these aggressive pockets of air scud over the surface of the water. Keoma shuddered as they reached us, but amazingly the anchor held in the sea bed. Other boats' anchors dragged and they had to reset them. From a distance we watched small wind lashed figures, running to the foredeck and winding the chain up, motoring forward, and then resetting it. We did not dare to leave Keoma.

In the evening the conditions subsided a little. Charlie persuaded the outboard into action and we went ashore, to a beach-side bar. Alice and Pip danced around like wild things, pleased to be released from captivity. Overnight we sat anchor watch again, but the next day conditions were calmer and we spent the morning on the beach. Juan and Charlie hired jet skis at huge expense, and zoomed around on them for half an hour. In the afternoon we motored back to Olbia. We didn't want to be late for Mr Guido, who we'd arranged to meet at 9am on Monday morning.

CHAPTER 36

We tied up to the old commercial dock and went ashore for the evening. Walking through the town, along mud roads, we found a restaurant where we could sit outside in the warm evening air. We ordered mussels, which, we thought, must surely be the thing to eat in Olbia. It was our final evening with Victoria and Juan, who had found their holiday with us quite eventful and I guessed they were wondering how we would survive a year of this.

We returned to the boat and passed a relaxed evening playing cards. The following morning Charlie radioed Mr Guidot at 9.00am, asking whether he was ready for us to come to his dock. Mr Guidot was strangely unwelcoming. He told us that he would call us when he was ready. Meanwhile, Victoria and Juan walked half a mile or so to the travel agents, to book their tickets to Rome. We waited for Mr Guidot to radio us, meanwhile supervising the children's school work. As Victoria and Juan climbed aboard they couldn't stop themselves from laughing. "It's *not* Monday, it's *Tuesday*!" With all the upheaval, distress and night watches we had somehow lost a day. How embarrassing. Charlie telephoned Mr Guidot and apologised, red-faced. "He thinks I'm an idiot," he concluded. He relayed the rest of the conversation with Mr Guidot; that he had agreed that we could take the boat over to the boatyard at 2.30pm. We walked to the ferry terminal, a dusty mile away, with Victoria and Juan. Hugging them, we said our goodbyes and they waved as they walked through the sliding doors of the terminal. Next time we'd see them, we would be back in England and they'd be parents.

CHAPTER 37

Back on Keoma we packed bags in readiness for several nights away. The boat was lifted out of the water and placed in a cradle in the boatyard. In fact the crack in the keel didn't look bad. A surveyor arrived with his young female assistant. They examined the boat externally and internally and took photographs. There was much earnest discussion with Mr Guidot, who was clearly highly respected. I talked to Mr Guidot's glamorous secretary about places to stay. Ideally, I would have liked to stay in an apartment, where we could cook for ourselves. She didn't think this would be possible and some telephone calls apparently proved her right. In the end she made a booking for us at a cheap hotel to the north of the town. The children had been playing around in the boatyard. They had assembled a collection of treasures. A washer, a screw, a stone, a piece of white plastic, a bottle top. Their hands were brown from the hot dust of the yard. Pip had tar on her favourite summer dress. At last the survey was finished and we called a taxi to collect us. It was 6 o'clock.

Our hotel room was a depressing box and I felt like a rabbit in the middle of a stack of hutches. The following day we traipsed all over Olbia trying to find a hire car. It felt as though we were a family of refugees. I started to feel despondent. Apparently next weekend was the busiest holiday weekend for the town and all the cars were taken. We received a call from Claudia, the receptionist from the hotel. She had found us a Fiat Panda, which could be hired at a cost of Euro 300 for one week. The car was barely worth that to buy.

Charlie went to work in the boatyard, to help with the repairs. I dropped him off at the yard and then drove the children to the beach. They counted the Fiat pandas we passed on the road. At the beach they were amazed by what they called the "wedgie bikinis". Even the big mamas wore their pants like this. As usual, the Italians did their promenade, walking up and down in the shallows, wearing the brightest swimsuits, plenty of jewellery, long dark hair and a mobile phone held to the ear as they walked. Beautiful men and women of all shapes and sizes.

CHAPTER 38

With time on our hands, we looked for activities that would get us out of the hotel. One day we got up early and drove for an hour or so and then parked the car. From here we could walk up a hill to an ancient village called Tiscali. We carried lunch and water in a backpack, plus hats, sensible shoes and suncream. I said to the children, "I'm not sure you'll be able to do this. It's a very long walk and if we don't get there and you're starting to get tired, we'll turn back." They looked at me with expressions of determination. "We *are* going to do this. Mummy." The first part of the walk was along rutted tracks, through woodland. The ancient gnarled trees gave us welcome shade as we followed the winding path. There was a faint smell of decomposing leaves. The track became more challenging, and at one point we had to scramble up a steep section covered with large loose stones. Some of these were anchored securely and some looked solid but skimmed away beneath our feet. We tested each one and pointed out to the children where to step. We fell into a line, Charlie first and me taking up the rear, often thinking of them falling and how I might brace myself to catch them.

The track had become less visible and we followed rough signs of red and white stripes painted on trackside rocks. The colours had faded and were reminiscent of the paint on an aboriginal's face. It became a game to hunt for these stripes, as some had almost been rubbed out completely. It felt like we'd gone back in time, that we were those first cave dwellers from 3,000 years ago, fleeing the Roman army to settle high in the hills. Then a woman in flip flops appeared ahead of us. "It's a long, long way," she said. "Your girls might find it a bit tough." I didn't ask her how she had managed to do it in flip flops; I couldn't have gone that far in them. She was with her husband and teenage children. "I hope you've brought some money with you because there is a man up there charging an entrance fee." I had not brought any money, but fortunately Charlie had some. We thanked her for the advice and walked on.

The path undulated, sometimes a slight incline, and sometimes very steep, with more patches of death trap stones, demanding hands as well as feet. We came to a narrow cutting between two high walls of smooth rock, which looked as though a bolt of lightning had cut through a huge standing boulder and driven the two halves apart with its force. Charlie climbed up a pile of rocks which formed a kind of natural step ladder, until he could pass between the severed boulder, and we followed. Looking back there was a stunning, vertiginous, view, of the burnt colours of Sardinia's landscape. The children still had plenty of energy, and we tried to explain how to conserve it. We told them to plod along, but they soon forgot and sprang about like caffeinated mountain goats again. Walking through the cutting, I put my palms against the rock on either side. It was so narrow that both my arms were bent at 45 degrees. I pressed outwards, feeling the stone, so cool and solid. Looking up, the sky was a sharp blue.

We emerged to a scrubby, rocky area, and walked downhill for a short distance. It felt unnatural after struggling uphill for so long. I was unwilling to give away the hard fought gain. We followed the edge of this hill, walking in a gradual curve, and came to a wall of rock. It had been carved by the wind into a long wave shape, and it was easy walking along the centre of the half pipe. Views of wide plains stretched down to the left, which seemed overwhelmingly beautiful, perhaps because we'd been at sea level for so long. Reaching the end of the rock structure, we rounded a corner and had a long steep slope of loose flat stones ahead of us. I wondered whether it was right to take the children up this. They didn't appreciate fully the dangers and might get injured. But they were enjoying it so much, I didn't want to force them to turn back now. Somehow we scrambled up to the top of the slope, and there we stopped for a drink of water.

We stood up and resumed our walk. Beneath us was a wooded area. Walking downhill for a short distance, I realised that we had come over the lip of the cave which held the village. We came to steps down, descending into the cave. It had obviously once been the most enormous underground area, but now most of the roof had fallen in. What remained still provided good shelter, and we found stone-wall edged dwellings beneath the remaining canopy. The roofs of these homes had disappeared, but we still had the impression of how they lived in these structures. The cave had a very definite atmosphere, like Stonehenge or some other ancient place. It was as though the air was heavy with history, and we didn't enter the ruined dwellings; it seemed disrespectful.

We ate our lunch sitting on the floor of the cave. I was so firmly in the mode of picturing lives lived here in ancient times that I thought of our forebears sitting on the same spot, eating. In my mind's eye they weren't eating paninis and thin-sliced palma ham, though, they were chomping into chunks of meat. I said to the children, "Think how long ago it was. It was 1,000 years before Jesus." There was a question mark over water supply to the cave, and the printed paper given out by the man at the entrance told us they believed the inhabitants had relied on condensation dripping off the ceiling and walls.

We started the long walk back, retracing our steps. It was more swimmingly vertiginous than when we went up, because we were looking down all the time now. My legs felt slightly less sure, from the efforts of the morning. The children were still energetic, and there were no complaints. It took around two hours to reach the car and we guzzled on our bottled water, warm from being left in the boot. After driving for a mile or so we stopped at a roadside spring. It felt wonderful to fill up two cupped hands and immerse my dusty face in the coolness. A small striped lizard came for a drink, its minute pink tongue lapping like a cat.

In our hotel room we showered in the tiny, chipped, cubicle and Charlie switched on the phone. Our house sale had completed. We breathed a sigh of relief and went out for a pizza to celebrate.

CHAPTER 39

The next day Charlie was eager to spend some money. We got up late, with stiff legs, ate breakfast in the hotel's depressing dining room and drove to the windsurfing shop. It was a colourful place with painted walls and boards and sails on display. Two car seats stood in the middle of the shop, which the children sat on. They looked like gypsies, with headscarves bought from the market, brown skin and thin strong legs. Their teeth looked white in their big smiles. Charlie spent *hours* looking at windsurfing gear, talking at length with the dudes who ran the shop. I persuaded him to think it over while the shop closed for siesta.

I was secretly hoping he would forget about the idea of going back there, but he insisted on returning later in the afternoon. However, the time to mull it over had been worth it because he had thought about the size of the board and calculated that there was nowhere on the boat it would fit. He didn't want to strap it to the manrail because it could be unsafe. If a large wave came over the bow, the water could be prevented from draining freely away, having the effect of pinning the boat down on her side or breaking the manrail.

At last he agreed on the boards, masts and sails that he wanted, and made the purchase, which the shop would deliver to the boatyard. We just needed to phone them and arrange a convenient date.

We visited one of the most exclusive marinas in the Mediterranean, at Porto Cervo. We went there by car and were relieved not to have turned up with the boat, as we could barely afford a Coca-Cola. It was the kind of place where the boat owners had a huge shiny yacht in the marina and also a house on the waterfront where they slept, showered and blow-dried their hair. If you had to ask how much it cost, you couldn't afford it. We headed to a nearby waterpark and had an afternoon blasting down slides and swimming.

The children and I spent the next couple of days on the beach. Charlie passed as much time as possible at the boatyard. He wanted to make sure the work on the boat continued to progress. I reminded him of something said to us by a friend who owned a boatyard in the UK. They had a pricing structure with three bands; the first, standard tariff, for when they were left to get on with the work, the second tariff for if the owner watched the work being done, and the third, most expensive, for if the owner helped.

I was not enjoying staying in the hotel. It was soulless, we had to eat out all the time, which we could not afford, and because we were all in the same room, we had to go to bed at the same time as the children. It was not as clean as I would have liked and our neighbours were often noisy. I couldn't wait to get back on the boat.

At last the day came when we could move back on board. We checked out of the hotel, with, fortunately, most of the bill paid for by our insurance company, and put our bags in the Fiat. When we got to Mr Guidot's boatyard the main gate was closed. We still weren't accustomed to the siesta. The small side gate was open and I went through to see if I could open the main gate from the other side. I couldn't, so I went into the building. The lights were off and it was cool and dark after the brightness outside. Mr Guidot came out of his office. He put a large hand gently on my bare arm and looked into my eyes. His dark brown eyes searched mine. Seconds passed. I felt a wave of heat, hurriedly asking whether he would open the main gate so that we could bring the car inside, closer to the boat. He smiled and backed away, leaning over to press the switch behind the desk. I thanked him.

CHAPTER 40

It was a relief to be back on Keoma again. We were home. Mr Guidot had said the repair would take 10 days and he had been true to his word. Our boat was floating in the small dock. An hour later a dusty van drove slowly through the gate, from which windsurfer boards and rigs were reverently unloaded. We stayed there overnight, and ate my Anglicised version of spaghetti bolognese in the open air. Mr Guidot came to see us to say goodbye. We invited him aboard but he could see we were about to eat. He seemed a sad lonely figure as he walked away, and we called after him with grateful thanks for all he had done.

In the morning we motored the boat back to the old commercial quay and went ashore for provisions. The children begged for one last visit to the night market, so we stayed. One street was lined on both sides with stalls selling nougat, leather goods, carved wooden ornaments, colourful clothes, candle holders, jewellery, and many other things. We dawdled, browsing the stalls. Charlie chose a frog carved in dark wood. It felt tactile in the hand and made a croaking sound when a stick, taken from its mouth, was scraped along its ridged spine.

We listened to the weather forecast on the radio. This was difficult to decipher because it was in Italian, and there was a numbering system for conveying sea states and wind in the ten or so different areas. It was often necessary to listen for a long time until our sea area was announced, and the voice was so repetitively mesmerising that it was hard to stay focused. Perhaps the forecast told us that there would be a force 7, but it was such a perfect day and we were so longing to get on the move again, that we set off. We weren't going far. The sail down river was perfect, bowling along with Keoma's effortless speed, and we emerged into the sea, then headed north along the coast.

Later we watched dark clouds welling up in the distance. They came towards us very quickly and the wind hit like a bullet, flinging the boat over on her side, until the lower rail was in the water. I released the genoa and wound it away, flapping, until there was only a handkerchief left. I wanted to leave a little of the foresail flying, to balance the boat. If there was no foresail the bow could have a tendency to point up into the wind, as the back of the boat was pushed away by the force of wind on the mainsail. It was a heavy job to wind it away, and it took me a few minutes to get the sail reduced. Next I climbed up to the high side and, bending over to hold on to the manrail with alternating hands, I moved forward to the mast. Clicking the boat onto autohelm, Charlie also moved forward, to the cam cleats at the front of the cockpit. We reefed the mainsail, to around half its previous size and the boat began to sail nicely in the strong wind. With the wind came waves, so the boat was now pitching up and down and Alice was feeling seasick. I cradled her in my arms and tried to comfort her. She sat quietly as I stroked her hair, then, without any fuss, detached herself and knelt down on the cockpit floor. Charlie removed one of the wooden boards covering the drain. He used the deck shower to rinse it all away down the drain. I took her down to her cabin, where she lay down, teddy held close, and went straight to sleep. It was a well-practised routine by now.

Back up on deck, Pip and Charlie were enjoying the conditions, grinning as the boat bounced on the waves. We were close to the Maddalena Islands, and heading for a bay called Cala Portese. A wall of rain was fast approaching. There was no time to grab waterproofs before we were hit by the blast of water. It wasn't cold, but rather like a warm shower. By now we were coming into the bay and putting the sails away. There was only a small amount of genoa to furl. Charlie switched on the engine as I released the mainsail halyard, dropping it into its bag. The bay was dotted with yellow buoys and we motored for a free one. I was on the foredeck with the boathook, pointing to the buoy in the water to give Charlie more idea of where to steer. Water was sluicing off my nose and my clothes were saturated. The fresh water on my skin felt fantastic. I picked up the buoy and the rain began to assuage. As the visibility expanded, we saw a familiar boat; the other Keoma. They must have thought we were following them around. They cast off the buoy and motored out of the bay, without waiting for the rain to stop.

Alice was up on deck now, laughing and spinning around in the wet. It had been so long since we'd seen proper rain, we were relishing it. We put up the spray hood and used it for shelter as we changed out of our wet things, before heading below for towels and dry clothes. Then the metallic clunk of the kettle being placed on the hob. Teatime.

The bay was beautiful but constantly windy and it rained often. There was a group of maybe twenty people who were probably in their late teens, staying on six yachts of around 24 foot long. The boats looked very basic and I could imagine they were damp inside. The group took the boats out sailing every day, practising their boat handling on courses rounding buoys and sailing out to sea. They returned and rafted up together in the evening. We heard them singing and playing music, clearly having a great time, constantly soaked.

One afternoon when it was dry for a couple of hours we went ashore for a walk. We climbed up the hill at the side of the bay, over rocky terrain. The view from the top gave a perfect picture of the bright blue water interrupted by odd shaped islands. There was a bothy on the top of the hill, full of graffiti. Charlie windsurfed for hours every day. I woke at night and breathed in deeply; the sweet smell of rosemary filled the boat, wafting down from the hills around the bay. We spent time on the beach and took short walks. I felt unsettled and was ready to move on. We tried several bays around the Maddelena Islands; Cala Brigantino, Golfo di Salina, Porto Punta, and Cala Massimo but the "Caribbean of Europe" did not yield anywhere that was sheltered from the fierce winds of the Bonifacio Straights. I felt pummelled, dried out. It was never calmer than force five, and usually more like force six or seven, and we were still having trouble deciphering the weather forecasts.

CHAPTER 41

We cast off the mooring and headed for Corsica. Before we left England, a friend had advised Charlie, "Don't miss Bonifacio". The wind was whistling along at force seven in our faces as we came into the channel. The journey would be around 15 miles, taking into account the need to tack. There were several small groups of islands that we had to avoid, or else meet the same fate as many seafarers before us in these waters, and Charlie went below to plot us a course that would minimise the number of tacks. The sea was rough but we made good progress. We had only the staysail and the mainsail with two reefs in, and Keoma was well balanced. We passed a red- and white-striped lighthouse. They were a rare sight in our home waters, and I enjoyed the reassurance of this beacon. It provided an immediate reference point, which helped navigation, as well as telling us that the rocks were over there and not too near. In the distance a geological phenomenon was coming slowly into view. White cliffs on a massive scale. Limestone that built and dropped in dramatic swirls and curves like a huge meringue. Closer in, we saw tall houses perched precariously on top, and then a ferry turning a corner and disappearing into the cliff.

The entrance was a narrow gulley between towering walls of rock. To our right, way up high, we saw the town fortifications, and then ahead, a collection of pontoons and boats of all descriptions started to unfold. An imposing castle loomed above us. I picked up the radio transmitter and began to negotiate a berth. We were now in France and suddenly communication was so much easier. A boatman approached in his inflatable dinghy, standing up. He was in a smart uniform of navy shorts and polo shirt, and now we saw that there were three or four of these individuals operating in the busy harbour. He helped us to dock the boat. It was rather a frightening procedure because the wind was so strong from behind. With no bow thruster we would have been out of control in seconds, but the boatman used his dinghy to push Keoma's bow into the gap, and then it was full reverse, all the fenders out, me jumping ashore as early as possible to push with all my might against 13 tons of boat keen to demolish the pontoon and anything else in its way.

We were in need of a drink by the time we were settled. Sitting in the cockpit, sipping a cold glass of Italian wine, we took in the surroundings. The high sides of the gorge were lined along the base with shops, restaurants, and further away from the water, houses. To one side, high up, was the castle fortress, square and imposing. A superyacht was reversing into the far end of the harbour, where the water came to an abrupt stop. The anchor was down and we could hear chain reeling out as it reversed to tie up the way we had in Giglio. Keoma was a very average boat here.

Later, we went ashore for dinner. We were ready to shake off pasta and pizza, although these were widely available. Tonight, we were going French and enjoyed white fish in a classic French sauce, with rice and a perfect salad. Two children sat with their parents at the table next to ours, although it was late, and I thought of how rarely we had eaten out with ours in England, especially in the evening.

In the morning Alice and Pip were determined to buy some croissants. They came into our cabin to ask if they could go off on their own. We decided that since the bakery was very close and it would be a good opportunity for them to speak some French, they should go. It was a blissful few more minutes in bed. Charlie got up and put the kettle on. He made some real coffee, using the plastic jug and sieve method that we had become used to. It seemed wrong to have a cafetiere on a boat. The children returned with croissants and baguettes. Pip was in awe of her sister, that she could speak French. We sat in the cockpit and enjoyed our breakfast, in the perfect sunshine of early morning.

There was plenty to do. Charlie wanted to get the watermaker sorted out, and he bought metres of tubing to replace the pipework that had been ruined on passage to Sardinia. I hit the local supermarket to replace the provisions we had consumed over the last couple of weeks in the Maddelenas, wheeling the ancient trolley over the jolting cobbles and uneven slats of the pontoon. I wasn't sure the eggs would survive. In the afternoon we all walked up to the castle and enjoyed hours of wandering through the ancient streets. We strolled along the famous cliff walk, where the views of the sea were uninterrupted. Enormous lumps of limestone had, at some time, detached from the cliff and plunged down to the water below. Some projected above the water, one balanced dramatically on one corner, a parallelogram 100 metres high, the rock deeply scored from the ravages of wind and water. Some lay at different depths beneath the water, creating a mosaic of aquamarine colours.

We walked down 187 steps, said to have been built in 1420 by the army of the King of Aragon while attempting to invade. It was tough walking up again in the searing white heat. We learnt about the numerous sieges of the town, one lasting for over a year, and we saw the dry wells in the ground where meat and flour had been stored. Finally I got to the laundry, with massive bags of dirty clothes, and a big purse of change for the washers and dryers. While the wash was on, I headed to the internet café and updated our website. It took twice as long as usual because the keyboard wasn't a "qwerty" layout. A few of the keys were in different places. Who came up with that idea?

CHAPTER 42

The following morning we made our escape, heading for a small river around ten miles from Bonifacio. The place we had identified as our next stop was called Pianottoli-Caldarello. We waited with a handful of other boats while one of the gigantic ferries departed and another entered. They passed each other with only a few metres to spare. I was enjoying a coffee made with real milk (recently we had been limited to UHT) as we motored through the narrow gorge. Coming out into the open sea we downed the last of the coffee, pointed the bow into the blasting wind and hoisted the sails. We sailed up the west coast of Corsica, and soon saw the wide flat entrance to the river, edged with rocks. A beautiful Norman castle stood near the entrance and our pilot book advised us to anchor just off. I was keen to go ashore here and visit the castle. But we could not get the anchor to hold. Again and again I dropped it over the bow and let the chain run. When we had let out three times worth of chain, Charlie put the throttle into reverse to test it. Bump, bump, bump went the anchor over the riverbed. I watched the chain bouncing. We tried with more chain. Still no success. Even more chain. Each time the anchor came up it was draped with weed. We concluded that the weed might be causing the anchor to slip over the seabed, preventing it from getting a hold. We gave up and I went below to consult the pilot book for alternatives.

Further up river the channel became very narrow and we followed it carefully. At a bend in its course we stopped. The book had told us we could anchor here, tying our stern line to large rocks ashore. We immediately got a good hold and Charlie swam ashore to attach the stern line. Keoma seemed very close to the river bank and I passed him his mask to check the depth. He concluded that the mud banked steeply, but far enough from Keoma's rudder not to be of concern. He swam to the front of the boat and inspected the anchor to see how well it had dug in. Pip was in her swimming costume, keen to get to the little beach that was just off our stern. Arms and legs flailed as she leapt into the water and swam for it. The sky was a little overcast and I wasn't tempted to swim in this silty river. Two bright yellow sea planes zoomed over, only just above Keoma's mast. They were coming in to land on the river, and practised landing and taking off again. Noisy, but interesting to watch.

In the evening a motor boat anchored near us. I woke several times in the night, sticking my head out of the hatch to check it hadn't swung towards us, resenting them. It was so still that the crickets on land sounded very loud. But the morning was windy and just as we were finishing breakfast it gusted strongly and we noticed the boat was being swept sideways towards the beach. The anchor was dragging. We couldn't motor off because the stern line was attached still and we were reluctant to lose a good piece of rope. Charlie started the engine, still with breakfast bowls and plates on the cockpit table. He released the stern line, throwing it overboard, well away from the propeller, as I went forward to wind in the anchor. Then I dived overboard and swam for the shore. I untied the line from the rock and swam back to the boat, now safe in deep water, holding the end of the line. The wind flicked small waves in my face. It felt like a long swim and the boat was huge in the water as I neared her. The swimming steps were not down and Charlie couldn't reach them from the helming position. I managed to push myself up high enough to reach the backstay with my hand, then heaved myself up onto the platform, where I sat, puffing, and pulled in the rope, coiling it up. The children were putting away the breakfast things. I showered off the salt and got into dry clothes, as Charlie pointed the boat down river. Once out on the sea we headed north, for another place we had read about in our book, only fifteen miles away, called Campomoro, a little further up Corsica's west coast.

CHAPTER 43

Another rough, short, sail and we were entering a huge bay and then turning right again, into a bay within the bay. The water flattened and I saw a crescent of perfect white beach. The high sides of the bay were studded with houses and there was good shelter from the wind. We anchored successfully. Yachts were only allowed to stay in one small part of the bay, and we were required to land in a particular place, a long distance away from the anchorage. Charlie pumped up the dinghy and placed the outboard engine carefully on its stern, back arched and arms sinewy as he screwed tight the clamps that held it in position. We stepped off the swimming platform into the dinghy as Charlie switched on the small motor's fuel, checked it was in neutral, turned the throttle to line up the arrows and pulled the rip cord. It was Alice's turn to drive and she drove at full speed. We reached the landing area and Charlie raised the propeller of the outboard as we jumped out into shallow water, all gripping the rope that was attached in loops along the dinghy's air tanks, pulling it up the beach away from the water. To preserve the bottom of the dinghy we lifted as well as pulling it forwards. The sand was fine and silky, like talcum powder between my brown toes, and as we emerged from the water it cooked our soles.

The exit from the beach was lined with palm trees, giving the place a Caribbean feel. Walking up the slight hill to the village's main road, we saw a post office and an épicerie, where we stopped and bought some fruit and a bottle of water. There was local wine for sale here at 2.30 Euros a bottle. In places the road was shaded by large trees and between these havens the heat was severe.

Back on the beach, we sat and ate the plums. There was not enough wind for Charlie to be interested in windsurfing. I took "Billy" out of my bag for a read. When the day cooled we picked up the items that we had scattered around; buckets and spades, towels, bits of windsurfer rig, books, and suncream. The dinghy was lifted and pulled back into the water. I held the boat steady in the shallows as the others climbed in and Charlie lowered the propeller of the outboard into the water. It started first time. I climbed into the dinghy and we were off, Pip at the helm, gunning it.

The following day we walked to the castle on the headland. I wondered to myself whether the days of being on the boat, where we did little walking, made it more of a treat to use our legs. The children ran on ahead, until they heard dogs barking fiercely along the rusty wire boundary fence of a roadside property, and then they scuttled back to us. The view from the top of the castle was 300 degrees of blue. Far beneath we could see Keoma, a toy boat.

Back at ground level Alice and Pip clambered around the rock pools, pointing out things of interest.

"Look, there's a crab in that one."

"Here's a sea anemone."

"Don't tread on it!"

Pip's skin was golden, her face dotted with freckles, but Alice was deep brown. Wandering past a jetty we looked at a fishing boat tied up, and decided this would be a good place for a meal ashore. On Keoma, the children put on their snorkelling gear for a swim. Recently Alice's fear of swimming in deep water had developed into a paranoia and Charlie was keen to cure her of this by getting her to look through her mask. "You can't spend the whole year *not* swimming," he said. She bravely agreed to give it a try. Charlie jumped into the warm water and waited for her by the steps. Shakily, she descended the ladder, then pushed away, limbs pumping frenetically. I threw in some small pieces of crust.

The bread was like a fish magnet and they arrived in their tens. She watched them through the mask and visibly relaxed. The tense sudden movements of limbs ceased and she breathed through the snorkel, becoming almost still, just a gentle flick of her fin or slight hand movement as she was enveloped by that underwater world. Emerging from the water her face was lit by a smile. She said excitedly, "The fish are amazing! And I could see the sand underneath the boat and the anchor chain."

When we'd dried off and changed, the school books came out. I was concerned about the lack of progress and we'd decided to make a real effort to do two hours of school a day. The children did all they could to avoid school, from the obvious, like taking a long time to get changed and not being able to find a pencil, to more subtle methods like being slow with their work, teasing and bickering with each other and claiming they were hungry. It was difficult to motivate them without peer pressure. When we told them they would be behind their classmates when they returned to school if they didn't do the work, Alice replied, "But we'll have learnt so much from the trip that we'll actually be ahead." We told them they still needed to learn things like spellings and times tables. The whole process put me on a slow boil of anger, and often ended in shouting. I caught Alice hiding her school books under the mattress in her cabin and I was furious. She replied, "I wish I had a proper teacher and not an, an, an abnormal mother!"

I opened my mouth to reply, but no sound came out.

Charlie stepped to my defence. "That's totally uncalled for and very rude. You mustn't speak to Mummy like that. You are going to be in big trouble if it happens again. Apologise to her."

"Sorry Mummy," she mumbled.

CHAPTER 44

Keoma lay peacefully at anchor for our entire week at Campomoro. I suspected that the anchor wasn't even used, since whenever I swam around the boat the chain seemed to be dangling over the bow, slack, some chain piled on top of the anchor, the weight of the chain alone sufficient to keep her stationary. We slept like babies, catching up all those broken nights, the hatch wide open above our faces. One night I woke and looked up to see an orange light high above us; Mars.

The following morning we watched the lifeboat leaving and a helicopter clattered overhead. We talked to people on the beach about it and they confirmed what we had feared. Someone had been lost at sea. Alice and Pip were grimly wide-eyed.

We ate lunch at a small table, sitting under one of the big trees, taking a break from the sun. The épicerie sold delicious salads, bread and olives, and we all tucked in, washing it down with plenty of water. In the afternoon we were back on the beach, the children collecting sea washed glass for a local woman who was making a collage. The previous night we had left our shoes on the beach by mistake, but they were still there when we came back this morning, four dusty, scruffy pairs.

Back on the boat, Pip placed her first lost tooth under her pillow for the tooth fairy. Charlie switched on the phone to find a text message from Victoria, saying it was the end of the summer holidays and she was going back to her teaching job tomorrow. I thought of our children and felt burdened by the responsibility of schooling them ourselves. What would it be like when they returned to school in a year's time? Would they be trailing their classmates?

We were starting to feel it was time to move on, and after the bread run in the morning, we did the washing up and wound up the anchor. The next port of call would be Ajaccio, Corsica's main town and a total contrast to Campomoro. Motoring through windless conditions, we trailed fishing lines fruitlessly. Upon arrival, mid-afternoon, we moored Keoma in the old town marina and went for a walk. There were perhaps 100 statues of the town's favourite son, Napoleon. According to our tour guide, he hadn't been proud of his birthplace, where he had spent the first nine years of his life. In fact, he was embarrassed about his provenance. But the Corsicans were not to be shrugged off and they embraced him at every opportunity. We walked past the house where he had been born; a tall square townhouse painted a mottled orange colour, with shutters of green peeling paint. It was said to have a secret passage leading from the cellar, which was the reason the family had escaped the lynch mob, and fled from the island, when he was a child.

We ate at a bistro overlooking the quay. Earlier we'd watched the fish being unloaded from the fishing boats and the boxes carried straight in to these restaurants, as it had for centuries. The fishermen sat on the quay mending their nets, the twisting rope spread out across the concrete.

In the morning I was focussed on provisioning the boat. Ahead of us lay our longest voyage yet. It was 230 miles to Menorca, which was likely to take us three days, and I was feeling a little apprehensive. At the far end of the quay a market had been set up. I was thinking of the market we saw in Olbia, which was beautiful but no use for buying food, and I expected to have to trudge across the town to a supermarket. As we entered the tented area the first thing I saw was a greengrocer's display. It was the longest stall I had ever seen and packed with brightly coloured vegetables. The classic summer foods of red, yellow, green and orange peppers, tomatoes, courgettes, aubergines, salads of all tones of green and pink, cucumbers, avocados, and on and on. A man in a beret filled a large bag for us. A beautiful lady with long dark curls hanging below her red gypsy headscarf caught our eye. She had a stall selling cured meats and laid snippets out on a wooden platter for customers to taste. We tried several, including the donkey meat, then bought a round parcel of pork tied up with cloth and string. The sample had been delicious and I hoped the piece we'd bought would be as good.

Nearby was a smell that we couldn't resist. Roast chickens on a spit, and we bought two. Next was a stall lined with small wooden vats of olives, and we bought four different kinds. Cheese, bread, olive oil, lurid coloured sweets for the children. Some wine and dried herbs. I stopped to admire the spice stall with twenty rolled-top sacks filled with exotic coloured powders. The only thing we couldn't get was milk, even UHT, and Charlie went to a nearby shop for that.

At 1.30pm, having eaten delicious hot greasy roast chicken stuffed into small baguettes, we motored out of the marina. Looking back at Ajaccio, the old town was at the forefront, with terracotta roofed churches, buildings and towers. Further back were modern white plastic tower blocks. The old and the new. Next stop Menorca. The wind was a light north-westerly beam reach, and Charlie set the autopilot to follow the course I'd programmed into the GPS. The children grudgingly did schoolwork and then watched a DVD as a reward. We spent a couple of hours on deck all together, eating supper, and then it was their bedtime.

CHAPTER 45

Charlie and I took it in turn to stand watches through the night. I wasn't sure why, but he found it much easier than me to be awake for 3 hours and then sleep for 3 hours. I began to feel as though I was badly jetlagged. He seemed to find it no problem. I hoped I would acclimatise to it.

At around 4.30 am Charlie woke me up. I had been fast asleep but I could tell by his voice that it was urgent, so I ran blearily up the steps in my pyjamas. "Get your camera!" Through the pink light of dawn I saw a pod of six whales very close to the boat. They glided serenely away. My camera clicked repeatedly. "I couldn't work out what it was in the water," he said. They were certainly big and I hunted for the book to check what exactly they were. I found it; the long flat head was a classic feature of sperm whales, but they were sleeping on the surface, so we didn't see the tail-lifting dive for which they were famous.

That afternoon we hoisted the spinnaker, which had become a friend now, and we called it "Big Blue". There was no sign of land, sea all around, hazy at the edges, a light breeze, and virtual silence. Just the occasional tinkle of water against the hull.

Another night at sea, alternating on and off watch. I was struggling with tiredness and forced myself to stand up as a way of staying awake. I was surprised at my body's reaction to this. My legs gave way beneath me as I dozed off. I was seriously tempted to wake Charlie early but, with extreme effort, I held myself back, telling myself that he needed rest, too. Occasionally I saw ferries and other small boats, and wondered whether they could see Keoma. Sometimes I had to change course to avoid them and I would then adjust the sails, shining the torch on them to see whether they looked right. I felt like we were invisible to ships and hoped this might help let them know we were there.

Another beautiful morning dawned and we saw the low line of Menorca in the distance, a cheering sight. Suddenly a dolphin leapt high in the air next to the boat. It was soon joined by three others and they swam, fast and energetic, at the bow. The water was a sparkling rich blue and the dolphins scythed through it, twisting on their white sides to look up at us with one eye. The boat was churning along, spinnaker up, autopilot on, and all four of us at the bow, brown feet on the hot teak deck, peering over the side.

Mid-afternoon we entered the river which lead up to the island's main town of Mahon. Structures with a shabby military look, built of the local faded pink stone, stood at intervals along the banks on either side. A stretch of wall interspersed with cannons, then a square building with columns, topped by a red and yellow Spanish flag, a building that looked like a large warehouse, in ruins, with trees and scrubby dark green bushes in between. A few houses started to appear, and then docks for boats lined the river in front of the buildings. Now we saw houses and restaurants, in a terrace. The river was widening and we headed for a man-made floating island in the centre, with yachts moored stern-to around the outside.

The bow line was attached to a thin rope called a lazy line, that was hooked over a post on the dock, and I had to do as in Civitaveccia; while Charlie reversed Keoma close to the island, I picked up the lazy line and held it, hand over hand, as I hurried to the bow, where I pulled the mooring rope as tight as I could and then, keeping the tension on, attached the rope to the cleat on the bow, threading the line under the pulpit, through the fairlead first. Charlie allowed the boat to drift forward slightly so that I could get the bow line good and tight, before he reversed against it and then we picked up the stern lines. I ran back to take one of these and attach it. We had given the children the job of "roving fender". In advance, we had attached six fenders; three either side. The other two fenders were taken by Alice and Pip and their job was to watch to anticipate where Keoma might touch another boat or the dock. They were not so good at the "watching" part of this, and would be looking at someone on the dock or on another boat, but they did leap eagerly into action when Charlie or I called them to go to a particular part of the boat. They held both hands high, gripping the fender's rope, to carry this tall, cumbersome plastic sausage, and it bounced against their shins as they shuffled along.

Once the boat was tied up we paid the very efficient dockmaster and pumped up the rib for a trip into the town. The architecture was Mediterranean, the buildings painted a rich ochre, tall bell towers dotted around. A wide swathe of ornate steps led up the hill to the town centre. Alice and Pip were desperate for ice cream, which was easily solved when we reached the first shop. We wandered through the streets, looking into the windows of the shops and bars. I was relieved that we had completed our first two night voyage, with no mishaps. It felt as though we were still just beginning to learn about the boat and how to sail her, but to have come this far was encouraging, and we chatted about the whales and dolphins that we had met.

CHAPTER 46

A couple of days later we motored out of Mahon harbour with a strong southerly blowing. I was keen to go south because there was a cala that I was interested to visit, but we knew it would be very windy and exposed in these conditions, so we decided to sail north, up the east coast of the island. The anchorage was behind Isla Colom, named after Christopher Columbus, and the bay was edged with a moonscape of black rocks. Some of the rocks were crunched into tiny sharp-edged pebbles, and some were enormous squares piled up on top of one another. The shapes seemed so geometric, I wished I understood geology. Exploring ashore, there was another of the round towers like the one we saw in Campomoro, but this one was not in good condition. There was a large hole in the ground and the walls were cracked. It looked quite unstable, perched on the edge of the steep cliff. I was looking out of the window, across to the boat, where Charlie was doing some jobs on board.

"Oh no! Mummy! I've dropped my camera down the hole!" It had gone down into the ground and I couldn't reach it, even when lying flat on the dusty floor. Alice had tears welling. I daren't get down into the hole because I was worried about the floor collapsing on top of me. I had a hand held VHF radio and I called Charlie, who patiently agreed to come across in the rib to help.

He brought with him a collection of useful things; the boathook, fishing rod and line, fishing net, torches. Using a torch we could see the camera in the hole and he managed tenuously to hook its thin strap with the fishing tackle and slowly reel it in. With a big sigh of relief the dusty camera was returned to Alice and the tears ebbed away. Outside, we climbed up and down the big boulders and enjoyed the view from above sea level. A line of black clouds was heading our way, and we ran for the rib, launching it quickly. We reached Keoma as the first big drops of rain splashed on her deck.

This variable weather became a feature of our stay at Isla Colom. The next morning dawned bright and hot, and we put on snorkelling gear and swam in and out of caves, over and around rocks, and under large overhangs, admiring bright purple corals and schools of small silver fish. Pip liked to swim right next to me when she was snorkelling, so our bodies were touching, making me feel like a mother whale with my calf. We swam back to the boat for breakfast. An hour later the barometer was dropping rapidly, with a dark sky approaching. Charlie and Alice had gone out in the rib, fishing with lines. There was a rumble of thunder and I could see lightening, and a band of rain sweeping towards us. I saw the rib, approaching at full speed, with Alice at the front and Charlie helming, bent into the angled rain, heads down. They were soaked and laughing. Alice was wearing a pair of orange bikini bottoms and a turquoise headscarf and her body looked like varnished wood. I was expecting them both to run for cover, but Charlie was reaching for his board. He wanted to take it out while the wind was strong. But it took him ten minutes to rig the windsurfer. The wind had been extinguished by the heavy rain by the time he was ready.

When the rain stopped we fancied a change of scene and moved Keoma across to the anchorage on the island side of the water. We went ashore for a walk along the beach and up to the top of the island's ridge. Underfoot was solid black rock, to which no plants had managed to cling, and the rock was deeply scored in straight lines. Coming back down to the beach, it was a surprising colour; a real contrast to the black rocks. I would describe the colour of the beach as ivory, but on close inspection, many of the grains of sand were actually bright pink.

The following morning Alice was fishing before breakfast. She and Charlie were becoming obsessed. Despite the hours spent and the different techniques employed, they were yet to catch a single fish. We knew there were fish in the Med because we swam with them every day. They were just too clever to take our bait. Suddenly she was standing in front of us holding up a small silver fish, a type of jack, shaped like a child's drawing of a fish and graduated silver with a black spot around the size of a two-pence piece just before the tail. She was smiling broadly. The first catch. Perhaps our luck would change now.

Later that morning I wound up the anchor and we set sail for a huge inland lake with an eponymous town next to it, called Fornells. Apparently the locals pronounced the name "Forneys". We passed the black- and white-striped Cabo Favouritz lighthouse and rounded the north east corner of the island. The weather was bright sunshine, but we had experienced so many sudden thunder storms recently that I didn't feel relaxed. We turned into the narrow channel that was the entrance to the lake. The entrance had a castle on one side; a perfect look-out point for defence against pirates. There were several unoccupied moorings and we tied Keoma to one. It was a slightly dangerous thing to do because the owner of the mooring might return at any time, and it was possible that they would simply cast Keoma adrift.

We dinghied ashore to explore the town. As usual, we ended up at the castle. Pip's national curriculum course included the study of castles. I hadn't realised how many there were in the Med; at some time in history it must have been a hotbed of unrest. This one had been beautifully restored and there were interesting booklets printed in four languages, including English. Walking back, we passed modern brick houses, painted white, then stopped to buy some provisions in a local corner shop.

CHAPTER 47

The next day we made our way to the island's south coast, to the place that I had been itching to visit, an inlet which, according to our pilot book, was considered by many to be the most lovely cala in the Balearic Islands. The weather still looked a little unsettled to me, but perhaps it was always like that here. On the way there we accidentally dropped one of the fishing lines overboard. We could see the hand reel (a chunky version of a reel used on a kite) floating in the water, but couldn't tell exactly where the line was lying, and there was around a hundred metres of it loose. It was tempting to leave it there, but it would present a hazard to wildlife and other boats, plus, line was expensive. We had to manoeuvre the boat close under sail; we didn't want to use the engine in case the propeller got the line wrapped around it. The propeller could only be de-snagged when the boat was stationary in calm conditions and someone could dive beneath.

We had several attempts at getting the boat close to the hand reel. Charlie was helming and I leant over the side. It wasn't easy because the waves were quite large and erratic and it was a long way down. I had to hold on to the man rail with my left hand and lean far out over the water, thighs on the deck. Finally, fingers at full stretch, I got a purchase on the reel. I took it into the cockpit to begin the job of winding it in. It made me think seriously about how difficult it might be to recover a person from the water, especially if they had been knocked out or were hysterical.

We arrived close to the entrance shortly after lunch. At least, our GPS was telling us we had arrived, but we couldn't see where we were supposed to go in. It looked like an unbroken cliff ahead of us. We furled the sails and motored gingerly closer. I went below to look at the chart plotter again. "It should be straight ahead," I shouted up to the cockpit. We ventured closer. Gradually, an entrance began to show. It was well hidden and tiny. I wondered whether we would be able to turn the boat around once we were inside. As the interior was revealed, we saw high pink-tinged grey cliffs all around the edge, pitted with rows of black holes. The pilot book explained that these were caves, rumoured to be 150 of them, dating from prehistoric times.

Inside the cala it was very quiet, warm and sheltered. We dropped the anchor and reversed towards the cliff, then Charlie swam ashore to attach our stern line to a large ring set conveniently in the rock. I tightened it up from the cockpit, winching it tight, and the boat was secure. Charlie was a little concerned that if the anchor should drag, the boat would hit the cliff, so he took our spare anchor, an old fashioned fisherman's anchor, from one of the lockers and attached a line to it. We had only one chain, so this anchor would have to be attached with rope, and he found an old piece of thin red rope that had been a halyard in a former life. He rowed out in front of the bow, where he dropped the anchor, and then tied the other end of the line to a cleat on the bow, tensioning the line as much as he could. It was blisteringly hot and the flat blue sea glinted invitingly. One by one we plunged into the cool water.

Some of the caves had ancient-looking faded paintings in them. Others contained tired matresses. We climbed to the top of the cliff and I stopped to photograph Keoma lying peacefully at anchor beneath us in her tiny patch of bright water, an oasis in the rock. We agreed it would be a magical place to spend the night. Back at the boat I dived off the side again, swimming down, down, down, through the cool crystal water, then turning to look up at three pairs of legs waving above me.

In the evening we sat in the cockpit with a glass of wine, enjoying the spectacular high rock walls and the gently lapping water, and then ate supper at the big table below. While we were eating a slight swell developed and slowly increased. We realised that the wind had veered and was now blowing directly into the cala, which was having a funnelling effect. The breeze was building, now pushing the waves in, which hit the cliff behind us and rebounded against the stern, lifting the back of the boat and then jolting her forward. Hopefully the wind would continue to swing and peace would return. The thought of moving the boat, negotiating the narrow rock entrance and ploughing out into the blackness, lurked in my mind. If conditions worsened, we would have to make a decision.

The boat began to buck around alarmingly. We became worried about the anchors. The children, perhaps sensing that it was best for them to be out of the way, climbed quietly into bed, as Charlie and I sprang into action. The priority was to let the stern line off and get the boat away from the wall of rock close behind us. Again, we had the dilemma of whether to abandon the rope, but it was the longest one we owned. Charlie stepped down into the pitching dinghy, standing as he pulled himself along the rope, hand over hand, towards the rock wall. As he disappeared into the noise and darkness I felt alone, responsible, even though he was less than ten metres away. Above the sound of the raging elements, I heard him shout, "The rope's too tight! I can't undo it!"

"Cut it near the knot!" I screeched. He always had a penknife in his pocket.

"It's cut!" He was holding the end of the rope and I pulled with all my might to get him back. In seconds he leapt onto the swimming platform and tied the dinghy to a cleat.

I ran forward to get the anchors up. Our main anchor would be hoisted by the electric windlass, but how was I going to get the other one in? That skinny red rope wouldn't be long enough to reach around the windlass. It was under immense strain. I wanted Charlie to stay on the helm because his boat handling was much better than mine, especially in a confined space like this cala. I grasped skinny red. It felt taught and wire-like in my fingers, as though it could slice through them like cheese. But I stood up and pulled with everything I had. Charlie had slowly motored the boat forward, feeling the way until I was standing just above the second anchor. "Stop now!" I bellowed at him above the sound of the whirling water. The boat pitched up and down, the surrounding rocks closing in. I had an enormous sensation of power as I felt the rope yielding. The anchor must be breaking out. The adrenaline release was like electricity coming from my spine, through my shoulders, as I pulled, and I kept on pulling. I couldn't feel my fingers, numb with tension, but ten slow seconds later I had the anchor on the deck. I felt like an Amazon. "First one is up!" I shouted over my shoulder as I pressed the button down on the windlass for the other. This one was an easy job, mechanical. The chain ground as it retracted.

"Both up now!" I called over my shoulder. Charlie motored the boat forward into the building waves. I couldn't carry the second anchor back to the cockpit locker in this weather, it was so cumbersome. I lashed it down. It had to be tied securely or it would grind into the wooden deck. I knelt, being thrown up and down, and did my best to tie it with the red line, but it was like a fairground ride without any restraint, and I was feeling physically drained. I steeled myself. I couldn't give up. As soon as I had done a temporary job I crawled back to the cockpit. Charlie donned a lifejacket, clipped on the harness line and headed to the bow to retrieve the anchor. I was on the helm now and we were out of the cala but the waves were worryingly steep. It felt as though the boat was climbing at an angle of 45 degrees as we headed up the oncoming waves, and I pushed the throttle forward for more power. Into the black night. Now I had time to reflect and I felt afraid and small in that large cockpit. The only consolation was that the children were in bed. How could they could sleep through this?

My hands gripped the suede covered steering wheel, knuckles white and fingers like claws, my calves pressed back against the locker beneath the steering seat. We'd never been through such waves. They seemed endless. Were we making any progress or were we being washed backwards towards the beach? I was craning my neck to try to see Charlie on the foredeck, but it was too dark and I needed to devote full concentration to the helming. I prayed he was still there. I didn't even know where I was going. I remembered, from when I had sat before the chart plotter earlier in the day, that there were no hazards in the area, and I started by taking the waves square on, with the intention of putting as much distance between us and the island as possible.

At last, I saw Charlie returning, bent over as he held on, moving slowly along the side deck, the safety harness attached. My knuckles loosened slightly. Gradually, the waves began to reduce, and I assumed this was because we were moving into deeper water. I turned the boat in a slow curve to the left, until we were running parallel to the coast. The next question was where to go now. Charlie took over the helm and I descended into the calm of the cabin, where I sat at the chart table consulting the screen for an up to date position, and the pilot book. I concluded that the only solution was to head back to Mahon. It was 24 miles away but easy to access, being buoyed for the cruise ships, and we had the confidence that we knew where we were going, having been there before. I plotted the course on the GPS, using our old waypoints. I clicked the button to activate it and then put on foul weather gear and headed back up to the cockpit, into the wind and spray.

Surprisingly, it turned into a lovely sail, a beam reach with medium sized waves. We came into Mahon at 2.30am and were amazed to see that the wooden island was crowded with people, who helped with our lines. Loud music was playing from the other side of the water and we were told it was fiesta time. There was definitely a carnival atmosphere on the dock as we cracked open a few beers and chatted with our neighbours. The perfect way to wind down after the night we'd had.

CHAPTER 48

Mid-morning, the harbourmaster arrived. We told him we had arrived that morning, which wasn't entirely untrue. Given that he charged 60 Euros a night for berths, we didn't feel so bad about it. We motored across to the town in the rib to do some shopping, and found some English newspapers. It was our first real news in weeks and the headlines were dominated by the wedding of Jordan and Peter Andre.

The town was very quiet, which we put down to the busy fiesta nights. The fringed decorations criss-crossing the streets flapped in the wind. We wanted to leave Menorca the following morning because a friend had left a message on our phone that he had just arrived in Majorca for a week's holiday.

At around 9.30am, having eaten breakfast and washed and stowed everything in its correct place, we motored out of Mahon and set sail for Majorca, a journey of around 30 miles. Earlier, we had listened to the Spanish forecast on the radio and had understood that the wind would be a gentle breeze, but the sea state was "agitated". In fact the sea was calm and the wind light and flukey, veering in direction and then dying away. All was peaceful on board.

During the afternoon I noticed an enormous black cloud, which seemed to be approaching fast. Within five minutes it was quite close and I suggested to Charlie that we should put the sails, the full mainsail and genoa, away.

He said, "For goodness' sake Juliet, just calm down. I don't think we're going to get much wind with this."

I felt furious, pent up, wanting to shout at him. I knew I was right. I felt he was putting us in danger *and* brushing me off like a panicking idiot. But, I did not want to frighten the children, so I held back from saying anything. It took a lot of self control. The skin on my chest, arms, face, stomach and calves felt tight, too tight, as though the anger had physically bloated me. I held it in, twisted it up, screwed it down. A minute later our attention was drawn to something over the port side of the boat.

About 100 yards away was a waterspout, a meteorological phenomenon where water was sucked up from the surface of the sea in a type of mini tornado, and it signalled that the weather was about to get extreme.

"Oh, actually, it *is* going to get windy," he said. I grabbed the furling line for the genoa and channelled my anger into pulling as hard as I could. Even using this level of energy, it took around 10 seconds to furl it all away. We were now in a strong wind. "Get the children down below!" Charlie shouted through the maelstrom. I wanted to get started on dropping the mainsail but I didn't want them outside, so I ushered them quickly down the companionway steps. Just as my feet touched the cabin floor there was the loudest sound I had ever heard and I waited to hear the mast crash down. It was actually a huge crack of thunder and simultaneous bright white flash. The boat rolled onto her side like a dog. I was gripping the steps behind me and the children lay on the floor. The windows along the port side were under water. Fortunately they were closed. Mortal fear had swept away my anger, but I didn't want to traumatise the children, who, so far, appeared, bizarrely, to be unfazed by the situation.

I looked up at Charlie, struggling to hang on and steer, bombarded by pea-sized hailstones, greyness all around. The boat slowly started to come upright again. Suddenly there was another massive crack of thunder and flash of lightning and the boat lurched violently again. I was gripping the steps to stay upright, but trying to look happy and relaxed. I pressed the molars at the back of my mouth together firmly. Pip said, casually, "Mummy, I'm not enjoying this." It was as though she was asking me to change the channel on the television.

I summoned the calmest voice I could, to reply. "Not to worry, darling, it will all be over very soon." It came out sounding quite strained and unnatural, but still they didn't seem to notice.

Another twenty seconds passed. Pip said, "What on earth is Daddy playing at, anyway? Can you tell him to stop it?" I thought about what to say in answer, then the boat swung upright again. As if a switch had been flicked, the hail stopped and we were in sunshine. Majorca lay ahead of us, beneath a clear blue sky. I remembered Pip's questions and laughed out loud.

We motored through the narrow entrance of the bay, Charlie speaking to Simon on the phone, arranging where to meet and getting advice on the best spot to anchor. Much of the bay was too shallow for Keoma, so we had to take care to find somewhere that was easily more than 2.2 metres deep at low tide, taking into account changes in wind direction that might make the boat swing around the anchor. We found the place he recommended and put the anchor down. As usual it took a few attempts to get the anchor to bite, and even then we were not entirely confident. We set the anchor drag and wind speed alarms, and placed one walkie-talkie on the chart table nearby. This meant that if any of the alarms went off, the walkie-talkie in Charlie's pocket would let us know, and it made us feel happier about leaving Keoma.

By the time Charlie had pumped up the rib and put the outboard engine on the back it was starting to get dark and the lights of the town looked inviting. At full speed we ribbed across to the town quay, weaving in and out of moored boats, all holding on tight to the dinghy. It took around five minutes at full throttle. Alice tied the painter rope to the ring on the wall with a confident bowline knot and we walked unsteadily up the concrete steps and towards the line of restaurants.

Five restaurants stood side by side, with tables and chairs spilling out onto the pavement. Charlie spotted Simon and his family, and they waved as we headed towards him. Simon had his three daughters, two sons-in-law and grandchildren with him. There were eight of them. After our harrowing day, combined with hunger and thirst, plus the strangeness of spending time with friends, I felt as though I was looking in on the conversation through a glass wall. For the last two months we had spent nearly all our time together as a four. Simon put us at our ease with a glass of white wine. We gave a rough sketch of our day but didn't dwell on the horrors of the afternoon. Charlie was explaining to Simon that somehow the batten that stiffened the bottom section of the mainsail had flown out during the storm without us noticing. The batten ran horizontally from front to back of the sail and measured around four and a half metres. We had to replace it and Charlie asked whether Simon knew where we could get another. Simon had a telephone number that we could try in the morning. He asked how strong the wind had been. "I saw the wind speed gauge register 55 knots when the boat was right over on her side," said Charlie. I refilled my glass.

At the end of the evening we arranged to meet on the beach the following day. We climbed into our dinghy and motored slowly back to Keoma, the town shrinking away to fairy lights.

CHAPTER 49

In the morning we swam to look at the anchor. It hadn't dug in particularly well; only two of the three prongs were in the sand. But the conditions seemed settled and we could watch the boat from the beach. We went ashore and enjoyed being sociable. It struck me how insular we had been for the last few weeks, and how we had enjoyed each other's company despite being in such close confines and stressful situations. I went for a swim with Pip. She wanted to get out to the diving platform a short way off the beach, and we began to swim towards it. But there were two women standing on the platform gesturing at us to go back. Suddenly I realised why. I saw hundreds of jelly fish in the water; small transparent mushrooms with purple veins in the centre. We turned back but Pip had already been strung and she was in tears as we walked up the beach. I sat on a beach lounger with her on my lap, a towel wrapped around her, comforting her while Charlie went off to find the lifeguard for an antidote. He returned with a small tube of ointment, which he rubbed on. "The lifeguard said we could only use this once. Not sure why. Maybe he was just making sure we returned the rest of the tube."

Simon invited us to his house in the evening and we knocked on the door at six. Jemma answered, welcoming us in. Simon was in the kitchen. "Have you heard the news?" He asked. We looked back blankly. "England have won the Ashes!" The mood was celebratory as wine was passed around and later we ate an incredible vegetarian meal cooked by Simon. The children were invited to stay the night. For the first night in two months, Charlie and I went to a bar without them and as a result we were out until 4.00am celebrating with the other Brits. We woke in the morning at Simon's house and I felt terrible about abandoning Keoma on anchor. I rushed to the balcony with a feeling of guilt and fear in case she had taken offence and slipped away in the night. She was still there. Relief. Hangover. Simon made us porridge, an excellent settler for the stomach. This was always Pip's cereal of choice. Even when the heat was 35 degrees centigrade, and we were sweltering, she would ask me to make hot porridge for breakfast.

The following day we invited the whole family for lunch on Keoma and we delved in a locker to retrieve her flags. For the ARC we had to have a full set of code flags, which were attached together (in the correct order) and this line of flags was hoisted from the centre point, on the main halyard. One end was then attached to the bow and the other to the stern, making the boat "dressed overall" which was a long standing naval tradition and gave a sense of occasion. We had not tried our flags out and so used this opportunity to do this. I made my speciality; mini pizzas, now a practised and perfected boat recipe. Except that I forgot about them while they were cooking and some from the back of the oven were a little charred.

CHAPTER 50

Another day a group of us went for a sail on Keoma, taking her to the nearby Cala Arsenau, where we anchored and swam. Some of the party travelled in Simon's small boat and they took our first photos of Keoma under sail. We had received emails from friends asking to see the boat sailing.

We had been reading in the guide book about the nearby Cabrera Islands, around 20 miles from Porto Colom, a nature reserve which may only be visited if a permit had been obtained in advance. We filled out the forms and faxed them off from the local grocery store. This small shop had a good selection of locally grown vegetables and various "deli" hams and cheeses, as well as olives. We had bought a lot of our food from here and they recognised me now. They gave me a free apron with the name of the shop on it. I was delighted, since it would protect me from hot fat spitting from the frying pan onto my bare stomach when I was cooking in a bikini.

Later that afternoon we went back to the shop, to discover that a response had arrived, approving our application and granting us three nights at Cabrera on mooring 24. That evening we were sitting in the cockpit, in the windiest conditions we had experienced in Porto Colom, when a local man approached in his motor boat. He told us that it would get very windy in the night, and suggested a sheltered place to move to. I was quite unwilling to move, as the anchor had held fast so far, but since he had taken the trouble to motor out and inform us, we felt it would be sensible and polite to take his advice. The spot he had suggested was rather shallow, but we anchored nevertheless. Later we lay in bed listening to the wind howl through the rigging, longing to abandon ourselves to sleep the way we could when we slept in a bed ashore. But it was hopeless; the best we could achieve was a kind of doze, which felt like sleep with one eye open, and then the wind alarm sounded. We both jumped up. The anchor was dragging.

I ran up to the foredeck and Charlie turned the ignition key. As he put the boat into gear and slowly motored forward, I engaged the windlass and wound up the anchor. We moved to a new place, maybe 20 yards ahead of where the anchor went down before and tried again. Charlie put the boat into a slow reverse, to allow the anchor take the strain and dig in. I hoped desperately that it would hold, but it didn't and we had to wind it up and re-set it again. Again, it didn't set. It was the early hours of the morning and we were in a howling gale in our pyjamas, we'd had no sleep and felt totally despondent.

I had a sudden recollection that there was a small marina in the corner of the bay. We took turns in going below to consult the pilot book. We also looked at the depth here, which we were not happy with, especially as there were now waves in the harbour. I was bracing myself for the crash of the keel hitting the rocky bottom when we dropped into the dips of the waves. Again the anchor came up and we motored for the marina, which was deep enough for us provided we could find a space near the end of the hammerhead. By luck there was a suitable space and we dropped the anchor and reversed slowly in, using fenders to keep us off the leeward boat beside us. This end of the bay was more sheltered, although there were still some small waves, but it was much better than where we had been before. We peeled off sodden pyjamas and towelled ourselves down, before dropping into bed.

CHAPTER 51

The following day it was still rough and windy, overcast with rain at times, and we postponed our visit to Cabrera. We talked to the man who managed the marina and he agreed that we could stay where we were for another night, prompting a sigh of relief that we didn't need to move the boat to another berth. We paid him. Anchoring was free, but we didn't fancy another night like the one we just had. We hired a car and drove inland, to a rain-lashed market in the centre of a picturesque old town. We weren't in the mood to buy anything, so we just looked at the stalls and falconry display and then stopped at a café for coffees and hot chocolate.

I was quite concerned and depressed about the trip so far. It had fulfilled our expectations in that we'd visited so many beautiful and interesting places, while spending quality time as a family, but we had had some nasty experiences with the boat and I was not relishing the idea of more of the same. In particular, the thought of an Atlantic crossing was a malevolent presence at the back of my mind.

I explained my feelings. Charlie looked down at the rustic table. He was quiet for a moment. He looked me in the eye for a few seconds, then said, "I know you might not agree with me, but I think the Atlantic will be much easier. We should at least give it a try. What about sailing down to the Canaries and seeing how that goes. Also, we could still email Nick and Amanda to see whether they would come with us on the Atlantic crossing." I felt a little less downcast, and we paid the bill and left, asking where the closest internet cafe was. We stopped at a steamy, crowded place a few streets away, and emailed Nick and Amanda, as well as updating our blog. We had experienced some extreme conditions in the Med, but I wasn't convinced that it would be easier in the Atlantic. I kept thinking of the vast distances involved and imagining huge waves.

After a siesta and an evening meal I was feeling more positive. We played cards in the saloon with the children. It was a rainy night but the boat felt cosy and secure. Alice was hopeless at playing cheat, always accusing others of cheating, when they weren't, and incapable of keeping a poker face when she was cheating. She struggled to hold most of the pack in her small brown hands. The following morning we would be off to Cabrera. There were only two nights remaining of our permitted stay but we were still keen to go. I lay in bed listening to the rain pattering on the glass hatch above my head.

The weather looked threatening the whole way there. At one point dark clouds welled up ahead and we feared another thunder storm. We immediately furled the sails, but it was nothing more than rain. I took the children below and left Charlie to get wet. Soon we were motoring in through the narrow entrance. We found mooring number 24 and picked it up, then ate lunch down below. When we emerged after the meal, the sky had cleared and we were in bright sunshine. The decks were dry. It was the most idyllic natural harbour, protected by high rocky walls, with a castle near the entrance topped by a huge Spanish flag, and a handful of other scrappy buildings.

We went ashore in the rib, tying it up to the wooden dock, and trudged up the hill to the castle. As we climbed the hill we heard frequent scurrying of tiny feet and looked to see black lizards of around 20 cm long, running for safety. A leaflet told us there was a particular species called the Balearic Lizard, which only lived in Cabrera. The summit gave us a view of the islands, topped with dark green foliage, and edged with a golden pink rock. The sea was a bright blue, graduating to aquamarine near the rising land mass of the islands.

Somehow, wild flowers flourished in the arid terrain, and I stopped to admire them and take close up photographs. Life must have been a struggle for them but they grew in abundance. I was gripped with an urge to photograph the lizards, an interest which had started on our first big walk at Tiscali, and I stalked them. I wanted to have pictures of their intelligent, inquisitive faces to study later, close up, and to capture the way they ran, spine flexible, bending in an "s" first one way and then inverting, legs moving in supple harmony.

After the walk we were hot, and stopped at the small shop to buy some ice lollies. Delicious coolness rolled over my tongue, sweeping the dust and fuzz away. There were a few national park employees and students here, but apart from them the place was almost deserted. The following day we went to the beach, the perfect crescent completely ours. Charlie strode off for a longer walk, to the lighthouse at the other end of the island chain. We were supposed to ask permission to venture off the designated route, but he ignored this rule and there was no-one here to enforce it. Sitting on the beach with the girls, we saw large fish swimming right at the water's edge. Alice wanted to go back to the boat to get her fishing rod, and I explained to her that no fishing was allowed here, because of the nature reserve status of the islands, and looking at the sea life, this rule seemed justified. Wading out into ankle deep water we saw a moray eel, an incredible find so close to the shore. It showed its ugly, green, angry face, like some miniature incredible hulk, and we kept our distance. We saw sea anemones with long green tentacles, tipped with bright pink. Alice and Pip went rockpooling and collected shell and stone treasures. They begged to take them back to the boat but we had a strict rule on this. All Keoma's floors were polished and would be badly scratched if shells and stones were walked into them. I firmly suggested they leave these beautiful things for other people to enjoy. They gave me a look that said they didn't give a stuff about other people, which I ignored. At last Charlie reappeared and we wandered back to the dinghy.

CHAPTER 52

There was no wind as we motored towards Palma. The water was flat calm. We sat beneath the bimini shade, an essential shield against the scorching sun. Unexpectedly, the engine stopped. Charlie went down below to investigate. He removed the engine casing and poked about. I unfurled the genoa but it just hung there. We were completely stationery. Charlie closed the engine up again, replacing the companionway steps. His voice was a little incredulous. "We've run out of fuel." I was annoyed. We would have to wait out here until the wind filled in, which could take hours, and then we would have to sail the boat into the marina. It would be very difficult to manoeuvre in a confined space under sail alone, especially as we were unfamiliar with the place.

"How could you let this happen?" I asked tetchily.

"It's ok, I've got a jerry can."

I deflated. He walked to the aft locker and removed a can full of diesel, then lifted the slatted wooden floor cover and unscrewed the fuel cap, and sloshed diesel in.

"I'm glad it's flat calm. This could be a hell of a job in waves," he said.

But the engine still wouldn't start. Charlie pumped the small handle on the engine to bleed the new fuel through. We were still stationary in the water, and I was casting around for another boat to radio for a tow. The nearest was a fishing boat. I was dreading having to try to speak to them over the VHF in Spanish. Charlie persevered with the pump. After a while he stopped and loosened a clamp on the fuel line, which did the trick of allowing the fuel through. To my relief, the engine fired.

Motoring into Palma, the city was surprisingly bland, with a long stretch of modern white buildings along the seafront. The marina had line after line of superyachts, which looked stunning. We headed to a dock called Pier 46, which was supposed to be less expensive. It still cost an extortionate 100 Euros a night, and that did not even include shower facilities. The dockmaster joked that we could use the hose to have a shower, while standing on the dock, which I did not find very funny, considering the amount we were being charged to stay there.

"Mummy, stop it," said Alice.

"What?" I asked.

"You're giving him *the look*."

"What *look*?"

"The one you give us sometimes."

We knew we would have to stay in Palma for at least two nights in order to get everything done. We needed to collect the replacement batten for the mainsail and we had decided to buy another as a spare, in case we had a similar incident mid-Atlantic. We needed to buy sewn canvas to make sea berths so that when the boat was healed over, two people could sleep comfortably side by side in a double bunk, without rolling onto each other. Charlie spent time measuring and sketching the design and then headed to a specialist to have it made up. We also needed deck cushions, since the long passages, particularly the night ones, had been hard on the bottom. We wanted to buy a light for the top of the mast that was red and green, as a back-up navigation light for when we were at sea. Our bow light, being quite close to the water, could be vulnerable to removal or breakage by strong waves, and was not as visible from a distance as a masthead light would be.

The other vital item was a Navionics Gold card. This was a plastic card that we inserted into the GPS chart plotter to give us detailed chart data on a particular location. We had the card for the Western Mediterranean, which we were currently using, but it did not provide coverage of the Canary Islands, where we would soon be heading. We had decided not to buy traditional paper charts of every place we visited, because they were expensive and difficult to find, they took up a lot of space on the boat, and generally we had found that the GPS data was more detailed and just as accurate.

Searching for these things was very dull for the children. They hated hanging around chandleries. Their boredom behaviour usually started with them picking up things which they would ask us to buy. We would tell them to put them back. Then they would play hide and seek in the shop. They would try to tickle us and then when all this failed, they would lie on the floor and roll around, arms and legs flailing.

I took them for a walk around the city while Charlie scoured the chandleries. The cathedral looked incredible from outside, tall and golden with intricate gothic stone masonry, but the officials at the door would not allow any children to enter! We met a man dressed as a Viking, complete with horned helmet and plaits, but sprayed bronze like a statue, and the children posed for a photograph with him. I put a Euro in his pot. We headed back to the boat, where I dropped the children off with Charlie, then I went to find a supermarket on my own, since these ranked as even more boring than chandleries for the children. I waited for a bus for half an hour in the heat. In the end I flagged down a taxi. The supermarket was enormous and had made a feature of having an "English" aisle selling Marmite and Bisto. From being hot and sweaty outside I was now freezing cold in this giant fridge. The hairs on my bare arms puffed up for warmth.

When I had paid and loaded up the trolley again, I asked the women on the "customer services" desk to arrange a taxi for me. They made a phone call and then told me I must go up to the top floor of the building to await the taxi. There was no lift, so this involved taking the overflowing trolley up an escalator. I had to hold the front wheels on the step, lifting the heavy back end of the trolley up and holding it there, back wheels suspended. Then I bumped the trolley up and down kerbs and repeatedly ran around it, to stop it rolling off downhill. I reached the waiting area and heaved the heavy trolley to a halt. I waited in the sun's glare for fifteen minutes, the food, and me, heating up rapidly. I was beginning to wonder whether the taxi was coming, and to think about how I would get the trolley back down to customer services to organise a taxi that *would* arrive. Given the trial I had had to reach the taxi pick-up point, I wondered whether I had misinterpreted the instructions and gone to the wrong place. Surely this didn't happen to every person who shopped here without a car. At last my taxi arrived. Thirty plastic bags went in the boot and I couldn't be bothered to take the trolley back, I just abandoned it there on the pavement. They didn't deserve it.

We drove the mile or so to the marina and stopped just outside the metal security gates at the entrance to our pontoon. I had to leave most of the bags on the sun baked concrete of the car park while I waited for someone to exit the security gate so I could get in (I had given Charlie our entrance card). I walked down to the boat to find Charlie to ask him to give me a hand with the bags. He had been wondering what had happened to me, but realised it was best not to pursue this line of enquiry. Instead he told me to put my feet up while he unloaded and stowed the food in the cupboards and impossible fridge. It was too hot to have a cup of tea, so I had a cold beer.

In the evening we went out for tapas, which the children loved. They especially liked the small green "surprise" peppers that we first ate in Majorca. Mostly these peppers were sweet and delicious, but approximately one in fifteen was hot and we watched each other closely to see who was pulling a face and reaching for the water.

In the morning Charlie went to collect the canvas for the sea berths. They were not ready and he was told to return later, which he did, only to find they were having their siesta. Third time lucky.

CHAPTER 53

After a restful night's sleep we were off, bound for Ibiza or perhaps Gibraltar. It was a beam reach and we zipped along. We passed the southern tip of Formentera in the dark, close enough to see disco lights flashing, but we didn't stop. The pilot book had discouraged us. It seemed that every stopping place I looked at had the commentary; "This was once a lovely anchorage but sadly it has been ruined by over development of the cala." We were enjoying the sail, effortless beam reaching. So we sailed on.

In the morning I was feeling the effects of a broken night. As usual, Charlie was bright eyed. The wind became light and progress slowed. We crept along through flat silver water, stretching as far as the eye could see, until it reached the sky. It was another hot day but the sails were still gently filling, pulling the boat along.

During the day we kept ourselves busy. A tiny bird perched on the man rail, turning its head from side to side as it took in its surroundings, and then it flew below. It perched on top of the chart of Giannutri on the wall in the saloon and had a good sleep. The children did their school work and then I read to them. We were all enjoying the Famous Five. Some of the speech just had to be read in a 1950's BBC voice. We were sitting beneath the bimini, the boat moving slowly through the water, when there was an unfamiliar scraping noise near the back of the boat. I stopped reading and we all looked aft. Quietly, as if not wanting to break the spell, Charlie said, "I don't believe it. We've caught a fish!" He wound the line in and slowly the fish was dragged towards the boat.

"It's a big one Daddy!"

"Don't lose it off the line!"

The fish was a medium sized tuna, and would be perfect for our meal that night. Charlie carried on winding. The fish was nearer now, mouth wide open, clearly in distress. There were only a few inches between the fish and Charlie's hand now and he lifted the last piece of line up so that the tail of the fish cleared the man rails. It was still alive but exhausted. I emerged from the cabin with the vodka bottle and unscrewed the cap. I tipped a drop into the tuna's gaping, hooked, mouth. It flicked its tail, body taught for a second and then the fish went slack, hanging loosely on the line. The children were wide-eyed with excitement and pride, as they posed, holding the fish up high, for photographs. I passed Charlie a chopping board and knife and he gutted it. I laid it on a baking tray. In the cabin I bent down to light the gas of the oven, fiddling with the lighter, one hand pressing and turning the knob of the cooker, and then slid the fish tray in. I boiled the kettle to cook some potatoes and chopped up tomatoes and cucumber for a salad.

Twenty minutes later we were eating the fish. It didn't get much fresher than this, and it tasted delicious. We sat in the open air, squeezing lime juice on the brown fleshed fish. The sun was still warm, low in the sky, and it promised to be another beautiful night. We didn't even consider putting on more clothing; t-shirt and shorts would be sufficient. The little bird emerged from the cabin and flew away. It hadn't eaten anything and seemed to be flying too close to the water.

I hoped it would be alright. It had left us some lucky on the map's glass case. I would leave it there for now.

CHAPTER 54

I was on deck alone, the rest of the family asleep below. The sky was so full of stars; if I looked closely there were stars in the gaps between the stars. The moon was full and I had a great feeling of contentment. I felt completely at ease and was relishing the peace and solitude. The boat was steering herself and all I needed to do was check the sails and watch for ships and items in the water. Even my bottom was now comfortable, seated on our new deck cushions.

In a split-second a double neon warhead screeched through the water towards the boat. I didn't have time to digest what was going on, but instinctively braced myself for the impact. I waited to hear the sickening tear of fibreglass and metal. But there was no explosion. On the other side of the boat two dolphins leapt out of the water, high in the air, synchronised. As they re-entered the water their bodies became sheathed in what looked like a pale green, close-fitting, veil. It was caused by phosphorescence in the water. They leapt and dived, cutting stripes through the water, all at great speed. Sometimes they swam so their dorsal fins broke the water's surface and it looked as if their fins were giving off white sparks. More dolphins streaked in and my head felt like it was on a swivel trying to watch them all. I shouted to Charlie to come and see, not wanting him to miss this amazing display. The dolphins played around the boat for maybe an hour; an extraordinary, uplifting experience.

When they left us, I headed for bed, feeling as though I would be asleep before my head hit the pillow. But I rolled around in a turmoil of sleeplessness, lying there as the cabin started to become lighter. The children got up and I might have been asleep by now but I could still hear conversations. It was as though my senses wouldn't all fade out together.

It was day three at sea and there were a few clouds on the horizon. It wasn't the solid blue sky we had yesterday. We'd covered 270 miles and had another 200 still to go to Gibraltar. As the day passed the weather and sea state deteriorated, the wind strengthening and swinging so that we now had a beat. We winched the sails in tight and the boat healed over, pounding the lumpy sea. It wasn't cold but we were in the mood for soup and I braced myself in the galley as the cooker swung on its gimbals, watching the soup slop back and forth in the pan. I put out "magic mat" to try to keep the plates and cups from sliding off the work surfaces. It felt like the cups of soup and buttered bread took half an hour to prepare.

In the early hours of the morning the scene was not a happy one on board. Alice had been seasick several times and was now confined to her bunk. The rest of us were tired and uncomfortable, and we decided to make for the port of Almeria, where there was a marina, for some rest before we embarked on the final 24 hour sail to Gibraltar. We motored into the marina at 4.00am, tied up on a dock near the entrance and slept deeply until 9.00am. Then we were off again, keen to get going. The Harbourmaster didn't charge us for five hours there and helped us untie our lines as we departed. The sea was calm and we had a beam reach again; next stop Gibraltar.

We made good progress, with speeds of 8 or 9 knots for most of the day, and in the afternoon we saw the hazy outline of "the Rock" from fifteen miles away. A thick cap of cloud hovered directly above it. A pod of dolphins appeared on the starboard side. They did not approach the boat to play, and then we noticed dolphins approaching from all directions. There must have been hundreds of them, arriving in groups of five or ten. Charlie had a theory. "I think they are hunting. I've read that they swim around in a circle and create a kind of wall of bubbles, to confuse the fish. Then they circle closer and closer, to get the fish trapped together, and then they eat them." They were circling very fast and it seemed purposeful; there was an energy, an excitement, to the movement. I wondered whether any fish would leap out of the water in an attempt to escape the hunt, and I watched intently but this didn't happen, the surface remained smooth and even.

Just as quickly as they had arrived, the dolphins dispersed. We continued to close in on Gibraltar. As we came into the lee of the rock we started the engine and a large, high-speed rib, approached. A very polite soldier asked if we could clear the area because they were waiting to perform a parachute drop. Charlie opened up the throttle and we motored away as fast as we could, heading towards the marinas. The sky was striped in orange, pink and purple, a dramatic backdrop to the silhouetted warships and tankers moored in the bay. We looked back to see a heavy black aircraft spit out a single parachutist, a tiny shape against the vivid colours.

It was dark by the time we entered the marina and we were keen to get the boat tied up and to eat something hot. Charlie radioed the marina office and asked for a berth. We could see many empty spaces as we waited. But we were told they couldn't accommodate us, and they suggested another marina to try. We followed the lights out and tried the other marina. They couldn't fit us in either, as they were hosting a regatta that week, and they told us the third marina was closed for refurbishment. I just couldn't believe our bad luck. I had expected Gibraltar to be well served with facilities, being the major port at the entrance to the Med. We were advised to anchor. The prospect of finding a space in the anchorage in the dark and then getting our anchor to hold was not a welcome one, but we had no choice. We had to stop here, to plan our exit into the Atlantic, which had to be carefully timed. We finished anchoring at 9.30pm, and I still had to feed the family. We were short of fresh food after four days at sea and the meal was a strange combination, neither healthy nor tasty. But at least I'd fed them something.

CHAPTER 55

Loud beeping in the middle of the night woke us. It felt like we'd only been asleep for 30 minutes. We stumbled around, disorientated, at last switching off the alarm on the chart table control panel. I flicked the anchor windlass switch on the panel and grabbed a torch. When we got up the steps the blasting wind hit us and it was clear the anchor was dragging. Charlie reached for the ignition key and I ran to the foredeck, a well-practised drill by now. The wind was howling. I pressed the switch to hoist the anchor. Several attempts to re-anchor later, we finally got a hold, and headed back to bed.

In the morning Charlie went ashore in the dinghy. He negotiated with the woman in the marina office, explaining that he had a young family on board. Eventually she relented and agreed to let us have a berth for two nights. We moved the boat into Queensway Quay marina. There were superb hot power showers and laundry services. We used tons of water. In the afternoon I took Alice and Pip up to the top of the rock, while Charlie hunted for the elusive Navionics Gold card. We paid £2.50 per person to board the cable car. Alice said, "Isn't it nice to be using English money again." At the top there was no view because the cloud was too low, and on the seaward side of the rock, the cloud poured up over the lip like dry ice.

Dirty brown monkeys with yellow teeth were dotted around. From time to time we heard screams as one jumped on the back of an unsuspecting tourist. Pip was nervous, saying, "I don't want one of them jumping on me," and we tried to keep away from them. We didn't even like the freaky tiny babies. I bought soft drinks and some crisps in the smoky pub and we decided to sit outside to have these. As soon as we were out of the door an alpha male monkey ran up to Pip, teeth bared, and scratched at her jeans with his filthy pincer hands. She cried out and dropped the packet, which he grabbed and ran away with. He climbed onto a low wall and tore the bag open, putting them into his mouth one by one, his actions so human. We walked along to St Michael's caves. These contained enormous stalactite and stalagmite structures. One chamber was large enough to have been made into a concert hall. It was believed that these caves extended beneath the Med to Africa, and had provided the monkeys with their passage across the sea when they first came to settle in Gibraltar.

We boarded the cable car to descend to sea level. Back at the boat, Charlie was unhappy. "The people here are unbelievably rude," he said. He had not been able to find the Navionics Gold data card. "I did buy a litre of whiskey for £5, though."

Alice was bemused that so many people were out jogging. We concluded it must be something to do with the military base.

I was looking forward to a rare night of unbroken sleep, without night watches or the anchor dragging. But, at 2.00am we were woken by incredibly strong winds. We had inadvertently left the wind alarm on and it sounded. Charlie got up to check the lines and bring in the last of the laundry that had come back from the service wash slightly damp. It had been pegged to the manrails, flapping. He noticed some activity on a nearby boat flying an Australian flag, and raised a hand in greeting.

The following morning we met the family on Whitehaven. Rob, tall, with George Clooney looks, was very amusing about his first impressions of Charlie. In his soft Aussie accent he said, "The night winds here are unbelievable! We keep losing stuff overboard. At 2am last night I was wrestling with some towels on the foredeck in my underpants and I looked over to see Charlie in his underpants doing the same thing!" Rob and Kerry had two daughters, and we invited Georgia and Emma to come and play. It had been like a long time since our children had socialised with their own age group, but they seemed to get along well. They threaded beads and chatted shyly.

Later we went to the supermarket. There was a Somerfield here, a British chain, and we bought real English sausages and bacon, which we had not eaten for months. It was comforting to recognise the cuts of meat on display. I bought two china cups. Charlie was disapproving, saying they would be smashed within days. But I was determined to have them. They only cost a pound each and I was sick of drinking plastic-tasting tea and coffee. We loaded everything into a taxi, enjoying the ease of communicating with the driver in English, and returned to the marina. After unloading the shopping, we went into the marina office to see whether we could negotiate more time in the marina. Kerry advised us to take the children in with us. But the woman was intransigent. We had to leave in the morning. I had hoped we could wangle a few more days, which would give us time to arrange for the Navionics Gold card to be couriered from the UK. But she gave us no choice, we had to leave. I was not prepared to spend another night in the anchorage, at the end of the runway. I would rather be at sea and navigate with charts and pilot books. The GPS would still calculate our position, so we wouldn't need to rely on the sextant just yet.

In the morning we took one last walk around the town. I bought some perfume, to replace mine, which had been stolen by the maids in the hotel in Olbia. Around mid-day we got ready to leave. Rob and Kerry helped us with our lines. "See you in Gran Canaria." Whitehaven would be following us south in a few days' time, with a crew of Rob's mates on board, headed for Las Palmas for the start of the ARC. Kerry had been organised enough to book the marina in Gibraltar several months before, safeguarding them against eviction for now.

CHAPTER 56

Earlier that morning we had checked the notice board for the weather report and we knew that the winds would be from the east. A tidal chart was pinned up which showed the straights divided into three bands, a northern section, a central section and a southern section, each around five miles wide. We motored out of the marina and headed for the straights, entering the northern section at the optimal time to enjoy a following tide as we headed towards the exit of the Med. The idea was to cross gradually into the centre band and then the southern one, before emerging into the Atlantic and pointing Keoma's bow south. These waters were not to be tackled if the wind came from the west, or the tide was against us. The combination of wind against tide could make that narrow stretch of water dangerously rough, especially when combined with the funnelling effect of the Med's narrow neck.

To begin with we were ghosting slowly along and in the light airs we hoisted the spinnaker. We didn't want to be going so slowly that we were still in the straights when the tide turned. Gradually our speed increased as we entered the central section of the tide. The wind built slowly and we were loving the effortless ride. There was plenty of shipping and we needed to keep a sharp look out to avoid collisions, frequently adjusting course. I kept the hand-bearing compass around my neck, so that I could keep checking the surrounding shipping. I felt a little disappointed that Africa was shrouded in mist. It was slightly eerie to think of that enormous, amazing continent so nearby, so mysterious. I kept looking across, hoping for a break in the whiteness. All the time the wind was rising, almost undetected. A collision course with a supertanker caused us to gybe. Charlie pulled the sock down over the spinnaker and then came aft to pull in the mainsheet. It was quite windy now and the full mainsail held a massive amount of power. We needed to be incredibly careful. The children went below. I started to inch the helm over, until the wind caught the back of the boat and spun us. As soon as I saw the mainsail come past the centre line, I turned the wheel the other way, full lock. The mainsail slammed across, the boat lurching over on her side, but the roll stabilised and I centred the wheel as Keoma slowly levelled out again, now on starboard tack. I reached for the hand-bearing compass again.

We felt confident to re-launch the spinnaker and I winched in the guy as the sock came off. The boat gave a rush of speed. In truth I was keen to get out of the straights, which were too busy with shipping for my liking. In retrospect, it was perhaps not a good idea to launch the spinnaker again. Some large waves came in from behind and we were careering along. It was exhilarating to feel the boat's power. As we neared the exit of the straights we expected the funnel effect to ease at any moment, so we carried on with the spinnaker. Then Charlie noticed the wind speed had reached 32 knots. This was too much for the spinnaker and if we carried on like this something would break. Getting it down was not going to be easy, though. Charlie went up on to the foredeck but as I eased the guy there was a problem. "Shit! We've got a wrap!" This was really serious. On being loosened, the spinnaker had gone into a frenzy and wrapped itself around the forestay. However, we knew what to do, because we had encountered this situation before, although not on a boat this size and not with just the two of us and not in the middle of one of the tightest shipping lanes in the world.

Somehow the atmosphere was controlled, calm. We knew that we just had to gybe the boat onto the other tack, so that the wind came from the other side of the boat. We did it exactly as before, ignoring the spinnaker. The pole would be on the wrong side but it didn't matter. Again I inched the wheel over, left hand down, down, down, down, down then hard reverse lock. The mainsheet flew through as the sail flicked across. We watched the wrapped fabric flap, flap, flap, over again, each flap unwinding the fabric, and when it was straight. Charlie ran to the foredeck, pulling the lines to get the spinnaker down. I clicked the autohelm on and let the guy and sheet run. It worked. I would have liked the sock to have come down quicker, but little by little, it came down. I watched for shipping, hoping we would be clear for a few moments longer. As soon as the sock was down, I called Charlie back. "We need to gybe again, there's another tanker bearing down on us."

Back on port tack, the boat was still surfing at 10 knots, with only the mainsail flying. At last, we found a clear patch in the shipping, and we sat down. Looking at the sail, Charlie noticed that our new replacement batten was poking out of the end of the boom. He thought he'd secured it but it was escaping. The wind was coming from dead behind, and it was strong, yet we had to winch the mainsheet in to remove the batten, or risk losing it. It was hard work and we worried about a destabilising gust, but we got the sail winched to a central position and removed the batten. We let the mainsheet out again and the rope flew through the block. Charlie stowed the batten down below, although there was no good place to keep it. At last we could take a rest, and look around. We were in the Atlantic. 570 miles to Lanzarote.

CHAPTER 57

Now we were in the open sea there was more room for everyone and we were no longer bothered by ships coming from both directions. We followed the coast on our left, gradually turning towards the south. I still couldn't see Africa, but I imagined that vast burnt continent just a few miles away. On our right hand side I had a sense of endless blue water, and Keoma was free as a bird, released onto the wide, wide sea, huge white sails spread out.

The instruments told us that the water was cooler here. The water temperature had read a consistent 30 degrees centigrade since the start of the trip, but now it had dropped to 24 degrees.

Feeling drained, I cooked sausages and mashed potatoes, which we ate in the cockpit. The children went to bed, and later, around midnight, I followed them. But the wind had dropped away to virtually nothing and the boat flopped around in the slight waves. Things clanked and banged with every movement of the boat and I couldn't sleep. Especially loud was the block which held the genoa sheet, crashing on the deck with every roll. I climbed out of bed and grumpily said, "Why don't you furl away the genoa and put the engine on, then at least it would be possible to sleep. The noise is unbelievable. Anyhow, all this banging can't be good for the boat." Charlie good-naturedly agreed and I lay in bed listening to the even throb of the engine.

I gave up trying to sleep and took over the watch. Charlie headed to our cabin and slept like a baby for three hours. Then he woke up, yawned and stretched, as though he'd had a full eight hours of silent slumber, and came up on deck to take over from me. There was still no wind, so he continued motoring and, finally, I managed to sleep for nearly four hours.

CHAPTER 58

During the day the wind picked up, as did the waves. They welled up behind the boat and then picked up the port side of the stern, raising the boat and then dropping her, in a corkscrew motion. Alice was seasick, but not unhappy. She sat in the cockpit eating a muesli bar. I put my arm around her. "Are you ok?" "Yes, I'm just going to be sick and then I'll finish this muesli bar." She passed the half eaten snack to me and leaned into the cockpit drain.

Towards evening the wind increased and the waves became more erratic. We took down the mainsail and used the genoa alone, slowing the boat down. The night was pitch black, with no moon. The waves seemed to be hitting the boat from all angles and I could not steer. Thank goodness for the autohelm, which did a much better job than I could. The ride reminded me of the "Black Hole" at Alton Towers. I could only sit there and hold on. What would happen if there were a hazard in the water? There was nothing I could do. Charlie had gone to bed saying we should see if we could hand steer because we needed to know we could do it, in case the autohelm broke. But I couldn't do it!

I saw two ships from afar but they were running parallel to us and I didn't need to change course. I was glad not to have to; the autohelm only needed a press of the button to change course by ten degrees in either direction, but the genoa would need to be adjusted and I really didn't feel like moving around the boat. At the end of my watch I went to bed and slept deeply. It felt heavenly and when I woke up there was bright sunlight. The wave direction had swung so that they were welling up directly behind the boat and propelling it forwards with a shunt. It was comfortable and fun, and we were all feeling relaxed. We ate cereal for breakfast and talked. We practised mental maths with the children. Mid-morning, the sky darkened and there was a partial eclipse of the sun. The waves were the same, but the atmosphere became quiet and strange. I was surprised how similar it felt to when I saw a total eclipse in England, soon after Alice was born.

Thinking back to that day, I recalled how the birds in our rural garden stopped singing, as though in anticipation of this seminal planetary event. My view was very different now, green hedges and fields replaced by a slate grey sea. The darkness now had a different quality to the fading light at dusk; it seemed somehow starker, blacker. I was surprised that we had not known there would be an eclipse today. Last time it had been all over the television, radio and newspapers, and generally impossible to miss. But we had not paid attention to any of those media in recent weeks.

Alice said, "We saw a jelly fish with a sail." I put this down to an over-active imagination, from too many hours at sea in a small boat. My raised eyebrows must have conveyed this, because she continued, "Really, Mummy, we did." Pip was nodding in agreement. I looked across to Charlie; he didn't believe it either.

The sun re-emerged. I'd taken over the helm and the children were writing their diaries in the cockpit. Charlie was sleeping. I was having a fantastic time with the big waves, which had spread out to distances of around 200 metres between each summit. When the boat was at the apex it was like looking down a mountain. I clicked the autohelm on and went below to make a cup of coffee. I put a cup of water into the kettle and lit the gas. I popped my head out of the hatch for a quick look around. I couldn't believe my eyes. A large ship was a hundred metres away, and I hadn't seen it until now. There was no risk of collision but I was shocked that I hadn't seen it. When Charlie woke I told him. He agreed that it was dangerously easy for ships to be hidden by these large waves.

Later in the day we caught a fish, which went into the oven. This one had flaky white flesh and a more delicate flavour than the tuna. The children followed their usual routine of going to bed around 7.30 pm, as we prepared for our night watches. For me it was a struggle to get enough sleep and I had a constant queasy feeling in my stomach from this lack, which was reminiscent of when the girls were babies. It didn't prevent me from doing anything, it was just that I didn't feel quite 100%. I knew I shouldn't complain, as Alice had far greater problems. She was seasick every day and she managed to ignore it. Charlie and I remained hopeful that she would find her sea legs.

CHAPTER 59

We travelled through the night with both headsail and mainsail up. The wind was much more constant than in the Med, where it would tend to die during the night. Here it just kept going. The waves had become smaller, now gentle rollers. We did not see any shipping. The only excitement of the night was that Charlie was attacked by a squid. The children found it on the deck, lying in a pool of ink that had stained the teak. Pip used her Tinkerbell ruler to measure this strange creature. It was around 20cm long. Charlie said, "Oh yes, I felt something hit my back and turned around to try and see what it was. I even got my torch out, but couldn't see anything in the dark. It must have leapt out of the water!" It was hard to imagine how something so small could have the power to jump that high. We talked about frying it, but by the time we found it, it had been out in the sun for a couple of hours. Pip threw it overboard.

When writing the blog, I found it difficult to describe the passing of time at sea. I wanted to let the readers know what it was like, but it was so hard to convey. I could never believe how little we did. We made meals and did schoolwork with the children. Sometimes this was activities like mental maths, which didn't require a pencil and piece of paper. Often I read to them. When it was rough, a malaise seemed to set in which meant that none of us talked much, or interacted. We just sat there, swaying with the movement of the boat, introverted. It was a time for thinking, for head space. Conversely, when we were surfing down waves we liked to hand steer and we whooped and sang, alert and happy.

Charlie noticed a dark line of land on the horizon. Lanzarote lay in the distance, under a cloud mass. We sailed into the cloudy skies as we approached. The winds lightened and progress was slow. A pod of curious pilot whales approached, their heads up, eyes out of the water as they looked at us. I was not totally comfortable with them swimming towards us, but they kept their distance. The sea became less regular and we were tossed around in the waves. Spotted dolphins appeared and lifted our spirits in the grey conditions.

Gradually, we closed in on the island, rounding the southern tip and furling the sails to motor into Rubicon Marina. Straight ahead of the entrance was the reception pontoon and a marina employee helped us tie up. Charlie went ashore to find out where our berth would be. Once we were moored up in our space, Charlie, Alice and I enjoyed a few hours of unbroken sleep. Pip did not sleep but she read and played quietly; very self-contained and considerate for a six year old. We woke and took a walk around the marina complex. It was silent and luxurious, with modern showers, restaurants, a supermarket and two swimming pools.

In the morning we downloaded and read our emails. There was a message from Nick and Amanda saying they were coming with us on the ARC. This was comforting; although we had enjoyed the sail to the Canaries and I had gained a lot of confidence, we had only spent four days at sea. It would be a different story to spend nearly three weeks out there.

There was also a message on our mobile phone that the mini-transat fleet was in Lanzarote, preparing for a race to

Brazil. These were 21 foot boats; tiny fibreglass pods with huge keels, that were sailed single-handed. We hired a car to visit the fleet, partly because one of the skippers was an old friend who we had sailed with a few years before. I was relieved not to have to drive, after so long off the road, and Charlie was happy to take the wheel. We drove to Puerto Calero, another marina around 15 miles away. It was less smart than the Rubicon, but had so much more atmosphere. The place was buzzing with sailors making their preparations for the 4,000 mile lone sail. Nick Bubb was not there; he was out sailing, practising.

We bought some sandwiches from the shop and drove up into the hills. The straight road cut through vast fields of charred earth clotted into ragged car-sized chunks, a barren, black, moonscape. It was hard to imagine how this topography had been formed. Charlie said, "It's so ugly, so awful, you would think it man-made." In a few places we drove through villages, where people had taken small plots and painstakingly broken the soil flat, then formed it into curved pits in which it was just possible to grow one vine. Often this had been done repeatedly and the earth looked, from a distance, like a huge, tarred, egg tray.

CHAPTER 60

We returned to Puerto Calero and waited for the skippers to emerge from their briefing. Nick seemed pleased to see us and told us that another friend, Geoff, was to arrive by plane that afternoon. Charlie phoned Geoff's mobile and offered to collect him in our hire car. We agreed to meet up with Nick again that evening and the rest of us drove to the airport. We felt like aliens inside the white plastic air-conditioned casing of the airport. As we stood in the arrivals hall I looked down; Alice was wearing flip flops, I was in dusty sandals and Pip had no shoes on at all. The pasty-faced English streamed through the sliding doors, but Geoff was nowhere to be seen. At last he appeared, carrying some extraordinary looking luggage. It was clear we were not the only people to fly with a spinnaker, although Geoff's was around half the size of ours. He also had a big wheel, around a metre and a half across, wrapped in fabric. It was replacement sail battens, which had been coiled as tight as he felt they would go without breaking. "I haven't been allowed to bring any clothes," he told us.

"What's in the holdall?"

"That's all Nick's dry food. They had a really good look through that at Stansted."

"We were going to offer you a berth on Keoma but I'm not so sure now we know you've not brought a change of clothes."

"Oh, not to worry – I've already accepted the offer of a sofa in one of the mini-transat apartments," said Geoff.

That evening we ate at one of Lanzarote's finest Irish bars, and enjoyed the ambience of Puerto Calero. The mini-transat skippers were partying hard, preparing for 3 weeks alone, with no alcohol and no sleep. We talked about their previous leg, from La Rochelle. It had taken seven days to sail to Lanzarote and Nick estimated that he had had a total of ten hours sleep. It sounded like very serious racing. The fleet had oversized spinnakers, which they flew even when it was very windy. His approach was to put on a harness and strap himself to the boat. He would sit in that position for hours on end, not able to use the autohelm when the boat was "on the edge". The times when he fell asleep at the helm, he would usually be woken up by the boat flipping on its side. They had enormous keels, so there was not really a danger of one turning turtle and staying that way, but they did semi-capsize.

CHAPTER 61

On Nick's last evening before the start he and Geoff came for dinner on Keoma. We had moved the boat to Puerto Calero and I cooked them roast chicken with all the trimmings. For some reason I had an obsession with Paxo stuffing. I'd bought ten packets of it in Gibraltar and it was lovely with these chickens. They were the smallest, skinniest chicken I had ever seen, and they came from the freezer in the marina shop. I was a little disappointed, since I had wanted to give him a really good meal before he embarked on three weeks of dried food. We had quite a few drinks, including the sloe gin that I had packed at the last minute into the crates we sent to Italy. There was a lot of discussion about the weather, and which course to take to meet the oncoming weather systems at the most opportune moment. Nick asked me whether I would take some photographs for a forthcoming article that The Times newspaper was interested in running about him. I agreed to take the pictures and email them to his agent.

The following day we took a close look at his boat. Alice and Pip were amazed at the size of it; below the space was roughly the same as one of their cabins. They asked him how he cooked and he pointed to the one ring camping stove. Alice asked him why he had a Barbie doll on board, strapped to the mast in the cabin. He laughed, blushing.

The mini-transats didn't have engines and they were towed out to the start line by ribs. Nick's was one of the first boats towed out and he experimented with his two headsails, to work out which would be the best for these conditions. The airs seemed medium, so he opted for his smaller headsail. This would be beneficial when he hit the acceleration zone winds that he was likely to experience to the south of the island.

Keoma had become the official support boat for all the British entries, taking family and friends out to watch the start, including the parents of Nick's friend Toby, another skipper. I had watched them say goodbye to their son; his father a stoic. His mother had to be guided away, father's hands on her shoulders, her pale arms outstretched.

We watched the confused mêlée before the start; 70 boats, each almost touching. Contact was not permitted, even from a sail or rope. The manoeuvring was careful, tactical. Somehow Nick popped out in front as the gun sounded, and sailed away slightly ahead of the pack, which was good news for my photography. I managed to get some good shots of his blue sail ahead of the others, the black mountains in the background and the water glinting in the sunshine.

We followed the fleet for several miles. It was a strange afternoon because we had eight adults on board and the men were trying to save me from having to do anything. I felt a little put out at not being allowed to sail my own boat, but I told myself that they were being chivalrous, and tried to persuade myself not to be so territorial. I found it hard to relax, though. This was my home and my life and suddenly it was crowded with other people. It was like letting someone else drive a "pride and joy" car. Charlie wanted to carry on to Brazil but I eventually persuaded him to turn the boat around. It was dark when we motored back into the berth. The marina was strangely empty without the minis, and without all the skippers. Not to mention their entourage, which seemed to have evaporated.

The minis had tracking units so that their positions could be followed on the official class website. Puerto Calero was one of the few places we had been to where there was a free wi-fi connection in the marina, and we logged on several times a day to check on Nick's progress. Each time we started up the computer with optimism and turned it off with sadness, as we witnessed Nick's lead ebb away and he moved down the pack. It was all a question of choosing the right course, a valuable lesson for us for when we set off on our own Atlantic race. Geoff flew back to England and we prepared to leave Puerto Calero.

Before departing, we visited the Whale and Dolphin Museum. Outside was a skeleton of what looked like a dinosaur. The plaque nearby told us it was not prehistoric, but a Brydes whale, which we might meet at any time. The museum was an interesting collection of information and artefacts. The curators were so enthusiastic that they walked around the museum with us, explaining the exhibits. Our guide described how she had been out in a small boat to try to see whales that had been reported in the area, but had been disappointed because none had been visible that day. We managed to restrain ourselves from talking about all the whales and dolphins that we had seen over the last few months.

Around lunchtime we slipped out of Puerto Calero, heading north to a small island that had been recommended to us, a little-known place around a mile off the northern coast of Lanzarote, called Graciosa. There was no wind and we motored along, arriving at the marina at dusk. The entrance was marked by two rough metal sculptures. It was difficult to tell what they were but we found them strangely welcoming. The marina was pretty full, so we rafted up next to a boat that was tied to a pier near the entrance. The skipper was a large Dutch man, who said, "You're welcome to tie up here but I must warn you that we're leaving at seven in the morning." We weren't worried about this; somehow we knew we'd have a good night's sleep. It was peaceful, with barely a ripple on the water and small lights dotted around amongst the boats. Occasionally we heard laughter from a nearby boat. We ate pasta and enjoyed a cup of real coffee in the cockpit as the girls pulled on their pyjamas and cleaned teeth. I'd used our new cafetiere to make the coffee. We'd given up resisting having a glass coffee pot on board, but I wondered how long it would last.

CHAPTER 62

We were not woken at 7.00am, and slept through until after 8.00am. There was no sign of life on the boat next door, but someone else was leaving the marina, so we started up our engine and cast off, taking the space of the departing boat. We were next to a Norwegian boat, called Blue Marlin. Alice and Pip were delighted because there were children on board, and they made friends straight away. There seemed to be no language barrier, even though the six year old twin girls couldn't speak English and Alice and Pip didn't know any Norwegian. We headed to the beach and enjoyed a day there. In the evening we lit a barbecue and ate sitting on the sand with a few cold beers. Blue Marlin was going to cross the Atlantic with the ARC, but she would then head for the Panama Canal. They were embarking on a three year circumnavigation.

The most impressive part of their story was that before they set off on the trip they had not sailed before. Rune and Idunn had decided they wanted to go sailing, so Rune, the father, went to England and bought Blue Marlin, a Dehler 41. He sailed her home with two friends, who had sailed before, and that was his pre-trip sailing experience. They left Norway in July of this year and sailed down through the North Sea and the channel and across the Bay of Biscay. It seemed to me like the proverbial baptism of fire; one of the busiest shipping lanes in the world followed by one of the roughest sea areas. They had stopped in Madeira on their way south. We told them our story; of selling everything in England and flying to Italy. Speaking of England, Idunn said, "But you must know Tim and Penny from Tamarisk. They're practically your neighbours!" We didn't know them, but heard they would be doing the ARC too, so it was only a matter of time.

Travelling with Rune, Idunn and their daughters was their sixteen year old nephew, Sondere. He spoke perfect English and was clearly a useful hand on the boat. He seemed mature for his years. I offered him a beer. "I'm only sixteen," he said. When dusk began to fall, Idunn said, "We must pick up all our things, otherwise we won't be able to find them in the dark." We gathered up towels, knives, tomato ketchup, the corkscrew, glasses and matches.

I got up early the next day because I wanted to take some early morning photographs of the village and marina. It was a perfect, still, morning and I relished the coolness of the air, the white sand and the mirror-like water. I walked along the main street of the village, passing a few ancient Land Rovers parked in the deep sand of the track. I came to a bicycle hire shop, which had a small sign, written on cardboard, taped to the window. The writing was naïve and faded, but written in three languages; Spanish, English and German. "If closed, simple put your returned bike in front of the door. If you want to rent a bike I'm in the restaurant "Girasul" (next to the little beech)".

I passed piles of fish traps, net, floats and rope, jumbled up. A beach ran around one corner of the marina, edged by fishermen's huts with blue peeling paint. Later Charlie searched for the Harbour Master in an attempt to pay for our berth, but he returned without success. Rune explained how it worked. "Sometimes he is here, sometimes not. You'd better try his hut tomorrow." It was a mañana kind of place; the marina had been fitted with electric sockets but they hadn't been connected to the mains so there was no point plugging in. The village had no running water, but it did have an internet café, with a cheerful queue at the door.

Charlie laid out the anchor chain on the pontoon and marked it with stripes of spray paint, every five metres, so that we could know how much we had let out when anchoring, rather than guessing, thinking this may help us to be better at it.

We enjoyed several days in Graciosa and then we were ready to be on the move again. It was around 120 miles to the island of Gran Canaria and light winds propelled us along. I made a sudden jolt of the helm to avoid a line of buoys suspending long nets in the water. Ahead I could see several more, and from that time on, we were extra-vigilant.

CHAPTER 63

The following afternoon we were around five miles from Gran Canaria, motoring through a windless zone. We passed a knot of rope and net in the water. As it passed our stern we looked behind, and saw that a turtle was trapped inside. Charlie turned the boat around in a circle and then I took the helm as we came close. Charlie reached for the binnacle knife. I slowed the boat until it was almost stationary and he kneeled on the swimming platform, leaning into the water to grasp the bundle. Alice stood next to him on the platform. When he had steadied himself she passed him the knife and he cut the net in several places. Fortunately the water was flat, with only the small waves caused by the stopping of the boat, as he needed both hands for the job. He took the turtle out of the net, but found there was another in there. Passing the first one to Alice, she held it to her chest while he cut the second free and they launched the two turtles together from the stern. Alice's thighs were scratched where the frightened turtle had moved its feet as she clutched it, but she was unconcerned and we were all elated by the experience. Charlie was worried about the turtles though. "They were so light, it felt as though there couldn't be anything but shell there. I desperately hope they survive."

We put the bundle in the cockpit to dispose of ashore, and motored on. Coming into the marina we tied up at the fuel berth, following the instructions in the ARC folder. We were told to go to pontoon 17. There was plenty of space on one side but when we tried to pick up the bow line, we realised why. The seabed anchors holding the line had been pulled out of position, meaning the whole line was too close to the pontoon and therefore useless for boats of our size. Other boats moored up here had used their anchors. But our anchor wouldn't hold in the marina sea bed. We spotted a place on the other side but it looked a little narrow. Motoring around there, a tall, moustachioed man stood on the bow of his boat and said, "You can get in there. There was a bigger boat in that space before." I couldn't quite place his accent, and we later found out that Rudy and his wife Lilian were Swiss. They were circumnavigating on their boat Shiva. It was hard to work out their age; they glowed with health and fitness, but had a gentleness that made me think they were slightly older than us. We reversed slowly into the space. The bowline worked on this side of the pontoon and Rudy helped us with our stern lines.

Las Palmas, the capital of Gran Canaria, had a huge marina. It needed to be large to accommodate 240 visiting boats at ARC time. There was an anchorage on the other side of the wall, where boats were crammed in as close as they dared to be. I was relieved we weren't there. Las Palmas was a sprawling metropolis and Charlie hit the chandleries as soon as he could. He ordered the Navionics Gold card, which we would need for the rest of the Atlantic. He researched anchors. When we were in Majorca, Simon had confessed to being an "anchor nut" and advised us to buy a spade anchor. But it seemed to be as elusive as the Navionics Gold. Charlie worked out what would be the right size and weight for our boat and the marina chandlery agreed to order it.

We walked around the marina and on the far side we found Whitehaven, with Rob and Kerry sitting in the cockpit.

"Come aboard and have a drink. We're just trying out some wine to put in the bilges for the crossing. Go below, Alice and Pip, the girls are watching a movie." They had bought a selection of wine boxes from a local supermarket and were conducting their own tasting. It was all pretty rank and cost under 2 Euros a carton, but Kerry thought it would be OK for Rob and his mates who would be flying up from Australia to do the ARC, Kerry taking their girls across by plane.

After a couple of glasses of red, Rob told us about his trip down from Gibraltar. "We set off from Gibraltar and within a couple of hours this head wind had set in. We were beating into it and I kept thinking it would die but the wind just kept building and building. I was so glad the girls were in London. We were healed right over for two days with the wind around 35 knots and it really wasn't fun, so we decided to head for Madeira, where we could get some rest and wait for the winds to ease. We tacked for Madeira and soon after we started to see all these black clouds welling up on the horizon. It looked like the end of the world. I said to Mike that I didn't like the look of the weather. Then I decided to go down below and see if Kerry had sent me any weather routing messages on the sat phone. I fired the thing up and the screen flashed up with thirteen messages, from Kerry and others, each one with a voice of increased urgency. There was a hurricane approaching. I knew what to do, which was to get the emergency gear ready and head south, and we immediately tacked and bore off. There was a ship around a mile away and I radioed them up. I couldn't see their name so I just said, "Big ship, big ship, this is sailing yacht Whitehaven," and they radioed me back. I said, "I just wondered whether you have any weather information you can give me." The only response I got was them shouting "GO SOUTH! GO SOUTH!" "OK, message received and understood. Whitehaven out." I got out the emergency drogue and lines to trail, got the liferaft ready and we all clipped on. But just having come off the wind improved the situation and within a couple of hours the wind was starting to slacken, and then I knew we were out of danger."

Although Rob's rendition of the radio exchange was hilarious, there was a moment when everyone stopped laughing and the conversation paused. We were all thinking the same thing. Hurricane. Out of hurricane season. Madeira had never had a hurricane before. Then Rob broke the silence. "And you know what the scariest thing about the whole episode was?" Rob started to smile, "Mike wanted to know what it would be like to sail through a hurricane! I've got to go across the Atlantic with this guy on board!" Mike was a huge bearded Welshman, formerly a bomb disposal expert, who had served in Northern Ireland. We all laughed and the wine was definitely improving with quantity.

CHAPTER 64

The next day we were regretting having drunk so much, and with a sore head I wandered around the local supermarket. I avoided the wine in cartons. I hoped that Rob's crew would be able to cope with it better than me, or it would be a miserable crossing. But they were tough sailors; some had done the Sydney-Hobart race and no doubt they were hardened Aussie drinkers too.

One of the items I bought in the supermarket was orange juice. We were trying all the brands before buying in bulk for the crossing. The juice we'd had so far had been disgusting. It tasted as though it had been left in the sun and gone off. Or perhaps it had been made with rotten oranges.

Later, we decided to visit the house where Christopher Columbus stayed when he was having his ship's rudder repaired on the island. We caught a taxi to the old town and the driver dropped us outside Casa de Colon. While Charlie was paying, I was trying to ask, "Are you sure this is Columbus's house?" The taxi driver didn't seem to hear me. Charlie said, "Casa de Colon?" while gesturing with his right hand. "Si, Si," the driver nodded as he pressed down hard on the accelerator. We were left standing on the kerbside, looking around. It wasn't the right place, although we couldn't be far away; we were in the old town. We walked up the quiet cobbled street, admiring the old houses with their muted colours and ornate carved wooden balconies. We passed some restaurants and became diverted by the idea of lunch. We sat down outside an Italian restaurant for a very average meal. Nearby stood a statue of a dog the size of a small pony, which the plaque told us was in recognition of the indigenous population of the islands, which had been packs of very large dogs. When the Romans settled here they used the word "canine" from which was derived "Canary". After lunch we walked further and chanced upon Casa de Colon, but as we approached the entrance, the heavy wooden doors swung closed and we heard bolts sliding across. It had shut for the day.

The following morning we went to the "rasto" market. If we had wanted to buy oversized polyester bras this would have been the place for us. They were swaying in the wind in their hundreds, cups lining up as though huddling together for warmth.

Charlie felt we should have a second pair of binoculars, in case our pair were dropped overboard or broken, so he bought a cheap pair. I found a stall selling fossils and bought a beautiful ammonite. The market was noisy and fast-moving and I could imagine a pick-pocket weaving in and out of the heaving crowd. We gripped the children's hands.

At Casa de Colon, the huge, old, heavy door was wide open and we spent around two hours there admiring the house and its artefacts. There were original maps from Columbus's voyages, models of the Nina, the Pinta and the Santa Maria, and many smaller items like plates and buttons. One room had been made into a scale model of the captain's cabin, and this included the boat's steering mechanism, a crude straight tiller attaching to the rudder which was pegged in position. The course was checked every four hours, when the sand timer ran out, and if it was felt that the rudder needed to be adjusted, it could be pegged to a new position. Quite different from our style of sailing, where we (or the autohelm) moved the wheel a few degrees every half second or so, to keep the sails filling to their optimum.

The star attraction was the house, which had been very sympathetically restored. It had a central courtyard, with balustraded walkways on the first and second floors and a well. The house had a cellar, with the essential escape route, like in Napoleon's home in Ajaccio. There were wonderful examples of the furniture; chairs, tables and chests, and we left with that boggled feeling of brain overload.

The marina laundry was in hot demand. It was a self-service affair and I collected together as many Euro coins as I could find in purses, pockets, and around the boat. We had hired a car for a couple of days and Charlie dropped me off with the bags of dirty clothes. The marina was so large that it was a ten minute walk to the laundry and a twenty minute walk to Whitehaven. The children had found a solution to the latter and they took the dinghy across to visit Georgia and Emma, which required five minutes of rowing.

I waited for the washing machines to be emptied and then loaded in clothes and filled the slots with money. One machine had the children's cuddly toys in. They had become filthy, from repeatedly being brought up to the cockpit, where they usually ended up on the floor. Alice and Pip sat in front of the machines and looked through the glass, saying, "Oh look, there's Fishy," and, "There's Toby. Hello Toby!" People came in to collect laundry and to wait for a free machine. There were a number of older men travelling alone with laundry that I dared not even look at as they loaded it into the machines. One bearded sea dog asked me whether I would mind moving his washing to the dryer once the wash had finished. I agreed to do it and later picked up his faded underwear, between a finger and thumb, quickly dropping it into a washing basket. Charlie returned from a search to find an internet café, fuming, having been sent all over town by different people, on a wild goose chase.

The car was a beaten up jeep with an open top and the children loved sitting in the back. From my guidebook we read about an area of sand-dunes at the southern tip of the island. On the way we stopped at a builders' merchants so that Charlie could buy some rods of wood to use to attach the canvas sea berths that he had had made up in Majorca. The sand dunes were called Maspolamas. We walked over them and wondered how they got there. It was like a small section of desert. The children ran down the dunes and then rolled down, laughing, covered in sand. At one end the dunes ran into a strip of beach called Playa d'Ingles. It was aptly named; the beach was full of fried waddling English people. Fast food shops divided the beach from the road.

Driving back to Las Palmas we took the mountain route. In many places the rusty brown rock was formed into tiers like giant steps up the slope, and the landscape rose and fell with the drama of the Grand Canyon. We climbed so high into the mountains that it became cold and the children found the towels in our beach bag to cover their bony knees.

Following the winding road, we passed Roque Bequia. In the middle of the island, it stood like a giant index finger pointing skywards, standing high above the others, commanding respect. We could appreciate why it was worshipped by the ancient people of this island. The tarmac ended and then we were driving on bumpy tracks, with a drop of maybe 500 metres, where the road seemed to crumble away, 30 centimetres from the passenger door. There were large holes in the track and wet patches. I was glad the car was four-wheel drive. As we started to wind downhill the road became solid again. We passed caves along the side of the road, that had had painted brick facades, so that they looked almost like normal dwellings from the front, except that behind they melded into the rough rock of the hillside. I wanted to know what they were like inside. We saw other caves high on hillsides that had had the coarse stone exterior painted white. The mouths were uneven black holes. I wondered who lived there, and how long it took to climb to the entrances from the road. The terrain looked unassailable.

We looked down over miles and miles of tomatoes growing under massive sheets of plastic. We had heard that these sometimes blew into the water and were a hazard for yachts. They were so large that I imagined they would be very difficult to free, once wrapped around a keel or rudder.

We drove through fields of sugar cane and then passed through rain forest and along a road lined with eucalyptus trees. The soil was the rich orange of central Australia. This small island, only 90 miles long, held so many flavours of the world.

CHAPTER 65

We'd had a big problem with lost shoes recently. I hunted around for Alice's trainers, only to eventually reach the conclusion that she'd left them in a car park on the other side of the island. "But I thought you would pick them up Mummy!" I cringed with frustration. Charlie put his shoes in the cockpit in a plastic bag and then accidentally threw them out with the rubbish, also in plastic bags. We visited El Corte Ingles, to try to replace these and buy sandals for the children. Their feet had been growing and their comfortable summer shoes now rubbed. The shops here didn't seem to measure children's feet. I was told that sandals were not on sale because it was winter, but they did have fur boots. We were still wearing just T-shirts and shorts all day and in the evenings. The shop displays were thick jumpers with snowflake patterns and pom-pom hats, yet I knew it rarely dropped to 15 degrees Celsius in these islands.

We found a pair of trainers that we guessed were the right size for Alice. For the first time since we left England, we all had haircuts. It was quite hard to communicate what we would like to have done, as the hairdressers spoke only Spanish. I was expecting a disaster but we all came out looking ok, in fact looking much tidier. By now my hair had bleached from mouse-brown to blonde and Alice and Pip had streaks of lighter colour. Charlie's hair had turned ginger at the tips, although most of this came off in the haircut.

Talking to Rudy and Lilian that evening, we told them that we would be leaving for La Gomera the next day, and apologised if we woke them with our early start, since we were planning to leave at around 4am. Rudy asked whether we would like help with our lines. It was kind of him to offer to get out of bed at that time of the morning for our sake. We thanked him, but said we'd manage, and we arranged to meet up at La Gomera, when they arrived there in a week or so.

We had trouble getting to sleep and then it was fitful. Around 3am Charlie said he had had enough and wanted to leave, so we dressed and slipped our lines, gently easing the boat from her space and out of the marina, the children still sleeping soundly in their bunks. Once we had cleared first the marina wall and then the long, high outer sea wall, we started to feel a gentle breeze on our faces, and unfurled the genoa and hoisted the mainsail. I slipped back to bed for a couple more hours of sleep, leaving Charlie on deck cradling a cup of coffee, the boat ghosting along over the flat water. When I returned, feeling better, a dazzling colourful dawn was breaking, and we watched the orange and purple stripes divide and expand, reflected in the water. The sky gradually lightened, fading out the colours. Charlie had hoisted Big Blue and we crept along. Dolphins appeared and swam along with the boat. I noticed that there were two large ones and two small, all bottlenose, and then it clicked that they were mothers with young. They zipped through the water, the young swimming beneath and slightly behind their mothers, slipstreaming them. Alice and Pip came up to the bow to watch, enjoying the dolphins' antics and the cheeky expressions on their faces.

Rounding the southern tip of Tenerife, the wind turned easterly, funnelled by the effect of the islands and we gybed. By mid-afternoon we were around ten miles from the dome shaped island of La Gomera, and the wind dropped completely. We snuffed the spinnaker and then lowered it into its bag. The boat was motionless in the flat water. We saw a line of water with a slightly rougher texture approaching us and then felt a zephyr. It was coming from ahead and gradually building, giving us an upwind end to that day's journey, the breeze created by the land mass of the island ahead. The dead patch we had just been through was where the wind from behind met this land breeze and they cancelled each other out. Now the breeze was taking hold and the boat powered along, heeled right over. Outside the marina we dropped the sails and motored towards the entrance. Five small girls waved at Alice and Pip from the marina wall. "Do you speak English?" they shouted.

"They've seen our ensign," said Charlie.

"Yes!" shouted our children, jumping up and down. I had the feeling they were going to enjoy La Gomera.

Once inside the marina, there was the familiar feeling of everything going quiet as we came into the lee of the enclosure, and Charlie radioed for a berth. We were allocated a space next to a large steel boat called Kormoran. She was around 50 foot long and deserted. She appeared to have been there for a while, locked up. We looked upwards at the imposing wall of stratified rock which ran along one side of the marina. I guessed it was around 50 metres high. Rock falls from this could cause serious damage to the boats here. Clearly no-one else was concerned. We took a walk around the marina to stretch our legs. Many of the boats looked as though they had been here for years. I imagined how difficult it must be for the owners to leave them, unsupervised. What if someone broke in, or just tampered with their warps? What if there were strong winds which wore or stretched the lines?

We ate on board and went to bed early, falling into a deep sleep. The hatch was wide open above us, as usual. I woke in the night with big drops of rain splatting on my face. With effort I reached up and grasped the handle, pulling it closed, falling back to sleep as my head hit the pillow. If only our night time awakenings were always so easy!

CHAPTER 66

We were supervising schoolwork with Alice and Pip when there was a knocking on the hull of our boat. It was three of the girls who had waved at us from the marina wall. They lived on Vortex, a South African boat in the marina, and we had met their parents briefly the previous evening. The girls asked whether Alice and Pip could come and play. I said they would come over as soon as they had finished school.

Charlie pumped up the dinghy and Alice and Pip climbed in. They asked to use the outboard but we weren't happy about them doing this on their own, so Alice rowed. I watched them climb aboard Vortex. Suddenly they seemed so independent. Over the next few days they began to treat the dinghy like the family car, and we gave increasing freedom. They loved being able to rove around the marina on their own. There were certain rules, like they had to keep together and they must not go on the boat of anyone we didn't know. The group of children grew and we watched them ferrying each other around the marina and having water fights. This gave us freedom too, and we tackled boat jobs. I cleaned and polished the hull. This protected the fibreglass and gave Keoma's blue a beautiful sheen. It was hard work, polishing a boat of this size by hand, particularly as some parts were inaccessible from the dock and I had to reclaim the dinghy. Then I had to hold myself close to the boat with one hand and polish with the other, using broad circular sweeping movements. While I was doing this, Charlie was servicing the watermaker. He had to wedge himself into the stern locker, which was restricting and very hot.

One day Alice got into the dinghy alone. Pip sat in the saloon, playing Game-Boy.

"Aren't you going off to play with your friends?" I asked Pip.

"No," she replied quietly.

Alice was untying the painter.

"Why?" I asked, gently taking the game from her.

"I don't want to tell you."

"If you tell me, you'll feel better. I might be able to help." I squeezed her shoulders.

Alice was still holding on to the side of the boat, listening.

"Alice, I think you'd better tie the dinghy on again and come down here," I said.

When she was in the saloon, I asked her why Pip was so upset.

"It's not my fault! We were playing dares and she didn't like it."

"What was the dare?"

Pip blurted out, "They dared me to lift my dress up and show my knickers." Tears welled. I rubbed her bony shoulder.

"Oh dear. That wasn't very nice. You don't *have* to do a dare, you know."

"I *didn't* do it! Then they called me a scaredy cat."

The tears were in full flow.

"I don't think you're a scaredy cat. I think you're brave for standing up to them and *not* doing it. And Alice does too. Don't you, Alice." I looked at Alice.

"Yes," said Alice slowly.

I fetched some kitchen paper and Pip dried her face. "Why don't you go and play, and Alice will bring you home if the game is dares. Alice will look after you. Won't you, Alice?"

"Yes," said Alice. "Come on, Pip. It'll be alright."

Pip followed her sister up the steps. I watched them row away.

Shoes appeared on the dock next to Kormoran. One was a pair of scuffed deckshoes, encrusted with salt, the other, pale pink beaded suede mules with low heels and elegant pointed toes. The boat's hatch was open and an ensign had been hoisted. We tried not to be too nosy.

The small town beside the marina was called San Sebastian. It, too, was keen to exploit its links with Columbus; there was a tall, square, tower where the island's queen was rumoured to have seduced Columbus. Next to the tower was a well, which was said to have supplied the fresh water for one of his Atlantic crossings. Many of the town's buildings appeared as though they were under renovation, although there was no evidence of any building work being done. Some of these looked as though they were once impressive town houses, and the antique balconies of Gran Canaria were replicated on a few buildings here. But the plaster was cracked and stained, the doors and windows boarded up. Thin cats wandered in the street.

Returning to the marina we passed another family. They introduced themselves and we had a brief conversation, during which they invited us to a Halloween party that evening, in the park next to the Columbus tower. We gratefully accepted and headed back to town to assemble some witch outfits. At home we would have had all sorts of things that they could wear and use as props. We found a shop called "Oriental

Bazaar", which was a pharmacy but also an Aladdin's cave of wigs, costumes and make up. The selection of stock was quite bizarre. We found a long, curly, purple and red wig for Alice and make-up to give them white faces, black lips and green nails. In a fabric shop nearby we bought three metres of black cotton, which we later made into smock type dresses. Back at the boat we put all this together, grabbed some bottles of beer and headed out to the party.

The Queen's tower was set in a park surrounded by shady trees and dotted with exotic plants. Hibiscus, strylitza and even English roses were in abundant flower. The children played games and the adults chatted. We met many English speakers, and were surprised how many were permanent residents in La Gomera. The children who waved at us from the marina wall when we first arrived were here. Two lived in the town with their mother. She'd left their father nine months ago and moved here for a new start in life. The children were at the local school and already fluent Spanish speakers. They were the only blonde heads in the school. The other three were from Vortex, which had been in the marina for six months. The eldest daughter was eleven years old and had never been to school. In one month's time they would return to South Africa, where they planned to settle permanently.

It started to get dark and we had to leave the park before it was locked for the night. We collected the empty bottles and headed home. When we arrived back at the boat, Alice asked, "Can we go and trick or treat Vortex?" We agreed to this, and watched them row over in their witches outfits. The parents came out, laughing, and found some sweets for them. Their children climbed out and jumped into the dinghy with ours. The five of them headed off to another boat (clearly friends of the parents on Vortex) and banged on their hull. We watched as the children were sent from boat to boat. They eventually came across to us. By now there were two dinghies full of children, dressed in costumes made of bin bags, parent's clothing, anything they could find. "Trick or treat!" they shouted and we passed down a bowl of sweets. We watched them go on to another boat, full of excitement, sugar high.

Two of the children we met that night were Ems and Ollie, from a boat called Blasé. The following day their parents came to see us, and we made some coffee. They had big smiles of white teeth and tanned skin. Paul was around 5'6" tall and thinning on top, although the wispy hair that remained had been bleached blonde and stood up vertically. Fi was taller, maybe 5'9", a mass of blonde curls. They were incredibly friendly. Fi confided her nervousness about the Atlantic crossing to me, which Paul overheard. "We'll be fine, Fi!"

That evening some familiar faces appeared in the marina; Rudy and Lilian arrived after a hard sail from Las Palmas. They had endured the slamming of endless square waves as they beat past Tenerife. It was dark and they were clearly tired and emotional after the trip.

CHAPTER 67

In the morning we walked to the market in the centre of town. It was a modern, purpose-built structure which from the outside looked completely soulless. But as we came closer we saw stalls lined up outside, selling all sorts of hand-made jewellery, purses, pottery and nick-nacks. We saved the browse until we came out again, although the children were keen to look straight away. Inside, the stalls were piled high with fruit, in a colourful display, with more in boxes behind. Pieces were cut up and given out, the stall holder explaining what each one was, handing it around, chatting with everyone in Spanish and English, painting a picture of life on the farm and enjoying the samples with us. We savoured the oranges and mangoes, which were the sweetest I had ever tasted, plus there were several fruits that I had never seen nor heard of before. We bought two large bags, plus herbs, the best home-made bread ever, cheese and vegetables. Walking along the street market outside, we chatted with the stall holders and Alice purchased a hand-sewn purse decorated with a red lizard. Charlie dragged us into a fishing shop. He had his eye on a large net. "It will make landing the fish so much easier," he said. He also bought some lures. The shop owner gave him a gift of an enormous lure.

On the way back from the shop I asked Charlie, "Do you think you'll ever use that lure. It's rather large. Surely we'd catch an enormous fish with it?"

He agreed. "Yes, I'm a bit scared to use it. Also, I'm not really fishing for big game, more to catch something large enough for our dinner. I think I'll give it away." He gave it to a boat full of macho men, who were preparing to leave for their passage home to the USA the following day.

Back at the boat we started to think about a net for the fruit. This was something that all long-distance cruisers had on their boats. It would save space in the cupboards, plus it kept fruit cooler and prevented bruising. This prompted me to think about the crossing. In less than one month's time we would be on our way. We worked on the boat. Charlie dismantled the winches and cleaned each cog and tiny spring, before greasing and reassembling them. I carried on polishing the hull. The children enjoyed playing with their gang of friends. The dinghy was in popular demand but Pip was tired of being rowed by Alice. She wanted to learn herself, and this marina was safe and enclosed, the perfect place to do it. Charlie gave her some tips and she set off for her first attempt, watched by many sitting in their cockpits and working on their boats. At first she went around in circles and one oar repeatedly slipped out of its rowlock. She lost her temper, face reddening, but remained determined. After an hour or so she had mastered it. When she came back onto Keoma I looked at her hands. The palms were sore and blistered.

We talked to our neighbours on Kormoran. Alex was 60 years old, practical, interesting and grumpy. Joy was around the same age, full of energy and wonderfully entertaining and kind. They invited us for dinner, which we gratefully accepted. The children climbed down Kormoran's carved wooden steps ahead of us. "Wow!" said Pip. "It's not a boat, it's a cottage." Joy had roasted a chicken, with couscous and a green salad. If there had been an AGA designed for a boat, Kormoran would have had one. Alex and Joy had good taste and the boat was decorated with art and photographs, a real home from home. We discovered that they lived, when not travelling, in the village where Charlie had been born, in Suffolk. They had a longer term plan than us; they spent around six months of each year on the boat, travelling the world.

Charlie phoned a hire car company the next day and rented a small car. We walked to the office to pay and collect the keys. It was a run-down house in the main street, and parked outside was a small red car, covered in dents. It looked like the victim of a hundred approximate drivers, which I found strangely comforting. If we caused another scratch I wouldn't feel guilty. It was just the kind of car that Charlie loved. We jumped in and set off. It was another beautiful sunny day and we wound uphill for several miles, parking in a lay-by. My guide book described a walk, which began with a tunnel through the hill to the next valley.

We found the tunnel but there was no way I was prepared to go through it. It was extraordinarily low; the children could have stood up but we would have had to bend over or crawl to go through, and it was maybe 200 metres long, plus the ground was flooded. I imagined Charlie putting his back out. We chose the longer route, around the outside of the hill, through woodland. The forest trees were draped in a dark green hairy growth that gave the place an ancient feel, and it looked like the kind of path that the hobbit might have passed along. After about a mile we emerged into a tree lined valley. We descended from the wood, past the other entrance to the tunnel, and walked down a road that led down to the base of the valley.

There was a strong smell of rancid milk. We were thirsty by now and spotted a rustic restaurant on the other side, which we made for. Ahead of us a narrow bridge spanned a river, and, standing in the centre of the bridge, was a large billy goat; the source of the smell. "There's Billy Goat Gruff," said Pip.

Charlie decided to take matters into his own hands, literally. He strode towards the goat, grasped its horns with both hands, as though holding the handlebars of a racing bike, and wrestled it out of our way. The goat was not very happy about this and it resisted, but he managed to hold it long enough for us to skitter past. Charlie released the goat and ran to us, laughing. We climbed part of the hill on the other side of the valley, and then took some rough steps up to the café. We had not seen anyone on our walk but there were several groups of walkers here. Sitting outside, we could see along the steep valley as far as the sea. It was warm and sunny and we sat on stools made of wide tree trunks sawn into sections and turned to stand on their flat ends. We ate the local speciality; watercress soup, and then chicken cooked in a sauce with potatoes. The chicken had a delicious flavour, and we agreed that it tasted as though it had lived on the farm down the road. We all ate well, and had several drinks and ice creams for the children. The bill came to 28 Euros.

Back at the marina we had drinks with Rudy and Lilian on Shiva. They gave us a tour of their boat, which was almost new and had been designed especially for them. The feature I was most impressed with was their washing machine. It would be so wonderful not to have to continually seek out launderettes and then scrape around finding the right change and work out how to operate the machines.

CHAPTER 68

The instructions for the return of the car were to park it in the road around the corner from the car rental shop, and lock it with the keys inside. We had the bug for walking now and took the road along the beachfront, before climbing the hill which led towards the tall white statue of Jesus. The path was rocky and ran along the lines of the rough terracing cut into the steep slope. It was difficult to comprehend the amount of manpower put into building this; every few metres there was a dry stone wall of around a metre high holding up the next level of copper-brown earth. I had read that in the past, when it needed to be self sufficient, the island of La Gomera could not grow enough food to sustain itself without the additional land created by these terraces. Along the route we passed enormous cacti. Some were comprised of pale elongated cucumbers, pentagonal in cross section, spiked along the five bobbled ridges which ran the length of each tube. There were sometimes so many of these tubes clustered together that the plant was around ten metres across.

Near the top of the hill the land became less steep and we came to a large pile of rocks. One wide, flat, rock was balanced on top of others, forming a low cave. We sat in the shade, enjoying some respite from the relentless sun, drinking from our water bottle. It was a perfect shelter with flat stone beneath. The roof was a little low, too much of a reminder that it could fall shut like a giant clam shell, crushing us inside. We emerged into the bright sunlight and continued our trek, reaching the top of the hill and gazing up to see the giant statue of Christ towering above us. Beneath was a small shrine. Inside it looked neglected, with dead flowers in jars and burnt out candles. We descended the hill on the far side. The stones were loose and Pip raced recklessly over them, despite my pleas to slow down. I held back from shouting at her, not wanting to spoil the happy mood.

Pip skidded and fell, cutting herself and bleeding profusely, bright scarlet blood gushing down her leg. I was worried about the amount of blood. All we had was a bottle of water and Charlie's not very clean handkerchief. We doused the cut and dried it, sitting on the ground in the blistering sun, holding her as she sobbed, and waiting for the pain to subside. I felt suddenly that we were very alone. There was no local GP, I didn't know where the hospital was, we didn't speak the language, and family and friends were far away. I dug deep to put on a brave face for Pip. A few minutes later the blood had stopped. She dried her tears on her dress and tentatively stood up again. She took one unsteady step, then another. We went much more slowly now, holding hands. The views of the marina, with Teide, Tenerife's mountain, in the background, complete with a sombrero of cloud, were inspiring, against the backdrop of the purest blue sky.

Joy and Alex had taken Kormoran to an anchorage to escape the marina for the night. We agreed that they were probably seeking some peace away from us, as we weren't the quietest neighbours. The anchorages in the Canaries were known not to be very protected and I hoped they would be ok. Rudy and Lilian came for a drink and we raved about the walks we'd done. Lilian, an anaesthetist, gave us some medical advice on Pip's injury. A rubber dinghy from across the marina came towards our boat and two people waving a bottle climbed up onto the pontoon. Charlie turned guiltily to me, "Oh, I forgot to tell you. I invited Bill and Mindy too." Over a couple of glasses of wine I heard the whole story. Charlie had rowed over to say hello to them because their boat had the word "Ipswich" written on her stern, which happened to be where they had bought her. He had said, "You must come for a drink," which they had taken to mean "this evening". It was an entertaining couple of hours as we swapped salty tales and discussed plans for "the crossing". Bill bemoaned his recent loss of his glasses overboard, without which he had terrible problems reading anything. He was kicking himself for having put them in the top pocket of his shirt, and when he bent over to tie the boat up, they fell into the marina and sank. He'd immediately dropped to his knees, trying to grab them, but couldn't get to them in time and now had a schoolboy graze on each leg. I doubted that he would find an optician in La Gomera, and this was their last stop before they set off on the long haul to the Caribbean.

CHAPTER 69

At last I finished the cleaning and polishing of the hull. It had taken several days of hard work and my arm muscles ached. I moved onto the chrome, armed with a can of Duraglit and a piece of old T-shirt. Charlie had ruined a few of his clothes with oil splashes and other marks, so we now had a useful selection of cloths. He finally got around to repairing the transom, where the boat had been blown against the dock in Italy. He mixed up the gelcoat, as recommended by the colour specialist he consulted in Majorca, then applied it to the hole, smearing it on in layers and rubbing down each layer when it had dried. The end result was a good finish, but the colour did not match at all. The new gelcoat was much lighter than the rest. Charlie was annoyed because he had spent an hour or so locating the colour specialist and then taking him to the boat, before going back to the chandlery to buy the materials. We agreed that he could have done a better job himself, just by guessing at the right blue.

The children had been playing with their friends and we broke the news that we would be leaving in the morning, heading back to Gran Canaria, via Tenerife. Our experience of La Gomera had been so good that I would have liked to visit the smaller islands of La Palma and El Hierro, but from what I had read they didn't have facilities for visiting yachts. I'd telephoned the port office on La Palma. They were extremely welcoming, saying, "Yes, we would love to see you. The marina is currently under construction and so we can not book a place for you, but please do come." It was over 50 miles away, and we decided that we didn't want to run the risk of sailing there and then not getting a marina space. Our conversation concluded that, in any event, we were keen to return to Gran Canaria for the final fortnight of preparations before we started our crossing.

The following morning we sat on the boat and waited for the fuel dock to become free. We didn't want to leave without filling the tanks, but there was a queue of boats waiting to do the same. It took maybe an hour and a half to get onto the dock, a frustrating wait. We said goodbye to Bill and Mindy, and Rudy and Lilian, and wished them "bon voyage". They were not crossing in the ARC but leaving from La Gomera in a few weeks' time. I wondered whether we would meet them again on our travels.

By mid-morning we were off. We began with light winds from behind, sailing gently along. The winds dropped and the water flattened and assumed an oily appearance. The colours in the water seemed to separate out into giraffe patches of different shades of blue. We were joined by a pod of pilot whales, including some babies, who escorted us towards Tenerife. The wind gradually built from ahead, and a gentle rocking wave developed, which became rougher over the course of several hours. Alice was seasick over and over, and then announced that she was hungry. I went below and was thrown around while I warmed up some chicken soup and sliced bread. I put the soup in mugs to try to keep it off the floor. While slicing the bread I needed two hands, so braced my legs against the back of the bench seat. I had to lean forwards and stretch my arms out because the work surface was now an uncomfortable distance away, and I wished for a "U" shaped galley. The meal helped morale a little but it was a cold, grey day and we sat quietly in the cockpit, feeling low, with just the noise of the wind and the crashing of the boat through the waves.

A group of dolphins appeared, as if they could sense the mood on board. I remembered the euphoria of the first sightings. We were more subdued now. The boat sailed on, up and down over each wave, leaning over on her side. In the evening I opened some cans of "emergency chilli" and put rice on to boil. The inside of the boat was still like being in a fairground ride and this simple meal took what felt like an hour to get ready. I passed up bowls to the others. Alice tucked in, saying, "Mummy, this is the best meal I've ever had." I thought of all the hours I'd spent chopping, making chilli, when I could have just bought this unappealing slop in tins. I consoled myself with the thought that it was dark. She may have a different view if she could see what it looked like in the bowl.

At around eight o'clock the children went to bed and I put the kettle on to make some coffee for Charlie and I. Our Tupperware box was currently full of chocolate biscuits and we tucked in. It was still rough and cold. We resorted to full wet weather gear for warmth. Neither of us slept, and we sat together on the high side of the cockpit, lifejacketed and clipped on, silent, miserable.

I wrote the ship's log every hour, recording our position, the wind direction, atmospheric pressure, and general comments. We knew it was essential to keep a track of our position, in case our GPS failed, in which event we would resort to paper charts. I unclipped my harness line and struggled down the steps in my bulky waterproofs. Holding the handles that were either side or the steps I swung myself into the bench seat behind the chart table. I kept my left foot wedged against the foot of the steps, to stop myself being thrown around. It wasn't the most graceful of positions. The boat rose and fell relentlessly.

I clicked the light on above my head and found a pencil. This morning, while we were waiting, I'd taped pencils to the top of the table, just inside the rim that ran along the edge, so that in bad weather I would be able to find them. There was one left.

The boat moved constantly and each wave was slightly different; a few more degrees of tilt, a more rapid drop. It was impossible to predict. Sometimes I craved stillness and felt like screaming at the elements, but I knew it would be futile, ludicrous! I opened the log book and started to fill in the boxes, looking at the GPS screen for our current position, tapping the glass of the barometer for a pressure reading. I checked the GPS for hazards in the surrounding sea area and worked out how far we had to go. Finally, I taped the pencil back into position and pulled myself out of the seat, reaching up for the hand holds on the steps with my left hand. The wet weather gear felt cold around the cuffs, heavy and uncomfortable. My booted feet climbed the steps and I sat down heavily next to Charlie for another grim hour until the next log-in.

At last we saw lights in the distance, and, hours later, we motored into Santa Cruz, the main town of Tenerife. We radioed for a berth and were told to proceed to the reception dock. The space we were told to tie up in was small and took some precision helming to get the boat in without hitting the boat in front; a huge superyacht. We just about managed it. It was 4.00am. The children were still sleeping soundly, and they would be awake at 8.00am, wanting breakfast. A figure climbed down from the superyacht and walked along the quay towards us. He introduced himself, "Hello, I'm Dave." It felt so cheering just to see another human being. He handed over two tins of Heineken, which we gratefully accepted. But we couldn't chat for long; we were totally worn out. As we climbed into bed we realised that we weren't tied up to a pontoon, but to a wall, with an ebbing tide. We set the alarm for two hours' time, when one of us would need to get up to check the lines were still tied correctly. For a short while I completely crashed out, then the alarm sounded and I got up to take a look around. The ebb was not too strong and the lines didn't require adjustment. I went back to bed for another couple of hours, but then the children woke and there was no hope of further sleep.

CHAPTER 70

The harbourmaster called out from the dock, to tell us he'd allocated us a berth for two nights, and we prepared to move Keoma. I felt groggy as I untied our lines. Charlie was concerned about how we would get into the berth; it was narrow and there was a boat with a big stern platform in the next berth, which limited our turning ability. The other factor was the strong wind that was blowing from behind, meaning it would be difficult for us to stop the boat. We wanted to avoid hitting the pontoon with the bow. We asked the Harbourmaster for help but he said he was too busy. We would just have to go for it. Charlie motored the boat towards the berth. A fat man dressed in a wetsuit was standing at the end of the pontoon. He started barking orders in Spanish and gesticulating at us. We ignored him and the shouting became louder. He was trying to help but we felt like telling him where to go. As Charlie swung the boat into the berth she narrowly missed our neighbour's aft platform, and I ran to fend off, pushing Keoma away from the other boat but also holding us there. Charlie had put the boat into neutral and he did the same as me; rushing up onto the side deck. We were suspended there, holding the other boat. We couldn't move.

Alice and Pip rescued us. They brought fenders which we squeezed into position between us and the next boat. I threw a line to Charlie, who had climbed over the other boat, onto the pontoon and walked around to the side where we would be tied. He took the line and we winched the boat across. We were still ignoring the wetsuited Mr Toad, who eventually gave up and walked away. There was no damage to either boat, but it had been a close thing. "We would have been fine if it hadn't been for that busybody!" said Charlie. We looked at each other and burst out laughing, partly at the relief at getting safely berthed, partly at the thought of the ridiculous man, and partly at Charlie blaming him.

The conditions were too windy to make it pleasant to sit in the cockpit, so we sat below, the children working at their diaries.

"Heello, heello, hello!" It came from the pontoon next to us. I stood up and stuck my head out of the hatch. I couldn't believe it; it was Mr Toad again. "Did you find some money?" he asked.

I was perplexed. "No, sorry, we haven't. Have you lost some?"

"Yes," he said in an irritated voice, as though it was our fault, and turned to stomp off, still in his wetsuit.

When the children had finished school they went for a walk around the marina. I knew they were looking for other children to play with. When they returned, Alice wanted to go and look at a boat that had just arrived, moored four spaces along on the same pontoon as us. We agreed, and she went off. She was relishing having some independence. After ten minutes she was back, full of excitement. "I saw Gypsy Moth!" she said, and told us about the historic boat. She was intrigued by the story of Sir Francis Chichester. We all tripped along the pontoon to see the boat, and were invited on board for a closer look around. The skipper told us they had had a difficult trip south, with strong winds on the nose and big waves. He had four crew: a first mate and three disadvantaged young people. They did not look as though they'd enjoyed the experience.

The boat was incredibly narrow and we understood the problems Sir Francis had had with the tiller in heavy seas; the cockpit was so small that the tiller was inhibited by the wooden coaming. I noticed that the boat's only compass was aft of the helmsman. It was the first time I'd seen a boat with a compass that was not in the helmsman's natural line of vision. A sailing boat was disorientating enough, with so much movement on different planes, to have to keep moving to look behind could not have been easy. The compass itself was a work of art; black and white triangles in a striking design. There was very little room in the cockpit and I wondered how they managed with five on board, since the boat was definitely designed for one. We descended the steps into the cabin. On the port side was the chart table, with the old fashioned VHF radio and depth sounder. "Those are just for show," said the skipper. "What we actually use is this," and he put his fingers under the base of the wood on which the instruments were mounted, and lifted. The board was hinged; once it was raised he fastened it in this position. Underneath was the most modern navigation equipment; GPS, SSB radio and electronic wind, speed and depth gauges. The rest of the cabin was spartan and small. In the forepeak were two narrow berths. The famous barrel of beer was there, on its stand, although I guessed it was empty now. "I can see why Sir Francis complained about the boat," said the skipper. "She's not built for comfort."

CHAPTER 71

We'd been advised by Rudy and Lilian to ascend the island's extinct volcano, Teide. But the weather was so overcast, we felt it probably wasn't worth going up there; all we'd see was cloud and it would be very cold and probably raining at altitude, so we headed back to the boat and got the playing cards out. In the evening we visited a restaurant recommended by Alex. Los Binchitos was in the backstreets of Santa Cruz, and the taxi driver couldn't take us the whole way there because the streets there were in the process of being turned from mud lanes into cement roads. We stepped over piles of kerbstones and walked along paths marked with metal poles linked by orange plastic netting.

It was the Canarian equivalent of a fish and chip shop, with wipe-clean table cloths. The waitresses wore baby pink crop tops, each one with a roll of spongy midriff on display. We took this to be a sign that the food would be good, and the counter display of the day's catch endorsed this. On the walls were photographs of fishing boats. The menu was in Spanish and we weren't totally sure what we were ordering, but the waitresses were patient and course after course of delicious fish arrived. Pip wanted to take a look at the kitchen. The food emerged from behind the counter displaying the fish. We had not really looked behind, and Pip got up to take a look. When she returned, she said, "It's not the kitchen there, it's just a cupboard." I stood up to look, and realised that it *was* the kitchen, a tiny bare room, and I explained this to the incredulous Pip.

We left the restaurant and crossed the mud roads, back to the place where our taxi had dropped us off. There was no sign of any taxis and the street was busy with groups of teenagers. A bus turned up, clearly headed for the City Centre, and we climbed aboard, handing over coins. The driver closed the doors and stamped on the accelerator. With a manic grin over his shoulder the bus roared off. We hung on to the seats in front and gripped our children, as the bus raced around corners. I looked out of the window to try to recognise where we were, but the city was unfamiliar and I couldn't pick out any landmarks or see masts. Thankfully, the journey was a quick one. Within a few minutes we recognised that we were close to the marina, and we rang the bell to disembark, exhaling as our feet landed on the warm tarmac.

The following evening we were invited by Dave, the skipper of Solaia, the superyacht, who we had met when we first arrived, to have drinks on board. It was exciting to see inside the boat. The crew, which included Dave's wife Fi, were welcoming. The owners were not on board and the boat was shortly to leave for the Caribbean for the winter season. She was 98 feet long and sheer luxury. One of the comfortable sofas in the saloon had a wide flat screen embedded in the backrest, so that at the press of a button the screen emerged. There were "surround sound" speakers all over the boat. We had some drinks and Dave had made a tomato dip that Alice loved. She asked him how to make it and he described the ingredients and method to her. Like so many of the other adults we had met on our journey, he treated her as an equal, not as a child, and I realised that we all had so much more time for each other.

Dave talked to the children about the sea life they had seen on their travels, and lent them his DVDs of "Blue Planet". The crew members had so many stories about whales and dolphins that conversation was lively. By ten o'clock the children were over-tired and we wandered home.

It was a slow start in the morning; Alice and Pip didn't emerge until around 9.30am. They did some schoolwork and then we took a walk around the town. It was a bustling metropolis, much larger than San Sebastian. We visited the market for provisions, which was well stocked and full of wrinkled old women dressed all in black. One hunched old lady with silver bristles on her chin hobbled up to the children and cupped both hands around Pip's face. In a high pitched voice she exclaimed, "Ah, los pecles, los pecles!" She was clearly referring to Pip's freckles; such pale skinned people were rare in these islands. She was so overwhelmed with Pip's appearance that she stroked her auburn hair and kissed her on both cheeks. Then she looked at Alice and was obviously thinking it would be unkind to leave her out, so she grabbed her shoulders and kissed her on both cheeks. The children smiled politely and we backed away slowly.

When we were out of sight, Alice muttered, "I didn't enjoy that."

"Nor did I," said Pip emphatically.

At one of the fruit and vegetable stalls we bought a big bag of produce. Alice added to it, selecting four beef tomatoes, a red onion, parsley, garlic and lemon juice. We bought a small bottle of Tabasco at another stall. These were the ingredients for Dave's dip. "It's 'Alice's dip' now," she said.

During the late afternoon Dave and Fi came over for a drink. Alice chopped all the ingredients finely and mixed them up in a bowl, with a teaspoon of ground cumin and some salt and pepper. She put tortilla chips in another bowl, as vehicles for the dip. Dave was encouraging, saying, "It's delicious, Alice." He added a tip, "Once I left it standing for a couple of hours before we ate it, which made all the flavours develop really well."

Our guests departed. It was the fifth of November and there were no fireworks. Alice and Pip thought of home, upset to be missing the party we usually went to. We cuddled up and put one of the "Blue Planet" DVDs in the player; we had missed this when it had been on the television the previous year and now it had special relevance.

CHAPTER 72

The following morning we dropped the DVD back with Dave and said goodbye. We motored out of the marina, bound for Las Palmas, Gran Canaria, around 50 miles away. It was a fine reach to begin with, a force 4-5. Again the sea was choppy and grey, and there was not much conversation on board. Some spotted dolphins accompanied us. We made the final approach in the dark. Rob had warned us that he had arrived in the dark and found it difficult to pick up the correct lights. It took us a while to work out where we were going, but the route gradually unfolded as we got closer. We stopped at the fuel berth again, and topped up our tanks. We managed to avoid being put on pontoon 17 this time. We were told to tie up on pontoon 15, and found a space between a boat from Finland and another from France. Near the end of the pontoon was a beautiful dark blue Swan 48 called Azure, with the letters HPYC on her stern. In England we were members of two clubs, one of which was Haven Ports Yacht Club; HPYC. We wondered whose boat this was.

Many of the boats were dressed overall, some flying a large "ARC 2005" battle flag. An atmosphere of incredible excitement pervaded. It dawned on me that we had only two weeks to go before we started our Atlantic Crossing. Nick and Amanda would arrive in ten days. There was so much to do.

The first priority was to tick off all the safety related items that were a requirement of the ARC. The list was long; it included obvious things like having the right sort of liferaft and an EPIRB, a device used by sailors in trouble. When activated it sent a signal to a satellite, which then beamed it to the rescue services. We had registered ours so that the signal transmitted was personal to us. Charlie secured it in a bracket in the companionway, where it could be grabbed on exiting the boat. There were other things that we had to buy or do, in order to comply. We needed another bucket, with a rope attached so that it could be dangled in the water, two fire extinguishers, a high power search light, a heaving line (a ring on the end of a long line that could be thrown to someone in the water), a particular first aid manual, and numerous other items. We had to write the boat's name in indelible pen on the lifepings on the stern. We drew a plan of the boat with markings to indicate where all the safety equipment was stowed. Charlie was at work installing the masthead three-coloured light that we'd bought as a back-up navigation light, and he planned to check all the lights to ensure they were working properly. We discussed what our emergency steering mechanism, and alternative method of navigation, would be, and what we would do if the rig came down.

A couple in matching polo shirts arrived on the dock behind our boat. They were there to carry out an inspection of the mast and rigging. This was a free service, as part of our insurance policy. The husband was wearing a bosun's chair, which he clipped onto the main halyard, and Charlie winched him up the mast. He spent around half an hour in total, suspended at different levels on the mast, inspecting the joints where the wire stays attached to the mast, the cross trees, the rollers at the very top and three quarters of the way up, that the halyards slid over, and the halyards themselves. When he came back down, he went below into the saloon and looked at the mast foot, set into the top of the keel. After all this he gave us a verbal report. There was nothing of concern, however he advised us to tape split pipe to the cross-trees as protection for the mainsail. Because we were likely to be sailing downwind, the boom would be out as far as it could go, and the mainsail was likely to be touching the cross-trees, which could cause wear on the sail. Or the cross-trees could be damaged by the rubbing of the running backstays, which would be loose while we were sailing downwind.

I was devoting considerable thought to the provisioning of the boat for the crossing, and walked with Idunn to the marina's conference room, to attend a seminar organised by the ARC. It was one hour long and packed with advice on how to work out what, and how much, to buy, as well as many useful tips on storage. It was suggested that pasta was a very good lunchtime meal, being quick to prepare and a good carbohydrate energy food. When we cooked the pasta, the best method was to bring the water to the boil and put the pasta in, bring the water back to the boil and then switch the gas off, with the lid on, and leave it for ten minutes. In the warmth of these latitudes it wouldn't cool down too much and would cook perfectly, which would save on precious gas. Pasta was also advantageous because after the first couple of days we wouldn't have bread, unless we made it ourselves.

It was suggested that we should have a go at making our own bread, and we were taught the Spanish terms for flour and yeast, for when we went shopping. I was not confident about this; having had a number of bread disasters in my time, I had given up trying to make it. But I resolved to buy the ingredients and try again, having a feeling that our diet could become quite boring during the crossing and we would need as much variety as possible.

There was much talk of fishing and it was suggested that some bottled sauces could be bought and used to make the fish less plain; a large fish might last for several days and some variation might be welcome. The ARC had an arrangement with El Corte Ingles that they would give us a 10% discount and put some English speaking assistants on duty in the shops, who would help us to choose soft drinks and meat. The meat could be frozen and vacuum packed on request, which they said would mean it remained fresh for 4-6 weeks in the bottom of a normal boat fridge.

The lecture was very interesting and I especially enjoyed sitting in a comfortable chair. I had not sat in an armchair for months. I almost dozed off in that warm velour cocoon. At the end we stood up to file out, slightly dizzy in the bright sun, and suddenly we were standing next to Penny from Tamarisk. Idunn introduced us.

Charlie had been looking after the children and they were waiting for me to come out of the lecture. He was going to a seminar on how to use a sextant, so I took the children and we headed back to the boat. Later in the day we did more sorting out of the safety equipment. We were going to be inspected in three days' time. We had yet to resolve how to comply with two of the requirements, but there was plenty of discussion amongst the boats on this. In the evening we went to the opening party of the ARC, involving free food and drink at a local venue. We walked into the courtyard where the party was to be held, to be greeted by two incredibly tall transvestites in thigh length platform boots. They had big beehive hair and were wearing lots of make-up. I asked Pip, "What do you think of those ladies?"

"Mummy! Can't you see they are men?"

She was certainly more switched on than I was at the age of six. I remembered when I saw Boy George on television for the first time, at the age of thirteen. I'd thought he was a woman, and only discovered the truth at school the next day.

At the party we talked to Penny and Tim. We discovered that they had attended the ARC presentation at the Boat

Show that we went to. They were at the show buying the last few bits and pieces for their boat. We told them that we hadn't decided whether we would go or not and didn't even own Keoma at that time. They must have thought we were incredibly disorganised.

Our reunion with Paul and Fi was like meeting up with old friends again. Paul told us how they had been hit by a rogue wave between La Gomera and Gran Canaria. I thought these were only a danger mid-Atlantic, but apparently not. The wave had broken over the boat, the top of it hitting the mast as high as the spreaders. Paul had been helming at the time and it took all the strength he had to hang on to the wheel. Ollie had been sleeping in the cockpit, fortunately clipped on, and his lifejacket auto-inflated. Fi and Ems had been below, and were woken by the noise of the wave engulfing them and, a split-second later, tons of water cascading down the companionway steps into the cabin.

Charlie introduced me to Dan and Susan, Canadians from a boat called Kosh Long. Apparently our children had met theirs in Santa Cruz. Charlie described a rather embarrassing situation earlier in the day when Pip had persuaded him to skip along through Las Palmas, holding hands. It wasn't the kind of thing that Charlie would usually do, but he'd obviously felt safe that he wouldn't meet anyone he knew, and his spirits were quite high. They were both skipping along when they met a man who said, "Hi Pip, is this your Dad?" It was Dan.

I was chatting with Rob and Kerry when Charlie appeared with the mystery owner of Azure, Stewart, who I'd met on a race to Ostende eleven years before. He was going to be sailing the ARC with his 22 year-old daughter and four friends. We talked for hours and everyone enjoyed the abundant Spanish white wine. There was lots of food, including the local speciality; mojo potatoes, which were spuds served with two colours of spicy dipping sauce, green and red. I couldn't tell any difference in flavour, but maybe the wine had made my taste buds as muzzy as my brain.

CHAPTER 73

The following morning was a slow start, but we had plenty to do. Charlie went to the chandlery to buy the rest of the safety items we needed and collect the spade anchor. I expected to see him return weighed down with this cumbersome item, but he held only a couple of light plastic bags. The chandlery had been unable to get hold of the anchor. "Maybe it's a good thing. We don't really want to take the extra weight across the Atlantic and we're going to be pretty pushed for space. We should buy an anchor in St Lucia," he concluded.

In the afternoon the children went to a party on the beach organised by some ARC representatives, giving us a good opportunity to spend a couple of hours at El Corte Ingles. I had asked the children to work out, as a maths exercise, how many cans of drink we needed. I was planning to cater for one can of soft drink each per day, four cans of beer each per day for Charlie and Nick and two cans of beer each per day for Amanda and I. We bought as much wine as we thought we could stow, because we had been told that wine was expensive in the Caribbean. We ordered crisps, cereal, biscuits, 15 bags of pasta, sweets, chocolate, flour, yeast, rice, couscous; all the dry ingredients. We bought a selection of different sized batteries, for our emergency GPS, torches and other small appliances. It was too early to buy fruit and vegetables, but we ordered the meat. Into the trolley went tinned tomatoes, baked beans, cooking oil, UHT milk, loo rolls, paper towels, washing-up liquid and sun cream. We didn't need tinned fruit, as we still had the tins we'd brought out from England. Finally, we put in a selection of different types of orange juice; we were still trying to find some that was palatable. This filled two trolleys to overflowing, which would all be delivered to the boat by the shop.

We raced back to collect the children from the beach, jogging through the dusty streets between tall buildings. The girls asked whether they could go back to Whitehaven with Georgia and Emma to watch a movie. Later, a man passed us a business card over our stern, advertising a hull scrubbing service. We agreed that it would be a good idea not to take Mediterranean weed to the Caribbean, as well as being fractionally faster, and we arranged for Edward to return in a couple of days with his scuba gear.

There was a notice board at the end of our pontoon, on which people had displayed advertisements offering themselves as crew. A few of these people found their way past the security gate, onto the pontoon, and asked at each boat whether they were looking for crew. It struck me that we would need to be desperate to ask one of these people to join us on the trip. Not only were they unknown strangers who we would have to spend time with in a confined space for the twenty or so days that we were at sea, but we would also be trusting them with our lives when they were on watch. I felt glad that we didn't need to worry; Nick and Amanda would be arriving in a couple of days' time.

Every morning there was a VHF announcement at 9.00am, outlining the events to take place that day. Today there would be a life raft demonstration, for which we were advised to wear our swimming things. Charlie was busy, still sorting out the safety equipment on the checklist, so I took the children along. I felt it would be worthwhile for them to find out what it would be like to be inside a life raft. When we arrived at the marina's open air swimming pool, two men showed us how to deploy the life raft. It involved removing any straps from the case, tying its long rope to the boat (here they used the swimming pool steps) and throwing it in. There needed to be sufficient jerk on the rope for it to activate, so it was sometimes necessary to give it an extra tug. The organisers made it clear that I was expected to get into the life raft with the children. I stripped down to my bikini and stood beside the pool, feeling self conscious in front of a hundred people. We lined up in groups of six to jump into the water. We were told to hold our noses with our right hands and fold the left arm over the top of our right and hold that position as we stepped off the edge.

We jumped into the pool individually, then swam to the life raft. With extreme effort I hurriedly dragged myself out of the water and into the life raft. Inside was darkness and a strong smell of rubber. My eyes slowly adjusted to the change from the bright sunlight outside, to the dim orange of the interior. I felt as though the colour alone could induce seasickness, even to a non-sufferer. I pulled myself across the saggy, flooded floor like a giant slug, to sit between Alice and Pip, who had climbed in before me. They found it a fun game, but the atmosphere cooled dramatically when I asked them what they thought it would be like to spend hours or days in here. Alice was feeling sick and keen to escape. We launched ourselves out into the sunshine and splashed around in the turquoise pool, liberated.

Upon our return to the boat we saw a huge pile of cardboard boxes in the cockpit. Our order from El Corte Ingles had arrived. The children went off in the dinghy to visit their friends, while we unpacked and stowed. Charlie unscrewed Keoma's floorboards and we secreted one layer of beer cans in the bilges, before screwing the boards back down again. We lifted up the seats and wedged in dry food, then opened the lockers behind the seats and at head-height. The children's schoolbook locker was reorganised, removing completed books (which we placed in deep storage beneath our bed) and tidying pens and pencils to free up space. We filled every available locker below and then reorganised one of the cockpit lockers to fit in the slabs of soft drink cans. We managed to find places to stow everything, although we were conscious that the meat, cheese, fruit and vegetables hadn't arrived yet.

I sorted treats into three separate bags, so that they would be more evenly distributed throughout the journey and to provide an element of surprise and variation. I sealed the bags and attached labels reading "week 1", "week 2" and "week 3". The children returned with some friends. Ems from Blasé said, "Mum won't let us eat *anything*! She says it's all for the crossing." I sympathised with Fi; it would have been easy to tuck in and make a significant hole into the provisions. Further, buying food for the crossing was enough to think about. It was impossible to plan meals as well!

Our neighbour on the Finnish boat next to us, Chris, was not happy about the cardboard boxes. "Keep them off your boat! And don't put it anywhere near mine!"

"Ok, ok," said Charlie.

"You know that cockroaches lay their eggs in cardboard, don't you?" asked our neighbour.

"Yes, I know that. But tell me something. Do you use loo roll on your boat?"

Chris looked perplexed, "Yes, of course we do."

"Well," said Charlie, "What is in the centre of each roll?" Chris's eyes crinkled up as he walked away chuckling.

Although Charlie enjoyed winding Chris up about the subject, we *were* careful to avoid an infestation. We had been told that many Caribbean boats had these uninvited guests on board, and that they were almost impossible to get rid of. I cringed at the thought of finding them in the food lockers or having them crawl over our pillows.

Later, it came up in conversation with Chris that he had recently received a letter from Halberg-Rassey, the manufacturer of his boat. "It says that no-one has ever starved on the ARC. So we shouldn't worry too much about having enough food on board," he concluded.

Kerry wasn't having much fun provisioning their boat. Whitehaven's crew would be six men, most of whom she hadn't met. She was concerned that she was buying the wrong foods. In the course of sorting out storage space on Whitehaven, Kerry gave Pip a pair of shoes that Emma had outgrown; expensive-looking Timberland sandals which Emma had hardly worn. They seemed to fit perfectly and soon became Pip's favourites.

The ARC parade was due to begin at noon and already a brass band was playing in the distance. I had thought these were a British phenomenon, but clearly they had them in Spain, too. There was a banner for each country that had a boat participating. As we lined up for the start, rapid drops of rain hit the ground, quickly building to a full downpour, drenching everyone, but we stoically marched on.

Back at the boat our safety inspector arrived. We were surprised to see that it was Chris Brooke, a former Commodore of HPYC. He was friendly and affable, ticked off the list on his clipboard, and approved of the way we'd dealt with the requirement to tie the mast down, one of the more tricky rules to interpret and one that had been the subject of considerable discussion over the last few days. Charlie considered that a mast was most likely to break at boom level, so he tied a strong strap to the mast, then through the moulded loop where the kicking strap attached, which would do the job of stabilising the mast in the event of such a break, making it less likely to pierce the hull.

CHAPTER 74

A pirate ship had recently arrived on the other side of our pontoon. It was the kind of vessel that Charlie had had in mind when he first pictured our boat. Solidly built, 50 foot long, high out of the water, two masts, a bowsprit with net beneath, and glazed windows along the stern like an old galleon. Children with bronzed skin and untamed, sun-bleached hair hung off the rigging and a naked blonde toddler grinned at passers-by from the well-netted rail. Two Arsenal pennants flew from the cross-trees. A scroll-effect wooden name plate read "Wild Alliance".

The relentless social scene continued, with drinks on different boats in the evenings. I was stopped on the pontoon by an older gentleman who complimented the children. "They were having the most wonderful time in the dinghies, with all the water fights and other games, but when it comes to seamanship they've definitely got it. They came into this pontoon and tied up the dinghies beautifully."

We found a novel way of calling the children back to the boat for mealtimes. All the families in the marina left their radios on, tuned to VHF channel 22. The conversation tended to go; "Whitehaven, Whitehaven, this is Keoma, Keoma."

"Hi Keoma, this is Whitehaven, over."

"Hello Kerry, have you got our children there, over?"

"No, Juliet, we haven't. Last time I saw them I think they were going to Blasé, over."

"Ok, thanks, I'll check with Blasé."

Fi chipped in, "Keoma, Keoma this is Blasé. They aren't here, but they did all go off together, over."

Susan's Canadian tones would then come over the airwaves, "Keoma, Keoma, this is Kosh Long. The kids are all here, over."

"Sue, great, would you mind sending them home, please? We're about to eat, over."

"OK, they're on their way! Over."

"Thank you, see you in the morning. Keoma standing by on channel 22."

"Kosh Long on channel 22."

One morning we watched a rescue demonstration. A helicopter picked up a man, using its sling and winch, from the deck of a motorboat in the water just the other side of the marina's external wall. The helicopter created a wide circle of deep ripples with the strong down-wind from its blades. Afterwards there was a flare display, with instruction on how to set them off. Some people brought their own flares to see what it was like to set one off. I wondered that gloves had to be worn to prevent burning from a hand-held flare; seemed like a serious design deficiency. Fortunately we had thick gardening gloves on board, which I'd bought in England, with fish-handling in mind. My second thought was, what would happen if we needed to set one off from a liferaft? Would the sparks melt holes in it?

In the afternoon I visited the launderette and filled a couple of the large machines with clothes and sheets. I was preparing Pip's cabin for our guests. She wasn't too happy about giving up her personal space, but there was no choice. We talked to her about sharing.

Early in the evening Nick and Amanda arrived. It was wonderful to see our old friends. Nick was incredibly excited. "You won't believe what we've got for you. Come on Mands, get the presents out, get them out!" Amanda produced a pile of T-shirts from her bag. She passed one to Charlie and one to me. I pulled open the clear plastic bag and laid mine on the table. The shirts had a logo of a sailing boat, the name "Keoma" and "ARC 2005", and they had also had small ones made for the girls. We were overwhelmed by their thoughtfulness. Then Nick produced a big Christmas pudding from his bag. I had been trying to buy one in Las Palmas, without success, and I had been warned that there was no hope of buying one in the Caribbean.

"Thank you Nick, but I had only asked for a small one!"

"Sorry, I don't do small. You'll just have to manage with this one."

Nick and Amanda had also brought CDs. "We were a bit worried we'd have to listen to your dodgy music the whole way, so we thought we'd better bring some decent stuff," said Nick.

After supper Kerry arrived with Georgia and Emma. "We wondered whether the girls would like to come for a sleepover, as a goodbye before we fly out to the States tomorrow?" Alice and Pip packed pyjamas and toothbrushes into a beach bag and, waving to us as they chatted away with their friends, wandered off to the next pontoon, where Whitehaven was now moored. We decided it was too good an opportunity to miss and we grabbed our money, found some flip flops and made for the marina bar.

The bar was heaving and the atmosphere buzzing. As usual, Nick met someone he knew from London. We had quite a few drinks before we wove our way home. Amanda was suffering with a bad cold, and the combination of feeling under the weather, excitement, tension, tiredness and the mixture of alcohol, proved to be a dangerous combination; she was sick into the heads. "I can't take you anywhere," said Nick.

In the morning we were woken by the sound of scratching coming from the underside of the boat. "It's Edward, cleaning the hull," said Charlie. Edward wore full scuba gear. He spent three weeks of every year in the slimy waters of this marina. I wondered whether he needed to work for the other 49. I collected the children from Whitehaven and we said goodbye to Kerry, Georgia and Emma for three weeks. Suddenly our departure seemed imminent. Nick and Amanda supervised the children's schoolwork while Charlie and I walked the mile to El Corte Ingles and bought butter, cheese and sliced ham. I had decided that I must have an iron on board and a non-slip tray, so we took the escalator up to the home-wares department. We purchased another two china mugs, for Nick and Amanda to use.

Charlie had found pipe to split and tape to the cross-trees and we winched him up the mast. He gave Nick and Amanda a full briefing on safety, from how the life raft was deployed to where the flares, first aid kit, EPIRB, fire extinguishers and grab bag were stowed. He passed them a lifejacket each and they put them on, adjusting the straps to the right positions so that they fitted snugly, Charlie explaining that we always wore these at night and showing them how we clipped the safety lines on to the boat's strong points. I was busy sorting out the galley. I removed all excess items and put them into deep storage beneath our bed. We kept only six mugs and six plastic glasses out. I marked each with a number, so we had one allocated cup and glass each, to cut down on the washing up. I'd marked the life jackets with numbers, too.

In the evening Nick and Amanda treated us all to dinner at a local tapas bar. There were ARC events every night, but we were feeling jaded and just wanted a quiet night. After dinner we returned to the boat with two tired children, and drank coffee in the cockpit.

CHAPTER 75

Other boats didn't have such a quiet evening. The following day Rob came to see us, needing to let off steam over his crew's night-time activities. Newly arrived from Australia, they had decided to prepare for their Atlantic crossing by sinking a few jars of the amber nectar. One, Mark, had drunk a tinny too many and fell over, hitting his head on the pontoon. It appeared quite a serious injury, and he bled profusely, so another of the crew, Greg, took him to hospital in a taxi. However, Mark didn't have EU medical cover, so he borrowed Greg's medical card. When the nurses asked Mark his name, the combination of the bang on the head, the alcohol and the deception caused him to become confused, so he didn't speak, leading the nurses to believe the injury was more serious than it actually was. The nurses checked him in under the name on the medical card and he was put in bed for observation. By this time Rob had heard about the injury and, as skipper, felt responsible for Mark. It was the early hours of the morning but he took a taxi to the hospital and asked which ward Mark was in. They answered that they didn't have anyone of Mark's name on their records. Rob wanted to be sure that Mark wasn't there, so he walked around the hospital, eventually finding Mark and ascertaining that he was not too badly injured. He told Mark to enjoy his night in a bed and discharge himself in the morning when the alcohol had burnt off.

It was the final day before departure and we all walked to the market to buy our fruit and vegetables. We had been told that the market produce was the freshest and the fact it had not been refrigerated meant it would keep for longer because the moisture in the atmosphere of a fridge initiated deterioration. I had a purse full of Euros, because we had to pay in cash. At the market we stocked up with all sorts, filling a shopping trolley. Susan was there, too, doing the same as us. Everyone carried bags as we returned to the boat. It had to all be carefully stowed and most of the fruit went into the net.

I cleaned out the fridge in preparation for the meat's arrival. This was one of my least favourite jobs; the fridge tended to collect a layer of putty coloured sludge in the bottom. I had yet to discover what caused this. Possibly, when we were sailing along things spilt and then went off, but it seemed to develop when we were in port, too. The sludge had to be rinsed out using Cif and a scouring pad. The smell was rancid and because it was a chest fridge I had to lean right over it to scrub the inside, inhaling the awful stink. I removed the shelves and washed them, and then gave the interior a final sluice with fresh water, to remove the Cif smell. With perfect timing, the meat arrived, and I put it in the bottom of the fridge. There wasn't much room in there for anything else, but we managed to squeeze in the butter, cheese and a few beers.

"Hello Keoma, Hello."

I'd just finished putting away the food. Charlie and I climbed the steps to see Ed Wildgoose looking over the stern.

"Hello Ed, come aboard. Thanks for coming," said Charlie, shaking his hand.

"Would you like a drink? Cup of tea, coffee, soft drink, beer?"

"Just a water would be great, thanks Juliet."

The purpose of Ed's visit was for him to explain about ways to improve the connection between our laptop and the satellite phone. We had managed to get them to communicate but it was a very fragile connection and sometimes failed half way through. Ed sold us some strange looking objects. One was an octagonal puck with a wire coming out of it, which would improve the signal. He suggested that we placed this on something metal, to improve reception even more. He fired up the computer and tested the connection. It worked well with the new equipment. We talked about our website, which he was hosting.

At the end of our conversation he said, "I must say, it's very calm on here. Most boats are in a total panic."

"Well, I think we're nearly ready to go. The majority of the jobs are done and the crew have arrived, so we feel in quite good shape." Charlie showed Ed our notebook, items crossed off.

"OK," said Ed. "That's me done then. Have a great trip."

Charlie and I walked to the marina office to pay for our berth, to avoid having to do this in the morning. On the notice board a list of handicaps for all the boats was displayed. The number allocated to each boat was based on an international system designed to give everyone an equal time on the water, if multiplied by each individual journey time.

Once we'd settled up, we walked to the "Skippers Briefing" where we were given packs of information marked with the name of our boat. There was a presentation from the ARC's meteorologist, Chris Tibbs. He showed us the pressure chart for the next 24 hours. A curved black line ran across the centre, with red semicircles and blue triangles attached to it. "This occluded front will pass through these islands during tomorrow night. We don't expect it to be particularly active." His voice broke and trailed off slightly as he said the last two words. No… I imagined that. I must have imagined it.

It was explained to us that an email or SSB message of the weather report for the following day would be sent to us each day. The SSB broadcast worked by a few boats volunteering to be group leaders. They had to communicate with their group to ensure that everyone received the ARC weather information, and that the ARC office obtained a record of each yacht's position. The positions would be relayed to the ARC office. For those using email rather than SSB (like us) we would email our position at 12 noon Central European Time to the ARC office. We were told that if we were not accounted for on any day, they would not launch a search party for us; our EPIRB was the tool that would trigger a search. I was a little disappointed at this news. One of the reasons I had been keen to do the ARC was the idea that they would search for us if we were unaccounted for, but, thinking back, this had been something I'd assumed would happen, rather than any assurance made. What I didn't know then was that ultimately we would be glad that they had this policy.

The positions for each day would be uploaded to the ARC website, which the public could access to see how boats were progressing.

We were given instructions for when we arrived in St Lucia. It seemed a long way away. As we left the briefing we met Dan, who was unexpectedly serious. "You know what they were saying about this frontal system. I've been talking to Herb, you know, the weather routing guy, over the SSB. He gave me the impression that it could be quite violent. Obviously Chris Tibbs is saying something different, but we used Herb when we did our crossing from Canada and he was always spot on."

During the afternoon there was a party on pontoon 15, next to our boat. One section of the slatted walkway sunk lower and lower with each person who joined the crowd talking and drinking. Water started to lap over the top, and large glossy brown cockroaches swarmed out from underneath. Chris had been worrying about cockroach eggs that might hatch on his boat, but the creatures themselves were only feet away! It would only take one to tightrope-walk a mooring line. We had been advised not to stamp on them because the eggs could attach to shoes and make their way on board as foot passengers. I put our music on, Madonna's "Confessions on a Dancefloor," playing through the cockpit speakers for the benefit of the party nearby. Stewart was disapproving, being a classical fan, and he cringed at my choice, but everyone else seemed to like it.

Later, the disruption of so much partying around the marina had calmed and most boats were having a quiet evening on board, finishing off final jobs. We enjoyed a last shower ashore and updated our blog. There was a reflective mood on the boat. Nick and Amanda went for a walk ashore and Rob came to see us for a final goodbye. "Well. It's been nice knowing you," he said, pessimistically. There was a slight undercurrent of tension as we exchanged hugs.

CHAPTER 76

As I drifted into consciousness I could hear music. It was sombre, old fashioned, simple cello music. Chris was playing it next door. The slow chords were soothing and I lay in bed enjoying the relaxation. When it ended, it was time to get up and we all sat around the saloon table for breakfast. I had been longing for toast and had now found a way to make it. I put a slice of bread into a hot frying pan, left it for a minute and then flipped it to brown the other side. Toast had not been something that I'd expected to miss. We ate cereal with real milk (something else that had become a rarity on board), coffee and toast with marmite and jam. We never found orange juice that didn't taste off, so we'd given up searching. After breakfast we washed up and stowed the cutlery and crockery. Charlie topped up the water tanks with the hose; we had to put the generator on to make our own, so we may as well take as much as we could from the pontoon hose. We took our credit cards and passports out of wallets and bags and put them into the grab bag. It was odd to think we wouldn't need to buy anything for three weeks.

Nick deflated the dinghy and we stowed it in the deep locker beneath our bed. He and Charlie removed the anchor and chain from the bow and stowed them in the aft locker. Amanda took down the code flags. I made sandwiches for lunch. We would cross the start line around two o'clock in the afternoon. I heard a brass band playing and when I stuck my head out of the hatch, the wall of the marina was lined with hundreds of people. Charlie and Nick were clipping the staysail onto the inner forestay. We helped Azure with her lines and waved them off. They were in the racing division, which left an hour earlier than our cruising division. I met Idunn on the pontoon but we didn't talk; her eyes were filled with tears and she looked away.

CHAPTER 77

It was our turn to leave and we were ready to be off. We slipped our lines and motored away from the pontoon. There was a traffic jam of boats leaving the marina, even though it was still early. Everyone seemed to want to be on their way. We coiled our mooring lines and put them away. The fenders were stowed in the bow locker, which was then locked. A heavy throng of people lined the sea wall, waving and cheering, and I sat with the children on the cabin top and waved back. The boats sounded their fog horns and the band was playing. From this distance the drum beat was distorted, too bass, the brass out of tune. It sounded loud and chaotic. We passed the end of the marina wall and the wind cut in, sweeping the noise away. We opened a bottle of fizz and ate our sandwiches. It felt almost like Christmas day; all the preparation was over and we were ready for the real fun to start. It was exciting and a relief, at the same time. Nick took a photo of Charlie and I standing behind the helm, arms around each other, dazed, grinning. The children came to our sides and we pulled them close. We had 45 minutes until our start gun and we relished the time to stop and think, to savour the moment.

Looking around, we could see the racing fleet sailing fast, already started. Six boats were in a pack, tussling to be ahead. On the start line was a huge grey Spanish warship. I wondered how she would compare to HMS Grafton. We put the mainsail up and unfurled the genoa, and did a few tacks. Nick and Amanda had never sailed on Keoma or anything like her, before, so there was great emphasis on safety. The loads on the sheets and halyards were much greater than what they were used to. We turned Keoma onto a run, heading back to the start line, sheets loose and sails out wide, then passed the line and turned again, onto the wind, winching the sails in tight.

We weren't on the line when the gun went off; holding back to avoid the scrum because we couldn't bear the thought of a collision, with the damage and penalties that could bring. There would be plenty of time to make up a few minutes' delay. At the start gun, the warship launched a maroon which exploded in the air, dropping a huge pressure of sound. Two seconds passed before the deep boom reached us. I felt it in my stomach as well as my ears. Suddenly, we were on the way to St Lucia, in the middle of a pack of two hundred white sails against a bright blue sky.

Within twenty minutes we were easing the genoa sheet by degrees, as the wind came gradually aft, until we had the right conditions for the spinnaker. The rigging and launch was so easy, with two extra adults on board. I called up Blasé on the radio. They had enjoyed the start and told us to look for their yellow cruising shute. All around us were triangles of colour as many boats hoisted their spinnakers. A mile to our right was the island of Gran Canaria.

Keoma sailed along over small waves, and for two hours we made good speed, steadily overtaking boat after boat. We gradually took the boat closer to Gran Canaria, thinking we would take advantage of the sea breeze created by the landmass off our starboard side. One boat had gone very close to the island, and this tactic had been a good one; they were steaming ahead of everyone. I thought back to that first sail in Italy and how we loved Keoma's movement. It was just as addictive now. The children were smiling, enjoying the sail. I hoped they would be this happy after ten days at sea.

There was much discussion about how close to the island we should go in order to get a stronger sea breeze effect, and to take maximum advantage of the wind acceleration zone at the southern end of Gran Canaria. But it was irrelevant because the wind began to wane and soon we were stationary in the water. We'd lost momentum, and with it, steerage, and were being drifted on the sea currents. The spinnaker hung, slack and crinkled. We sat on the side-deck on the low side to tilt the boat slightly to leeward, which could help the sails to set in very light winds. The boat hardly moved. We, and the boats behind, were in a windless hole. We waited and waited. I made cups of tea. All we could do was be patient. Dan's conversation with Herb popped into my mind. Looking ahead, boats were beating with reefed mainsails. This made us think the wind would fill in for us in the same way, so Nick and Charlie went up to the foredeck as Amanda let the spinnaker halyard run. They packed the sail away and stowed the pole in its clips on the side deck.

They'd just got the pole away when the wind hit us, filling in from the other side this time, the island side. The wind was funnelling around the southern end of the island and we'd now come into this band. Charlie and Nick gripped the rails on the foredeck as the boat rolled onto her side. Suddenly the noise of the wind was in our ears and we held on to whatever we could get a hand to. Charlie and Nick reached the cockpit and we unfurled some genoa to balance the boat. Then Nick moved forward to the base of the mast to reef the mainsail. Charlie took the helm from me, and steered the boat so that she was head to wind, relieving the pressure on the mainsail. I let the main halyard drop a few feet and Nick hooked the ring stitched into the sail through the metal prong. I tightened the halyard up again and then winched in the reefing line that ran through the back end of the sail. The boat was under control and we were making good speed over the water.

CHAPTER 78

It was starting to get dark and I lit the gas stove for our supper. We had bought two new lighters for the stove. Matches were fiddly and could easily get damp, but press-button cooker lighters tended only to work for a short while. We weren't sure why, they just never lasted. It was a treat to have a new one that worked well, especially as I had to reach right inside the oven to light the line of flames at the back, and the boat was bumping around. I had made a shepherds' pie for our first night at sea and I slid this into the cooker and slammed the door. The cooker swayed on its gimbals as we were hit by wave after wave.

The meal was well received; it was exactly the kind of comfort food we needed in those conditions. We were all wearing full wet weather gear and life jackets. The boat slammed and crashed in the rough sea, healed right over on her side. These were not the kind of conditions we had been expecting for the ARC. We furled the genoa away and hoisted the staysail, which would enable us to point higher on the wind and prevent unnecessary strain on the genoa. I took Pip down below and helped her get undressed and into bed. I told her she could take a night off brushing her teeth. Then I took

Alice down, and got her clothes off her as quickly as possible; I needed to get her lying down before she started to feel sick. She was annoyed with me for helping.

"I'm not a baby," she said. "Why are you doing this?" I felt frustrated with her that she couldn't appreciate the urgency. She must have known that spending time below in even quite small waves made her feel sick.

I tried to be calm, "I'm only trying to help. If you don't want help, do it on your own, but do it quickly." I was thinking it was probably better not to mention the word "sick".

I headed back up on deck and we decided to put another reef in the mainsail. The wind was rising and the sea seemed to be getting rougher. We followed the same drill as before; Nick was harnessed and clipped on this time. He had attached a three shackle strap to his lifejacket, and clipped onto the webbing straps that lay on the sidedeck from the bow to the stern. He stumbled along the deck. Then he clipped his free shackle onto the loop at the mast, before reaching down and unclipping the other shackle. He stood at the mast and shouted back to the cockpit. Rain lashed down and the boat rose and slammed. We had put the spray hood up several hours before. It was useful for keeping the front part of the cockpit dry, but the halyard cleats and winches were beneath the hood, obscuring my view of Nick. Amanda looked over the hood and relayed what she could see and hear of Nick and the mainsail to me, as I was bent over, beneath the hood, winching. Nick returned to the cockpit. We decided that for tonight we should split into pairs, with Charlie and Amanda taking the first couple of hours while Nick and I got some rest, then we'd swap over.

I headed below, grateful for the shelter. The boat was still jolting around and I held the handgrips firmly as I clambered towards the forecabin. I peeled off the wet layers and lay in bed, a towel over the pillow for my soaking, salty hair. Lying in bed it was difficult to relax with such movement going on, but I knew I needed to get some rest, for the sake of everyone on the boat. I felt a strong pang of guilt for how Nick and Amanda must have been feeling. The conditions were very unpleasant and it would be natural to feel fear, but I hoped they weren't terrified. Amanda was quieter than usual and Nick's ebullience had been replaced by seriousness. But their decision making was as spot-on as ever. They were unfamiliar with the boat's controls and it was hard to see much in the dark. For example, the cam cleats which held the halyards were labelled, but you needed to switch on the torch to see them, and then they were in Italian; something that we'd grown used to and forgotten to change. They must have been wondering whether the entire three weeks at sea would be like this. I told myself this must just be the front coming through and tomorrow would be better. My throat felt dry all the way up to my nose. The strong taste of salt didn't help. Somehow I dozed off.

I woke when my body was rolled against the wall of the leeward side of the boat. The boat was leaned right over on her side. It felt wrong. I leapt out of bed and pulled on my waterproof trousers, boots and heavy coat, which I zipped up. I was stumbling a little, put off balance by the angle of the floor. The lifejacket was helpfully attached to the coat, and I fastened the clip at the front. The clothes felt cold where they touched my skin. They were perfectly waterproof and I was grateful for that, but the fabric felt plastic and clammy.

I clambered through the cabin, clutching at the handgrips. There was a smell of sick. I looked up to Charlie and Amanda on deck. Amanda looked pale and her eyes were big. I climbed to the top of the steps and called up to Charlie, angrily, "What's going on? Why are we right over on our ear again?"

He answered, "I thought it had calmed down and we took the reefs out."

I shouted, "Look! This is madness! Why are you racing in conditions like this? We need to sail conservatively. We're out here for three weeks. If we need to go slowly for a bit with sails that are smaller than perfect, then we should. We need to appreciate that the conditions are very unstable right now, thanks to this frontal system." By now I was in the cockpit and Nick was behind me. I was quite surprised how vocal I was being but all things combined had pushed me over the edge, and the children were asleep.

Charlie answered, "Ok, ok, let's get some more reefs in." So we went through the process again. Nick crawled up to the mast, Amanda told me what she could see and hear, and I adjusted the halyards.

Nick and I took over and we kept the sails reduced. I apologised to him for throwing my toys out of the pram. The conditions quietened down but we didn't shake out the reefs, we just accepted a slower pace. I went below to write the log. This morning I had written, at the top of the page, "From: Gran Canaria. Towards: St Lucia", which now seemed wildly optimistic, tempting fate, even. The cabin still smelt of sick and my boots slipped on the tilted floor.

"Blimey, it's like an ice rink down here!"

"Oh yes," said Nick, a little embarrassed. "That was me. I climbed into bed and it was weird. I had this sudden urge to throw up. I got out of bed but didn't make it to the heads. It went all over the floor. I have cleaned it up though."

I said, "That shepherd's pie can't have been too nice, second time around."

"Actually, it was all right. When I was cleaning it up I noticed that all the goodness had been extracted from each morsel. So it wasn't a wasted meal." The thought of him analysing his vomit in the middle of a howling gale made me laugh. He paused, and then he laughed too.

The rain had stopped but the sea was still rough and we had some strong gusts. I wondered how everyone else was getting on. I ran through the ARC weather advice again in my brain. Presumably if they had advised us to delay our departure, what might have happened was the whole fleet would cross the start line and then motor back into the marina. It would have been chaos with all those boats trying to come in at once and the marina had probably taken bookings for spaces that couldn't then be honoured. The anchorage outside the marina had been so full that I imagined quite a few boats were waiting to come into the marina to provision for their crossings. Anyhow, we had started and we weren't going to turn back. Nick went below to wake Amanda and Charlie for their watch.

CHAPTER 79

The morning dawned much quieter, with a west-south-west wind, and we all enjoyed breakfast in the sunshine. We were on a fine reach, on starboard tack, and our course was taking us towards the west coast of Africa. On the chart, the arched coastline stretched welcomingly towards us. It was clear that the frontal system had passed and we shook out the reefs. Gran Canaria had disappeared from view and we were surrounded by sea, only broken by the horizon. Pip helmed the boat competently for nearly an hour. She looked tiny behind the wheel, standing on the bench behind the binnacle, a big smile on her face. I passed up the first bag of treats and we switched the boat onto autohelm. Amanda opened the bag with the children. They excitedly pulled out chocolate bars, sweets, biscuits, crisps, nuts and a bottle of sparkling wine.

At midday I put a marker on the GPS and wrote down our position in the ship's log. I started up the computer and wrote an entry for our blog. I was keen to continue to make it an honest account, but I was having to temper my words with a consideration for the grandparents, who were anxious about us, so I described the start and glossed over the details of our "tiring night". Charlie laughed at my euphemisms.

My writing was cut short by cries of "Fish! Fish!" from the cockpit and I raced up the steps. Nick was winding in one of the long lines. We could see flashes of yellow and green in the water, and as it came closer we saw that it was a dolphin fish, also known as dorado or mahi-mahi, around 50cm long. I lifted one of the cockpit seats and reached into the locker for our new big net, and Alice passed up the vodka from below. We held the net next to the swimming platform and Nick gently flipped the fish into it. Following Rob's advice, Charlie took a sip of vodka and spat it into the mouth of the fish, killing it instantly. Nick posed with the fish and the children for photos. He couldn't stop chuckling.

I wrote an email to the ARC office stating our position, and sent this, with the blog, via the satellite phone. We received emails, including the ARC daily weather information message. There were good luck messages from parents and friends. Victoria wrote, "A friend of mine, Lucy, is on Spellbound, which is in your class. You'd better make sure you beat them!"

The wind had become moderate and we moved slowly through the water. After the previous night we were glad of some easy sailing conditions. Charlie gutted the fish. I cooked it in the oven with potatoes chopped up into chips. It had a flavour and texture not unlike sea bass. As we sat around the saloon table, Pip picked up one of the eyes and placed it on her tongue.

"What the..? Pip!?" said Nick.

"Delicious," she said, patting her small round stomach. "You should try one."

"Err...OK then..." He tentatively put the other one into his mouth and chewed, pulling a face. "Hmm... don't think I'll be rushing to eat another one of those. Good party trick, though, Pip."

My head felt heavy and I still had the sore throat. It felt as though I was coming down with a cold, for the first time since leaving England.

Charlie had decided to run the generator every evening, for a couple of hours. This would give us sufficient power for the following day. It made sense to run the watermaker at the same time. He switched it on and it clunked into action, but he was concerned. It sounded perfectly normal to me, but he could tell there was something wrong. He opened up the casing, to discover that it was only producing a tiny amount of water, not the 21 litres an hour that we should have been getting from it. Charlie switched the watermaker off and considered the problem. From our previous issues with the unit, he knew it intimately; he had spent several hours stripping it down and examining it. There was no visible problem. He reassembled the unit. If he couldn't fix the watermaker we would be reduced to the water in our tanks, which would mean strict rationing of drinking water and very little for washing. Showers would be out of the question. I hadn't worked out exactly how much we had, but now I thought about it. I knew the tanks held a thousand litres and we had some bottled water on board. Maybe twenty bottles. We knew we were supposed to drink 2 litres a day in this climate. Hopefully there would be enough.

We spoke to Blasé over the VHF. The reception was amazingly clear, even though we were around 50 miles apart. They had caught two fish, also dolphin fish. Ems told me they'd caught a male and a female at the same time, although on two separate lines, which they thought were a courting couple. Apparently the males had larger, squarer heads than the females.

Charlie had been pondering the watermaker problem. He pointed to the bubbles coming out beneath the back of the boat. "I think those bubbles are interfering with the watermaker. They come under the hull at the bow and then pass all the way along, close to the hull. Maybe some of them are going into the inlet hole. If I stuck a piece of pipe into the watermaker inlet it might part the flow of bubbles and solve the problem." He rummaged around in a locker and found a piece of the dinghy repair kit that he thought would fit, and stay wedged in place. "The only other problem is how to fit it. I think I'm going to have to choose my moment and take a swim." I was very unhappy about this idea, even though it felt as though the boat was stationary and he had swum beneath many times before when the boat had been at anchor.

Charlie decided that now was his moment. We furled the sails. He looped a rope beneath the stern and tied it to the manrails, so that it formed a belt around the underside of the boat. Grabbing his mask and snorkel, he jumped in. It felt as though we were a long way from land to be doing this kind of thing, but it may solve the problem. He reached up to take the piece of pipe and the hammer. Pulling himself beneath the water on the rope, he descended to the inlet. We heard a dull thudding from beneath the bottom of the hull as he hammered it in. He emerged, gasping for breath, then went under again and hammered further. His head reappeared, puffing, and he swam to the steps. "Well, I've hammered it in. I just hope it stays there."

At six in the evening we had "happy hour" with drinks and snacks. I wasn't feeling like alcohol tonight and opted for a cold relief drink instead. We had no tissues on board as we hadn't needed them for so long, so I was using toilet paper to blow my nose. Charlie talked about his swim, saying that even when we all thought the boat was completely still in the water, it was actually moving quite fast, and he had to hold firmly onto the rope.

Overnight we used a different shift system than the previous night. We had only very light winds and the sea was calm, which was a great improvement. We each took our own shift of two and a half hours. The autohelm did most of the work. It was so easy only having to break the night for this short watch. I enjoyed the time alone, sitting, reflecting on life. The sky was heavy with bright stars, and I wished we had a book on astronomy on board. I felt like a pointless speck of dust amidst this show of silent brilliance.

CHAPTER 80

I could hear someone shouting in the far distance. Alice's voice slowly came into focus and I opened my eyes. "Dolphins!" Feet slapped on the floor and pattered towards the steps. I waited to climb up into the cockpit and then we all made for the foredeck. Four spotted dolphins leapt and dived in the water, playing around the bow. They spun on their sides to look up at us with one eye. Their faces looked intelligent and expressive. "Look, they're smiling!" said Alice. But they didn't stay with us long and a few minutes later they peeled away and soon merged into one with the blue waves of the ocean.

Amanda and the children were peeling fruit to make a fruit salad for breakfast. They couldn't resist eating some as they chopped. Pip crammed an orange quarter into her mouth, covering her front teeth and the juice dripped down her chin onto her bare legs. I stood on the seat in the corner, feet pressing into the spongy velour, and sorted disappointedly through the fruit net. Several pieces of the market fruit had gone soft with a patch of green mould on one side and I piled them up in my hand and then took them up to the cockpit and lobbed them overboard. It was a different feeling from when a piece of fruit went off at home. I couldn't bung it in the compost bin and make a quick trip to the shops to buy some more. I felt let down by the market trader who'd sold the fruit to us. He'd known where we were going and that we were relying on its longevity.

The boat drifted along slowly under spinnaker, the wind a gentle north-easterly now. I stared at the sea. I had often heard the sea described as some kind of higher being or giant creature, gently inhaling and exhaling, but looking at it now brought to mind the appearance of a vast rolling moorland. With the impact of each puff of wind, the grass would undulate. Charlie switched on the watermaker. It started its regular dull mechanical thud, and when he removed the pipe to test the rate of production, it was working perfectly. 21 litres an hour, the elixir of life!

At midday I went below to put another marker on our chart plotter, and log our position. I typed the email to the ARC office giving them the chart co-ordinates. Then I climbed the companionway steps and stood in the cockpit holding the enormous telephone high above my head, to get the best possible signal. I felt like the Statue of Liberty in a bikini. A wire connected the phone to the laptop, which we had to keep down below at all times, to protect it from rogue waves. This meant I couldn't see what the computer was doing. It tended to behave like an errant child. As soon as I took my eyes off it, the screen would display a message about timing out, and then, sixty seconds later, it would halt. Nick and Amanda sometimes helped me by holding up the phone, so I could sit below and watch the screen. It was slow and frustrating and often I needed several attempts just to get a connection, let alone to complete the whole routine of sending and receiving without the satellite switching off or going behind the sail.

After around fifteen minutes the phone eventually connected and emails left us and flooded in. We received a message from Kosh Long, telling us that they crossed the starting line and then motored back into the marina at Las

Palmas for a relaxing first night with a few other non-starters. They had left the following day, after the conditions had settled. Sensible people.

Charlie analysed the positions of some of the other boats from the previous day and we saw that Azure was twenty miles away. I radioed them and the response was almost immediate. I was cheered to hear Stewart's voice, and that they were all well and in good spirits, although they had bad news. Their watermaker was not working, meaning they were each rationed to two litres of water to drink and a cup of water for washing each day. Of course, salt water could be used, but it left the skin itchy and dry, with a crust of salt that rubbed off onto bedding and clothes.

As usual there was a weather update from the ARC organisers. Today's forecast was disturbing. "The following Tropical Weather Outlook was issued from the National Hurricane Center, Miami FL. A strong and large non-tropical low pressure system over the central Atlantic centred about 1100 miles southwest of the Azores islands is moving slowly south-south-westward. This system is gradually acquiring tropical characteristics and could become a tropical storm later today". I didn't want to upset everyone and I called calmly to Charlie, "I think you ought to come and take a look at this." He read the email and scratched his stubbly chin.

"Hmm. How strange. This is extraordinary. But the track *has* to change. The direction the world spins means it has to loop back up towards the North-East. I don't think we should worry just yet. It has to turn. This would explain why we're having such light winds; the trade winds are being disrupted by the storm."

Scrolling through the emails there was another message from the ARC office, which gave me further discomfort. It alerted us to an event the previous night. A boat called Miss Charlotte had been approached from behind by a boat which was not displaying any lights. It had followed closely behind them for several hours, and gave no response to shouting or radio calls. The email reminded all boats of the need to be careful. We were currently passing through a zone which was known to be an area frequented by pirates from Africa. I thought of all the times we'd talked about pirates when we were in the Med. They were always so firmly in the past tense, and it was shocking to think that there was a modern-day equivalent, as brutal as ever.

The email continued; "Falmouth Coastguard advise that if boarded, yachts should set off their EPIRB and contact MRCC Falmouth 0044 1326 317575." We felt a long way from Falmouth right now. It ended with the words "Yachts were advised to keep well clear of the African coast."

The radio was alive with conversation. Three Norwegian boats had converged to form a convoy. We sat in the cockpit discussing what we would do in the event that a mystery boat approached us. Amanda was very cool about it, saying "It's probably just a fishing boat with no lights." I didn't feel so relaxed. Charlie explained his plan, that if a motor boat were to come up from behind, he would sail a winding course to prevent them being able to board Keoma. In addition, he would throw a spectre rope into the water, with the intention of fouling their propeller. Spectre was a nylon with the strength of wire and unstretchable. After much deliberation we decided the safest approach was to join the "Norwegian convoy" and we started the engine to catch them up. Running through my head was the music of a song released in the 1970's called "Convoy", which I found bizarrely comforting.

It took us a couple of hours to catch up with the group of, by now, eight boats. As we approached, the wind started to pick up. We hoisted the sails and switched off the engine. For an hour or so the speed was ideal, keeping us at the back of the convoy. But then the wind began to freshen and soon we were sailing faster than the rest of them. I wondered why they were continuing to motor, as we now had a perfect beam reach and were achieving consistent speeds of between 8 and 8.5 knots. The stars were bright and the water sparkled with phosphorescence. Behind the boat was a trail of glittering bubbles that made me think of a vapour trail and I felt as though I was sitting on a rocket ship. I was alone on my nightwatch, and couldn't resist giving the boat her head. We cut through the water. I took Keoma around the outside of the group, overtaking them one by one. They didn't switch off their engines. As we sailed along with these other boats close enough to give a feeling of security, I heard a panicked voice over the VHF.

It was an oriental-sounding man, radio protocol abandoned. "If anyone can hear me I am at (he gave a position around 50 miles behind us) and there's a boat at my stern with no lights on. I don't know what to do and I'm really frightened. Can anyone help? Please! Help me." It was distressing to hear. But help was out there and other boats near to his location radioed up and arranged to sail towards him. It would be a few hours before they met up, but he seemed comforted to know that reinforcements were on the way.

Amanda's head appeared at the top of the steps to take over the watch, and I headed for the forepeak. I cleaned my teeth, undressed and lay down on the berth, but I was wide awake. At this speed the water swooshing past the bow made a loud noise. I was thinking about the distressed radio message and the storm. What on earth were we doing here, with our young children and beloved friends on board? I lay in the darkness listening to the water, two centimetres from my head, unable to switch off. Charlie stirred and rolled out of bed, dressed and left the cabin for his watch. If we were to hit an object in the water, such as a semi-submerged container accidentally lost from a ship, it would mean instant death. The bow would hit it, the boat's fibreglass tearing open like a wet cardboard box, sea water gushing in, and then my skull would smash against the metal box. I tried to think more comforting thoughts, and as dawn came, I began to drift off to sleep.

CHAPTER 81

When I awoke it was ten o'clock. I didn't feel refreshed in any respect, and my eyes felt red and scratchy. Lying in bed in the forepeak, I could tell we were moving slowly. A gentle tinkling of water sounded at the bow. The breeze from the night before had expired and the boat was creeping along, with only a zephyr from behind. Charlie was tweaking the spinnaker to keep the boat moving at three knots of boatspeed. I felt hot and sticky and I indulged and took a shower. It was only the barest spritzing of cold water, but it brought my thoughts back into focus.

The others had eaten breakfast, so I just poured myself a bowl of cereal with UHT milk. To begin with I had thought UHT was disgusting but now we had become accustomed to it and couldn't taste the difference. It reminded me of an old diary of my father's that had I found in the attic years ago, describing one of his holidays on a small boat in the 1950's. One entry read, "Ran out of food. Had to eat cornflakes without milk. Blew away in the wind." It wasn't all tales of hardship though, another day they, "Donned blazers and slacks and ate a very good dinner at the local yacht club," which we teased him about whenever the opportunity arose.

There was a cry from the cockpit. "Fish! Fish! No... Two fish! Two fish!" It was a double strike, with a fish on each of the two trailing lines. Charlie grabbed one reel to wind in and Nick reached for the other. Charlie had started winding the line in, but before Nick touched his the line went loose. The fish must have broken the line and taken the lure and most of the line away. It was a shame to lose so much tackle, and we were nervous of losing any more, or the fish on the other line. Charlie wound slowly, sometimes letting line out to tire the fish. "It's putting up a good fight!" he said. When, fifteen minutes later, we landed it into the net, it was another dolphin fish, but bigger than the previous one, at around a metre long. The head was very square; maybe we had a male this time. I imagined him swimming along without a care in the world, his girlfriend by his side. They both spot a tasty meal ahead, take a bite, and, disaster! They're hooked. But she was the Serena Williams of the fish world and with sheer willpower she broke the line and was off. The hook would dissolve in a few days and she'd be on the lookout for a new mate.

At midday I logged our position as usual. The email download included an email from Victoria, who had sent me a recipe for cheese scones. This recipe was more straightforward than the one my mother had sent a week before we left the Canaries. I had emailed Mum back, asking, "What is cream of tartar? It sounds to me like the kind of thing that people cooked with during the war, along with powdered egg." I couldn't imagine finding it in a Las Palmas supermarket, or what the Spanish translation would be, so I'd given up on that recipe.

We were anxiously watching the weather. Because of the potential seriousness of the tropical storm we'd decided to buy a forecast which showed a satellite picture. The ARC forecasting had generally been good but it was a very brief email forecast, setting out a sea area according to a code name (these were defined in the ARC folder) and assigning a wind strength and direction. It was a simple and effective forecast, and one which could be conveyed via radio well, for those using SSB for receipt of weather forecasts. However, we wanted to see a visual image of the storm, and to see the peripheral weather systems.

The ARC's special weather email told us the following: "SPECIAL WEATHER STATEMENT Deep low now at 25W 40W classified as Tropical Storm Delta moving SSE at 8kts. Then is expected to decrease in speed and move North with some initial strengthening at first. Max winds forecast 50-60 kts vicinity of centre with higher gusts possible in squally showers. The forecast area of concern is a circle north of 20N, west of 30W, east of 50W, south of 37N. Yachts are advised to avoid this area."

Thankfully, we were outside the area of concern, at 22N, 19W, and we were also relieved to hear that the weather experts anticipated that it would start to track north. The conversation on board Keoma turned to recent weather events. The hurricane that Rob almost sailed into in Madeira was a first, too. Was this a result of global warming? Had we reached a "trigger point"? There had never been a tropical storm that had tracked across this part of the Atlantic, headed south-south-east. This year there had been so many named storms that the alphabet had been exhausted, which was why the Greek alphabet was now being used. The ARC was supposed to be timed to take place outside of hurricane season. What would happen if a hurricane ripped through the ARC fleet?

The email pressure chart (that we ordered from the Ocean Prediction Centre, at a cost of $10) gave us a more graphic view of the storm. The email arrived with a pdf attachment of a line-drawn picture showing isobars for the whole of the North Atlantic. The storm seemed to have stopped heading South-East, and appeared to be on an Eastward course. This track would still bring us within its skirts, however we were optimistic that it would continue to swing in direction, until it was on a North-Easterly track.

Now the serious business of logging in and analysing the weather was done, the girls made cheese scones for lunch. It was hot down below with the gas cooker on, but the result was delicious, even though we had no scales or cutter. I felt so encouraged that I was considering having a go at the bread recipe tomorrow.

My cold was taking its toll and Charlie, Nick and Amanda kindly extended their watches so that I could have a full night's sleep. I dosed myself with some night nurse and slept like a baby. It was a quiet night, with not too much water noise on the hull and no radio calls. The panic of the previous night appeared to have calmed.

CHAPTER 82

In the morning the wind began to pick up. We still had Big Blue flying, and with the sails set on a beam reach, the wind a constant 18 knots, gentle waves of around 3 foot high regularly swooshing us forward, it was perfect sailing. Keoma was in her element, stable and comfortable, light to the helm, riding the glittering water at a steady 10 knots of boatspeed. The sky was a perfect blue, dotted with small puffy clouds. We really felt as though we were in the tropics (we had now crossed to the south of the Tropic of Cancer) with the sun warming through to our bones. We all looked bronzed. The boat felt spacious, even with six of us living in a small space, because we were outside virtually all our waking hours, and the view was an open expanse of sea until it met the sky.

The day had its usual punctuation and I went below to log our position and collect emails. Before embarking on the trip we had discussed whether we should do the crossing without sending and receiving emails. However, we all so enjoyed receiving messages from family and friends, as well as the therapy of relaying our own experiences, that I was glad to have it.

We had some sad emails from the ARC office giving details of a boat that had been forced to make for the Cape

Verde Islands for repairs, and two others that had retired and returned to Las Palmas, also needing repairs. There was an email about the storm, and I took encouragement from the final sentence. "Delta could reach hurricane strength for a brief period during 25/11 but is expected to start to weaken. 50kt winds extend about 60 miles from centre of low. It is expected to begin moving to NNE in 24 hours."

We also had an email from Amazon with some "great offers for Christmas". I mulled over what the delivery address would be. Victoria emailed, saying, "Lucy's boat is way ahead of you – Hurry up!"

The radio had stopped picking up anything at all, probably because the boats were now dispersed over a wide area, and it was blissfully quiet on board, with just the sound of the water on the hull. There was now a great feeling of peace and tranquillity on the boat. Amanda and Nick were sunbathing on the foredeck and Charlie was in the cockpit with the children. For the first time in ages, I reached for my novel. The boat's shelves were groaning with books which had mostly remained untouched by me. I had thought there would be plenty of time for reading on this trip. The only time when I seemed to have hours to spare was on night watch, when it was too dark to read.

Mid-afternoon I spooned dried yeast into a cup of warm water. I set the yeast on the top of the unlit gimballed stove (in case of an unusually large wave) and left it to start to ferment. I poured flour into a plastic mixing bowl and added a lump of butter and a teaspoon of honey.

Within a minute or two the cup had a frothy, almost beer-like, head on it. I'd never had this happen with yeast before, and concluded it was something to do with the air temperature. I added it to the other ingredients and mixed it around, adding some more warm water and then gave it an energetic kneed for five minutes. That was about all I could manage in the heat of the enclosed cabin. I put it into the baking tin (which I had bought especially, in Las Palmas) and covered it with clingfilm. But the result was very disappointing. It just wouldn't rise. I left it for hours on top of the cooker and nothing happened. I felt like throwing the whole thing overboard.

"Look at it!" I complained to Amanda. "Such a waste of time. I just know it's going to be like a brick when it's cooked."

"Well," she said tactfully, "If you're planning to bake those potatoes, why don't you stick it in the oven at the same time and see what happens?" I knew what she was saying made sense, and grumpily agreed.

Half way through cooking the potatoes and the bread, the gas ran out. Charlie quickly changed the bottle. The food was unaffected, and the bread looked alright. It wasn't exactly puffy but it hadn't sunk and it did have a nice golden colour. I put the loaf on the breadboard and cut into it with trepidation, bracing myself for statements like: "We could always use it as an anchor," and, "Did you drop a winch handle into the pan with the mixture, by mistake?"

But Charlie was concerned about something different. "We've only got two more gas bottles on board. We need to be really careful with it. Let's try not to use too much." This was quite difficult for me, because I had bought the kind of food that kept well and could be shoved in the oven and forgotten about, in case of bad weather. I hadn't bought salads because they wouldn't keep. The next few meals would have to be pasta, cooked using the ARC method, with a simple sauce.

The evening happy hour had become a daily institution. We took turns to choose music and sometimes it was loud; the Kaiser Chiefs were a favourite. Sometimes it was Jack Johnson for when the mood was mellow. Very little alcohol was drunk, mainly because of the stinking colds, but we enjoyed the cans of soft drink. Amanda had great plans, "We can have a massive session one night!" But that never happened, because we all felt a tinge of responsibility. We had to take our turn to drive and there was a great feeling of sharing the burden and needing to be alert in case anything went wrong.

The winds seemed to have become more stable and we decided to leave the spinnaker up all night, giving us a distance run over 24 hours of 186 miles. I stared at the water, mesmerised, for hours. It was like watching a log fire. The boat was surfing along with a lovely following sea, still heading south. We kept reading the phrase (which apparently had to be said in the voice of an old sea-farer) telling skippers to, "Steer south until the butter melts," after which it was supposed to be ok to point west. I had reached the stage that if one other person said it or wrote it, I thought I would scream. Also, we were going further south than normal because the trade winds were unusually far south right now, disrupted by the hurricane. AND, we had a fridge.

The good news was that Delta had turned to a north-easterly heading, so we were in the clear. A cause for celebration. We put on some loud music and poured rum punches. Charlie and Nick went onto the foredeck to get big blue down and when this operation was complete we unfurled the genoa, in preparation for a windshift that the ARC forecast had warned us of. The wind was expected to fill in from SSW, and this happened on cue in the early hours of the next day.

CHAPTER 83

The following morning Pip found a flying fish lying on Keoma's deck. She picked it up by the tail and examined it. It was around 20 cm long, with a boxy head, bulbous black eyes, and delicate fins of around 7cm in length. It was silver, with a white underbelly and it smelt. We had seen plenty of these leaping through the air, just above the waves, but none on the boat until now. Unusually, the conditions were damp and overcast, but within a couple of hours it had burnt off and the heat began to build again. The wind changed direction, to the South West, and we were close hauled, for several hours. Those settled conditions had disappeared again. We longed for the trade winds!

I was conducting my daily inspection of the fruit. I was sad to say that the market fruit had not survived well. Perhaps we bought a batch that had been left in an open truck in the sun. The chilled fruit from El Corte Ingles had lasted much better.

We played a game of Scrabble in the cockpit, which, unexpectedly, the children enjoyed immensely. I took a photo which I downloaded and sent to our website and to the ARC office with our daily position reporting. The good news amongst the emails received was that the ARC forecasted that trade winds would set in on Tuesday; the day after tomorrow.

Later on we caught another dolphin fish, and I fried it (using minimal gas) for our supper. The evening sky gave us clear sitings of Mars and Venus, which we looked at through the sextant, although we couldn't be bothered to analyse the data. I had the feeling that if we had no GPS on the boat we would take astral navigation more seriously.

Again, I was having difficulty sleeping, despite having put a sheet onto the seats in the saloon, which was quieter than the forepeak. So many thoughts ran through my head. In the morning the wind had swung to the South East, but it was light and flukey. Around lunchtime it disappeared and we decided to take the opportunity to go for a swim. Having talked about swimming for days, if the trade winds were to fill in tomorrow, we may lose our chance. Charlie rigged a long line with a float on the end and tied it securely to one of the boat's cleats. Individually we ventured into the deep blue water. It felt cool, although it was 30 degrees centigrade. Strange to imagine that directly beneath our bodies could be all manner of sea creatures. A mile or more down there could be a sperm whale. A grimacing, ugly grey head and 11 metres of body, lurking in the depths. It felt fantastic to be immersed in the water, as the coolness encased our bodies, cleansing, so good that all negativity dispersed. There were no waves, only a very gradual rise and fall on the surface of the endless blue.

We took turns to swim, conscious that if we all jumped in at once, the boat could catch a breath of wind on her hull, and move off faster than we could swim, despite our precautionary furling of the sails. At last the final swimmer hauled up the dripping ladder and stood in the sun to dry. We had long since given up using towels for salt water drying. It was worth relishing every drop of coolness for as long as possible, because the only escape from the heat now was the shower. Even at night it was hot, and we wore only shorts and T-shirts. But no-one was complaining. Perhaps our bodies had adjusted, but it hadn't reached the point of being unbearable. We never sweated, and the emails from home describing snow on the ground helped to keep things in perspective.

The boat sat still in the water, gently clanking. Maybe the top of the mast swung ten centimetres from side to side; not enough to call it rocking. The children sat below and watched a DVD, relaxed and not fidgeting and bickering, thanks to the swim. "Let's get to where the wind is," said Charlie, reaching for the engine key and waiting, poised, for an answer. We all agreed, but the sound of the engine was so alien, so violent, in such a scene of perfect tranquillity. It was like sitting close to the lawnmower on a perfect summer's day.

Everything had to be louder when the engine was on. The music, the radio, our voices. I felt less in tune with the boat.

Around 8pm we started to feel a zephyr of wind, and took the throttle back to neutral. It was amusing to watch the adults, sitting up, faces pointed into the wind, poised, assessing, feeling it. We looked like meerkats. There would be a pause and then someone would say, "Yes, I can definitely feel it, it's filling in." Nick headed up to the foredeck, untied the spinnaker bag and started clipping the lines on. Up went Big Blue, we tightened the sheet and guy, tweaked to get it pointing exactly right to catch the most wind, and Keoma did the rest. Enough breeze to give us five knots of boat speed and with a relief the engine went off. Peace.

The spinnaker stayed up all night, although the wind was very light in patches. Progress was slow. We were down to around 3 knots of speed. We ate breakfast beneath the bimini as the boat drifted. Charlie and I reflected that the Atlantic had, so far, generally proved to be a far gentler beast than the Med. I shuddered to remember those dark lines in the water, those five seconds' warning of an approaching squall that would knock the boat on her side and send everything that was not stowed crashing onto the floor, as we leapt to shorten sail.

CHAPTER 84

At 10.30am the spinnaker filled properly. It was a solid, constant, wall of easterly wind and somehow we knew we'd found the trade winds. It felt as though this air would take us all the way and that finally we were off. 2,000 miles to St Lucia. The frustration of light changeable winds had gone and it was so satisfying to be romping along. The entry in the ship's log read, "Boat is going like a train".

Our increased speeds took a toll on the fishing. Two fish fell off the lines as we wound them in.

In the evening we sat around the saloon table and ate roast chicken with all the trimmings, including stuffing and gravy, on normal flat plates. All six of us were relaxed, the boat steering herself. Every ten minutes or so one of the adults would get up from the table and climb half way up the companionway steps, just to check there were no vessels in sight. When it was my turn to look out, I also glanced at the digital read-out above the chart table. We were travelling at 11.6 knots. I stuck my head up out of the hatch and saw the spinnaker filling perfectly. I looked around for lights of ships, and anything else that might be visible, but there was nothing, just a black void. My eyes would take several minutes to adjust fully, and then I would be able to see the water surface, but my roast chicken was calling and I stepped below again, leaving Keoma to it.

Below it was like being in a huge burrow, safe and protected. The music was on and a few glasses of wine and beer were drunk. Nick was talking about my sleeplessness. "I'll be sitting there, on watch, with everyone asleep, and suddenly I realise I'm not alone. There's a dark figure standing on the steps. Black Shuck is lurking around." Everyone laughed, including me. I realised he probably thought me a bit strange, but maybe they would have children of their own one day, which might make my behaviour more understandable. I remembered those carefree sea passages that I did when there was only Charlie and me; I was totally relaxed and could always sleep, whatever the weather. "The amazing thing is," Nick continued, "You always seem to catch me just as I'm dozing off!"

"You see, I'm the sleep police!" More laughter, and the conversation moved on to the emails that had come in that day.

We'd received another amusing email from Azure, which included an instalment of a series of articles that one of their crew was writing for Yachting World magazine. He was a well-known horseman, but had never sailed before, and so gave a newcomer's perspective on the peculiarities of sailing. I said, "I think the only thing lacking from Alec's articles is some kind of title. The series should be headed 'Horseman on a Boat' or something like that."

Charlie said, "What about 'Norfolk Goes to Sea'?"

"No, no," said Nick, 'It's got to be 'Norfolking Idea on a Boat.'"

There had been several emails telling us how much the senders were enjoying reading our blog. It reinforced my opinion that it was right to be using email while at sea. We were also told that the picture of us playing Scrabble had been posted on the front page of the ARC website.

Charlie and Nick decided to remove the staysail from the foredeck, now that we had trade winds, since it was unlikely to be used and it should be protected from sun and spray. A job for the morning, they agreed.

In the morning the sea had built slightly, giving lovely waves which shunted us along from behind. Keoma carried on like a good workhorse, never tiring or complaining, and we realised we had covered 200 miles in 24 hours, with a top speed of 12.5 knots. The wind remained a steady easterly. The heat felt a degree or two higher and we were lethargic. I nagged at the children to drink more water. If a half full glass was left on the table, I would know, from the number on the glass, who to call back.

Charlie climbed up the steps and stood before us in the cockpit. "I've got some very serious news. We're down to our last seven loo rolls." There was silence all around the boat. I knew I had bought 25 rolls for the crossing. How were we getting through so much?

The usual daily routine of being on watch, bread making, games, daily position logging, blog update, emails, schoolwork, fishing, cooking and reading continued. The boat rolled on relentlessly. In the afternoon the waves became less uniform, slightly more unpredictable, gently jolting the boat now and then. The VHF radio was silent and we saw no other boats or shipping.

CHAPTER 85

I was lying in the children's cabin, with Pip sleeping next to me. Alice had taken to sleeping in the forecabin, enjoying the solitary splendour of the big bed, seemingly unaffected by the noise of water rushing past the bow. The children still kept to their regular routine of going to bed at 8.00pm and getting up around 8.00am, a sharp contrast to the adults' irregular sleeping habits, disrupted by having to sit a two and a half hour watch in the middle of the night.

Pip looked completely content, breathing deeply, eyelids loose and relaxed, her skin a light tan, dotted with pretty freckles, a white crumpled sheet over her legs. Her strawberry-blonde hair lay in waves across the pillow. The boat rocked gently from side to side, and sunlight streamed in from above, where we had the ceiling hatch open, for maximum air circulation.

Something flew in through the top hatch and landed on the floor. It flapped around on the small floor space, creating a strong smell of fish. Pip suddenly awoke and we retreated to the end of the bed. I banged on the ceiling. "Charlie, Charlie! Help! We've got a flying fish in here!" Laughing, he descended the steps and bent down to grab the fish. I was so relieved that it hadn't flapped itself into bed with us. He carried it up to the cockpit and lobbed it overboard. I couldn't imagine that it would survive, though. The floor was covered in scales and it must have had a sore head after the crash landing and the thrashing around.

I climbed out of bed and plodded across to the galley, then started spooning flour into a measuring jug, followed by a good measure of milk and two eggs. Using a small hand whisk I whipped it all together. I put the frying pan on the heat and added a knob of butter. When it was bubbling I ladled in some of the mixture and swirled it around in the pan, setting it back on the heat. The jug stood on top of the fridge, to my left. I watched the pancake begin to bubble, but something caught my attention out of the corner of my eye. Another flying fish was lying on the worktop, which must have come in through the side window and only just missed my jug of pancake mixture!

I made pancakes for everyone, which we enjoyed with squeezed limes and sugar, sitting in the sunshine of another perfect morning. Scanning the endless horizon, it wasn't quite even. There was a boat there in the distance, and they must have seen us at the same time because a voice came over the radio. It sounded alien after so much silence. "Boat flying a blue spinnaker, this is White Heron." We replied, and discovered that they were having difficulty with their satelite phone. The problem was a familiar one to us. We agreed to email the ARC office with their position and to email some family and friends, whose email addresses they spelled out over the radio.

We received a shocking email about another ARC boat, Caliso, which read "ARC Fleet Message: Caliso. Situation on board has deteriorated. Yacht is unable to lay Cape Verdes due to weather conditions. Water ingress is becoming worse. Skipper is concerned about state of keel and has decided to request evacuation. MRCC Falmouth are coordinating. At time of issue, it is not known if any commercial shipping is able to assist. Any ARC yacht in the area, that is able to either

1. Rendezvous and evacuate crew, or, 2. Standby Caliso until other assistance arrives, is requested to contact the ARC office directly."

Putting together a picture from other emails, it transpired that Caliso had previously suffered keel damage which had been repaired, but, it was now clear this had been done ineffectively. The yacht had started to take on water near the Cape Verde islands (presumably when the winds had picked up and they started to move more quickly). Those on board had been sleeping on deck, afraid that the keel might detach, and the boat turn turtle, at any moment. Charlie felt guilty because we had passed near Caliso that morning while he was on watch. He had not seen or heard anything amiss with the boat, so had carried on, sailing much faster than them because they were using only white sails. By the time we received the email, we were 60 miles away. We were comforted that we could see from the emails that other boats were standing by.

Another email, headed "Have you heard, the Fat Controller has lost his rig?" told us that Oystercatcher, the largest, newest, shiniest, boat in the ARC, had been dismasted and was heading for the Cape Verde Islands for repairs.

It was the first of December, and we delved deep in lockers to find advent calendars, thoughtfully bought by my mother and Amanda, for the children. We sat in the cockpit as they peeled open the doors marked with the number one. It didn't feel remotely like December. We sat in the blistering sun, in bikinis and sunglasses, surrounded by glistening water and blue skies.

While eating lunch at the cockpit table, the spinnaker guy released. This caused the spinnaker pole to ping forward and hit the forestay, placing a lot of weight on it, which I knew could sometimes cause dismasting. Nick steered the boat directly down wind, to slow the boat down and relieve some of the pressure. We snubbed the spinnaker and examined the guy. The rope had worn through. It was a lesson in the need to regularly inspect all the lines. We soon had the guy re-tied onto the shackle and the spinnaker flying again.

Finishing off lunch, Charlie and Nick agreed that they'd exerted themselves enough for one day. The staysail could wait until tomorrow.

On the day we'd left Gran Canaria we'd marked a waypoint on the chart at the point where there were 1,400 miles to go to St Lucia, our notional "half way point". We had just reached that point, which was a cause for celebration and meant (probably) another eight days at sea. The conversation turned to what we would do when we arrived. Nick and the children were longing for ice cream. Amanda would like a swim. Charlie wanted a beer in a bar and I would like to go for a long walk, through trees. An avenue of English oaks, with a backdrop of green rolling hills would be ideal, but I supposed a few palm trees and a white sandy beach would be ok…

The boat rolled on and we continued our routines. The red crosses on our chart plotter had spread out as the daily distances continued to notch up around 200 miles per day. The children built boats from pieces of wood, tin cans, tape, string, anything they could find, and trailed them from the stern. We were more relaxed about the gas use now that we were making fast progress and the second bottle had not run out yet. It had been difficult to know how full the bottles were when we had them refilled in Gran Canaria. I had reverted to putting the oven on for an hour each day to bake bread, and, today, at the same time I cooked potatoes and pork chops for supper. The bread making was now a well-oiled machine. I knew how to produce a loaf that was perfectly risen, with a golden brown crust and an irresistible aroma.

Every other day we put a supermarket bag full of rubbish in the anchor locker. We threw organic waste overboard to try to cut down on the rubbish we carried, and everything else was thoroughly rinsed and crushed before going into the bin. There was no smell from the locker at present, although I wasn't looking forward to emptying it out when we reached St Lucia. Three weeks' worth of rubbish, festering in the heat.

There was more news of Caliso. Those on board had been evacuated to a cargo ship, MV Endless. This couldn't have been easy, as those ships didn't generally have facilities for boarding people from the sea, and if there were any waves at all, the ship and the boat would have been knocking into each other. I really felt for the owner and crew, but no doubt they were thankful to be alive. It used to be that boats left in the Atlantic would have their water inlets opened, so that they would gradually sink to the depths of the ocean, and therefore not present a hazard to other boats and shipping. But Caliso's owner had been told by the insurance company to leave the boat floating, with her engine running and navigation lights on (which would shine until the diesel ran out, the engine stopped and battery power ran down). The insurers were intending to arrange for a Cape Verde company to undertake a salvage operation. It must have been heartbreaking to stand on the deck of the ship as it motored away, leaving Caliso floating there, dreams in tatters.

The emails indicated that we were doing fairly well in the race. Victoria emailed, which read, "Thank goodness you've got some speed on. You need to do better if you're going to catch Lucy's boat, though." The ARC website had a tracking device which drew a different coloured line for each boat. We were circumspect about this, because we couldn't know how much other boats had been motoring, something which would be factored in when the final results were calculated. And anything could happen between here and St Lucia.

It did feel like we were going fast. With a constant breeze of around 20 knots, and waves generally from behind, the boat was flying along. We had set the boat up to steer herself, using the 'wind vane' setting, which meant she kept herself pointing on a constant angle to the wind, avoiding the need to adjust any of the lines. The other option on the autohelm was to set the boat to steer a set course, however this meant that if the wind veered, it could result in an involuntary gybe. Wind vane steering meant we did need to check, from time to time, that we were going in roughly the right direction, but we never found that the wind swung by more than a degree or two.

CHAPTER 86

There was good news on the loo roll front. The latest count showed there were still six and a half rolls left. Now the colds had ended, consumption was back to normal levels. We all breathed a sigh of relief.

We received an email from Whitehaven. It sounded as though life on board was generally harmonious. They described how they were 1,000 miles from land when a tiny, beautiful bird landed on the boat. He hopped wearily along the sidedeck and cocked his head on one side to look at them. They so enjoyed having this little visitor. The message ended with the words (which Charlie read out in an Australian accent for full effect); "and, I must say, it tasted delicious."

Our staysail still had not been removed from the foredeck. There was a definite feeling of inertia on board. I had not nagged. I couldn't be bothered.

Earlier that morning we had enjoyed steady 10 knot winds from the East. We changed the clocks, moving them back one hour. This would help to keep the mornings and evenings with the right amount of light and dark, and would mean not having to change our clocks by four hours in one block when we arrived in St Lucia. I now had to remember to record our midday position at 11am. I wrote it on the notepad in big letters. My handwriting looked like that of a ten year old.

I sent and picked up the usual early afternoon emails. The phone cut out while I was receiving them, and I stood in the cockpit with one arm aloft for what seemed like ages, trying to persuade the phone to reconnect. I checked the computer and the connections and tried again. It still wouldn't work. I began to suspect that the phone was out of credit. We had bought $500 worth of phone credits at the outset, thinking that this would last us for the whole trip, but we'd used a lot of credits while working out the foibles of the system. When we had been preparing to leave Las Palmas I asked Charlie what would happen if the phone credit ran out mid-Atlantic, and he told me that it could be recharged by telephoning an international freephone number, at any time.

I now phoned that number and heard a recorded message. I couldn't believe the timing. It was 4.00pm our time; 5.00pm UK time. The office had closed for the weekend and I was asked to phone back at 9.00am on Monday. This meant that we wouldn't be able to report our position or receive weather or other emails for two days. I was annoyed with Charlie, with the Iridium office, with the bloody thirsty phone, and with myself, for not anticipating this. I had a sudden urge to throw the phone overboard. But I didn't. I put it carefully back in its case and back in the locker. The children were arguing. "Stop that pathetic squabbling and get on with your diaries!" I shouted.

CHAPTER 87

The fridge was starting to give off a smell. I opened the lid and removed the things that I suspected may be causing the whiff and threw them overboard, removing the packaging to put in our anchor locker. We still had lots of food left, but the fresh was disappearing rapidly. We were down to the last lonely tomato. We had no green vegetables. The vacuum packed meat had lasted well, and in the evening Charlie and Nick prepared a spicy chicken dish, made to their own recipe. It was nice for me to have a night off and they found considerably more enjoyment in the galley than I did.

Later, on nightwatch, it felt supremely peaceful. There was no moon but this seemed to have the effect of making the stars appear bigger and brighter, against an even blacker sky. I sucked in a deep breath of the night air. It smelt so pure, with just a slight hint of salt. I kept sniffing on it in, just couldn't get enough, it was the most delicious perfume.

The morning brought another perfect day. It was quieter than ever on the boat, and we felt isolated without our communications hub, but I had come to accept the situation and was no longer annoyed, just slightly anxious that our families and friends would be looking for a web update today and tomorrow, which wouldn't appear. I didn't know what they'd make of this, but hoped they wouldn't launch a Tony Bullimore-style rescue effort.

Nick and Alice were sitting in the cockpit, and he was patiently helping her with her maths. They counted out on their fingers and debated the answers to the questions. Behind them the ocean was spread out, a vast wide, wide sea, blue and sparkling in the sun. As usual, Keoma was doing all the work, big spinnaker pulling, carrying us to St Lucia.

At last the staysail was removed from the foredeck and put away. Charlie and Nick needed a lie down and a beer after the effort. We dug out the second bag of treats, which Nick opened with the children, teasing them that he was going to keep it all for himself.

Sunday was another calm, pink, dawn and sun-drenched morning. In the afternoon a front of heavy black clouds swept into view and I wished we had an up to date weather forecast. We could see that it looked nasty, and we ran through the routine of getting the spinnaker down. As usual the children went below for this operation, and when I passed the spinnaker bag down the hatch they were waiting at the bottom of the companionway steps. Alice's brown face looked up as she said, "The umpa lumpas are ready to take the spinnaker through to the forepeak!" What a team effort.

CHAPTER 88

Nick's hair was standing on end. He looked as though he'd been touching a Van der Graaf generator in a science lesson. There was definitely something in the atmosphere. The skies ahead looked dark. Miniature lightning strikes flashed at regular intervals all along the horizon. Nick went on deck to put a couple of reefs in the mainsail. We checked that everything was stowed in the correct place. A fork of lightning struck the water near the boat. It was too close and we were all thinking the same chilling thought, that the boat might be hit. If lightning connected with the mast it could fry all our instruments, including the GPS. I had read that it was extremely unlikely for lightning to strike a boat, even when the mast was the only high point for miles around, but that wasn't much comfort right now, and I pictured the boat, blackened and charred, instruments smoking, melted and irreparable. Would there be damage to the keel? I knew that a lightning strike ought to earth in the water, but might it take the easiest conductor, straight down the mast and onto the keel where the two touched? What about us? Was there anything metal in the bunks that the children might be leaning against? Should I hold onto the metal steering wheel? I clicked the boat onto autohelm. I wasn't wearing any shoes; perhaps I should have been standing on an insulated sole. There were several strikes near the boat and deafeningly loud thunder claps. Our mast seemed to pierce so high into the night sky, as if inviting a bolt to connect. But the storm was not with us for long; we were travelling in opposite directions.

In the morning we hoisted the spinnaker again. I thought I detected something not quite right about the helm. It seemed heavier than usual. It felt as though there was a judder beneath the boat when we were travelling at more than eight knots. It was almost imperceptible, and we all sat quietly, listening, trying to feel it, trying to understand, trying to work out if it was worsening. Could we have got something wrapped around the rudder or the keel? Charlie's first instinct was that a rudder bearing could be failing, which would be an extremely serious problem for us. If the rudder became inoperable, we would not be able to steer. Without steerage, we couldn't continue on Keoma. We were 800 miles from St Lucia.

Charlie telephoned Iridium and arranged a top up of phone credits. I held my breath that they wouldn't ask for a password that was in a storage box in England. They didn't and it worked. Charlie typed an email to Alessandro, describing the symptoms and asking for advice. Alessandro's response came in the next time the phone was fired up, minutes later, which read, "I have spoken to the factory, who advise that in the event of a rudder bearing failure the boat should immediately be lifted out of the water for inspection." That was not so easy in the middle of the Atlantic.

We adults had our attention focused on the rudder. We took down the spinnaker, to cut down our speed and ease the load. We steered by hand, to try to get more of a feel for it, and because we didn't want to break the autohelm by over-stressing it. Everyone was quiet and thoughtful, conscious of what this might signify.

When it was my turn to helm, I noticed that the display screen which indicated the degree of turn on the helm was not reading correctly. It was showing the helm to be turned by 30 degrees even when the wheel was pointing straight on. I mentioned this to Charlie. "Oh… brilliant. That might just be the answer," he said. He opened up the locker beneath the helming position and looked inside. "Alice, pass me up a torch, would you?" Bending over the locker, he said, "I can see what's happened. It's OK. I'm pretty sure I can fix it. The radius arm on the rudder post has dropped down and needs to be lifted up and re-keyed into position." He might as well have been speaking Japanese as far as I was concerned, but I was elated that he could fix it. He climbed into the small locker, as Nick opened one of the side lockers and lifted the heavy tool boxes out.

"I'm impressed you can get in there," said Nick.

"I couldn't have done it a year ago," replied Charlie. For the next half hour he was like a rather cramped surgeon, performing an operation, ably assisted by nurse Nick, who passed and received tools.

It was mended. Huge relief. Back to normality. Now we had no storms, no juddering rudder and no lack of satellite phone credit. We hoisted the spinnaker again. The emails flooded in. Clearly there had been some consternation that we'd had a media blackout for two days. I posted the web updates that I'd prepared over the weekend, and emailed the ARC office with details of our positions, explaining the problem. As I read through the emails, there was one from the ARC office, telling us of another hurricane in the Atlantic, named Epsilon. It was around 1000 miles away and not expected to head in our direction.

During the afternoon the waves began to build. It was superb sailing, with rollers coming in from behind, giving us that now familiar push as the boat was picked up and surfed along for a few seconds. Nick put the Faithless CD on loud, blasting from the cockpit speakers, perfect for the conditions, as we sped along, the music raw and rough.

The waves became gradually larger and larger, welling up in great pointed mounds of water behind the boat. I felt very relaxed, which surprised me. It wasn't disconcerting because the waves never gave the impression that they would break over the boat; they always ducked beneath the stern when they got close.

Around 9.00pm we took the spinnaker down, replacing it with a small amount of genoa. It was too gusty to risk keeping it up all night. We could see more thunder storms; small wisps of lightning along the horizon, against a pitch black sky. I wished for them stay at a distance. For perhaps two hours they lurked there, then gradually fizzled out.

CHAPTER 89

The first thing I did today was to look at the GPS. As I sat at the nav station, I had to hold myself in there, the boat being buffeted around by the waves. Looking out, they were even larger than the previous day. When we were sitting in the cockpit they were like a brazen nosey neighbour, welling up behind, as if trying to listen in on our conversations from behind the garden fence. Then they grew too tall and the peaks began to topple. I loved the colour occasionally seen on the top of a wave, when sunlight started to shine through the crest, a bright aquamarine. It was only visible for a second or so and only on the very tallest, most pointed, waves.

The spinnaker was up again but the wind was blowing 24 knots and everything was under pressure. We hurried to take it down, in case the wind built further. It was the usual drill, and the children scampered down below. Nick went up to the foredeck, Charlie steered the boat downwind. I let the guy run at the critical moment and Amanda eased the sheet, as Nick pulled down the snubber. But something went wrong. A big gust of wind hit us just as a big wave healed us over and the spinnaker filled with Nick hanging onto the snubber line. He slid across the foredeck on his backside and then let go, at which point the sail dropped into the water, the top section still filled with wind and pulling. Charlie stopped the boat by throwing the helm across to steer the boat into the wind and she rolled over on her side even further, the spinnaker acting like a giant sea anchor. The keel must have been out of the water, we were so far over.

I reached into the water and grabbed the sodden spinnaker and tried to pull it in, my fingers clutching at the damp slippery fabric, but the force was too strong and I could feel myself being dragged towards the sea. I let a little of the sail run and then grasped again, trying to hang onto the boat by pressing my thighs against the side of the cockpit. The angle of the boat was disorientating. My head felt like it was pointing downwards, and that I might topple in at any moment. The boat was still on her side, making it difficult to move around. Amanda came to help but she was being pulled in too. I looked at her and she was wide eyed, pulling with all the strength she had and shouting, "We're not clipped on!" We didn't want to lose the spinnaker, but it was running through our hands, we just couldn't hold it. Charlie and Nick clambered to us and grabbed the sail. With all four of us heaving as hard as we could, we were slowly making headway getting it in, but it was heavy, wet and slippery. We were all soaked through with salt water. I hoped the fabric wouldn't tear before it was in; it was under serious tension. After fifteen minutes or so we had pulled the whole drenched spinnaker into the cockpit and the boat had swung upright again.

We sat in the cockpit recovering, subdued. A small head appeared on the steps. "Look at this! It went down the loo!" Alice was holding the satellite phone. A pang of dread went through me. "I've dried it off as well as I can, using loo roll." The boat had been at such an angle that the phone slid off the chart table and landed on the other side of the boat, in the toilet bowl. It started to rain. We packed the spinnaker into its bag; it was such a large piece of fabric that it would be in the way if left loose, so it had to be packed wet, to be dried out when the weather improved, before the sail began to rot. I took it below, to the forecabin, where it would be out of the way. As I placed the bag on the floor, I felt as if I'd captured the beast and I knotted the top of the bag tightly.

In the saloon everything was a mess. All sorts of things had left their places and scattered around. The books in the children's room had cascaded out of the shelf and landed in a large pile on the bunk. Wearily, I began to tidy up. I started to think about lunch, feeling that a meal would restore some energy. It was difficult to have any enthusiasm for food because we seemed to have eaten everything of interest. But we still had some bread and cheese and I heated up some of the emergency soup retrieved from the depths of the lockers. Just to look at the label, from an English supermarket, seemed comforting.

Later we collected and sent emails, the phone behaving in its usual temperamental way. There was another email from the ARC office about hurricane Epsilon, which was supposed to be decreasing in force and moving away from us. It actually felt to me like we were catching it up. From the email, it looked as though the towering waves and squally weather would continue until we arrived in St Lucia. We had 472 miles to go.

When I returned to the cockpit Charlie and Nick were discussing the genoa. It had a horizontal tear near the foot, around 40 cm long. We didn't know how it had happened. Charlie went below and rifled through his locker of spares. He found some heavy white tape, and took a pair of scissors from the galley. Alice wanted to help, but I was reluctant for her to go up onto the foredeck in these conditions. She persuaded me, until I agreed, so long as she stayed clipped on. I asked her not to be annoyed if she couldn't really help but had to just watch, and she agreed. The three of them crawled to the bow, one hand on the deck and one on the manrail, holding on firmly as the boat rose and fell, leant over and then came flat again. The movement was erratic and relentless.

At around 11pm the boat was hit by a squall. It was 30 knots of wind, and stayed with us for 10 minutes. The boat blasted along; at one point I saw 16.4 knots on the speedometer. It was exhilarating but felt a little out of control, on the edge. The wind subsided slightly, to between 20 and 25 knots, but the noise of the water roaring past the hull still made it difficult to sleep anywhere in the boat. It was not so much the noise, but the thought of so much water rushing past us. Somehow it invigorated the senses. There were other noises, too. The blocks on deck were rattling and squeaking as they came under pressure. The cups and plates shuddered in their wooden holders. The cutlery clinked around. The pencils rolled, contributing to the cacophony. Even with the cabin door shut, it was difficult to block it all out. I pictured all these items dancing around as if animated in a Disney film.

We took the mainsail down completely, for a little less speed, a little more control, all agreeing that it would be heartbreaking to do some serious damage now, and jeopardise the last few hundred miles. We were still doing a regular eight knots, sometimes ten, with only a small patch of genoa unfurled. The genoa was a slight cause for concern; we'd done a quick repair but it could easily tear further. It would need to be professionally repaired when we arrived in St Lucia. As, no doubt, would the spinnaker. We hadn't allowed it out of the bag but I was sure it couldn't have escaped undamaged. It needed to be dried out soon but we were unwilling to unleash the beast in such conditions.

The boat careered on, through the night. In the morning I had the usual game of making coffee and tea and getting each cup to the cockpit without it spilling all over me. This meant making separate trips for each cup, passing them up to the cockpit. It wasn't far to walk, but when each step was a stagger, it took four times as long as when we were on flat water. I couldn't find the non-slip tray. Drinking, the cup had to stay in the hand. As soon as it was put down on any surface, it would tip over.

Later, I sat at the chart table, writing an email. We were 329 miles from St Lucia, which we calculated would take around 40 hours. The boat lurched and suddenly I was lying on the floor. I hadn't been holding on or braced against anything. Luckily the laptop was a survivor. It clung to the chart table, those small rubber feet sticking like glue. The computer had taken a dousing of salt water the previous day. In the heat, I had opened a window to get some air down into the cabin. But a wave found its way in and landed on the keyboard. I'd dabbed it with kitchen paper and it seemed to be working fine.

It was exciting to be so close. We were longing for some fresh food, and for the company of others. We were keen to hear how people had fared on the crossing, and that everyone was ok. The last we had heard of Blasé was that their boat had been attacked by a sperm whale. It was thought that they somehow ended up between a mother and her calf. The mother rammed against the underside of the bow, lifting the boat up a few centimetres. She injured herself in doing it; their email said the sea was red with her blood, but fortunately the boat seemed fine and they had carried on.

The powerful waves continued to hurl us forwards. We scanned the horizon for a sign of land. All I could see was a grey sea and an overcast sky. I kept opening my nostrils, expecting to smell something different, but there was still just the salty perfume of the sea.

I opened the chart table for the ARC folder, to read up on the procedure for finishing. It would have been a shame to get this far and then forget to cross the finish line. We tied the boat numbers back on the manrails. I worked out a course for the final approach to St Lucia. It felt alien to be navigating again, after so many days of just recording our position. In the afternoon I updated the blog. We had only 105 miles to go. There were so many encouraging emails from friends and family. "We're within range of helicopter rescue now!" Charlie joked. I didn't find it funny but it was a comforting thought.

The children were reaching a fever pitch of excitement. "Ice cream, ice cream!" they shouted. Their usual routine of bed at 8.00pm, for twelve hours of uninterrupted sleep, was shattered. They snatched a few hours, as did we. I was looking forward to a good sleep on a flat, quiet berth, as much as a salad, some fruit, getting drunk in a bar, a walk and a swim. Not necessarily in that order.

During Amanda's watch there was a violent rainstorm. I sat at the chart table as she was lashed with water. The wind speed instrument hit 46 knots at one point. It was a great test for the autohelm, which coped with no trouble, and she didn't need to intervene. I feel bad that she was out there in such awful weather but it was her watch and there was no sense in us all getting wet.

After this gust, the wind steadied at around 30 knots. We were all awake and one by one everyone climbed up the cockpit. It was just too exciting to stay in bed.

CHAPTER 90

There was a light! It peeped through the darkness from far away, a weak, teasing, pinprick low in the black sky. It represented the first land we had seen for 19 days. We knew St Lucia was mountainous but we couldn't see any contours. Hopefully our GPS hadn't been playing tricks on us and we weren't somewhere off Brazil or the USA. The hours passed painfully slowly as we gradually closed the island. We didn't talk. None of us could think of anything to say. We didn't listen to music. We just sat and waited in the darkness. Every second was extended, stretched out, an elastic band at breaking point.

Still we just sat there. I went below to make coffee at around midnight. Within a few seconds I was back with the steaming mugs. It hadn't taken enough time. A mumbled "thanks" from everyone and then we were back to more hours of silence, swaying with the motion of the boat.

Hours and hours and hours. Water torture.

CHAPTER 91

The island had some strange lights that we couldn't work out. We just needed to get closer and hopefully it would all become clear. We had to round the northern tip of the island to enter Rodney Bay. We could now see that some of the lights were from two large ships which were anchored off the end of the island. We wanted to go between them and the island, rather than around the back of them, which would have been much further. The moment we were committed to going in front, one of them started to move, heading towards us. We were unaccustomed to making decisions like this and felt disorientated. The ship was headed straight towards us, and was quite close. Fortunately it had only just weighed anchor, so was moving slowly. Then, gradually, the bow began to turn, and the ship started to swing around, until it was heading away from us. Something flew down the open hatch. Charlie went below to retrieve another flying fish.

At the Skipper's Briefing in Las Palmas we had been reminded to leave Pigeon Island to port as we approached Rodney Bay. Since Pigeon Island was no longer an island, but at the end of a causeway attached to the main island, it would have been difficult not to, but we felt so dizzy right now that anything was possible. We were five miles away and I radioed the ARC finish boat to tell them we were close, as instructed. Charlie rigged the St Lucia flag to our starboard cross trees, with the yellow customs flag beneath it.

The wind had lessened but there was still plenty to take us to the finish line. We sailed around the corner, into Rodney Bay, beating on port tack, looking around for the Committee Boat. It was dark in the bay, with a kaleidoscope of lights on the shore but no sign of the Committee Boat. I radioed them up again and they replied that they would shine a light on us. But there was no beam shining on us. We bore away. Then we spotted a light on another boat that was also finishing, and this led us to the line. We tacked onto starboard to make it. Over the VHF came the words, "Welcome to St Lucia, and congratulations!" A photographer flashed us. We were all in full foul-weather gear and we'd been up all night in howling wind and rain. I had imagined it would be glamorous arriving in St Lucia, and had pictured us arriving in blazing sunshine, the sound of steel drums wafting across the water, but I wasn't disappointed. I didn't care about the conditions. We'd arrived.

The Committee boat gave us instructions to get the engine on, sails down, warps and fenders out. It was a good thing they were organising us, because we were away with the fairies. Somehow we found the warps and fenders and managed to attach them. The small amount of genoa was quickly furled away. As we motored through the narrow cut into the marina it was blowing a howling gale. No wonder I hadn't been able to detect any smells; they had all been blasted away. The island looked like a hurricane scene from a newsflash, with bent over palm trees and flattened shrubs. It was chilly and grey, the water like slate, and it was 6.00am.

Incredibly, three other boats arrived at the same time as us, and this sent the ARC organisers into a state of panic. They were trying to work out which berths were reserved for our boats, and to help four boatloads of incompetents to tie up. We chugged towards our allocated berth but had to wait while a catamaran in front struggled to manoeuvre, blown sideways by the wind as it tried to turn into its berth. Eventually we made it into the berth, and Nick jumped heavily ashore to fend off as the boat was blown towards the pontoon. Someone appeared with a tray of rum punch and, thoughtfully, some lemonade for the children.

It was an extraordinary feeling, leaving the capsule that had been our lives for the last 19 days, leaving our Atlantic crossing behind us, as we stepped off our mother-ship. It was probably a combination of tiredness, sea-legs, weak muscles and the relief and emotion of arriving, but my legs felt wobbly as we stood there, sipping rum punch at 6.00am. I took a few grey photos, including one of the children which became entitled "the ragamuffins". They looked bug-eyed with tiredness and their hair had formed its own dreadlocks from all that wild wind, but they were smiling from ear to ear, very proud of themselves.

It was quiet. The sound of water, varying in volume between a whisper and a roar, that had been our backdrop since we left that becalmed state near the Cape Verde Islands, had gone. It was as though a radio had been on in the background for ten days and now it had been switched off. There were many empty berths around us, soon to be filled. The boats that had already arrived were silent, with crews aboard, sleeping. A few recent arrivals walked up and down the pontoon, taking a walk just because they could.

Alice turned to me, suddenly anxious. "How are we going to get Keoma home again?"

"Well," I said, "There are several options. We could put her in a cradle on a big ship and have her shipped home. Or Daddy and I could sail her home, maybe with some other friends, and you could go home on an aeroplane, or maybe you could come with us. Do you think you would like to do another crossing?"

"You're not taking Keoma home without us on board. No way. We're definitely coming home on the boat." I was surprised to hear she wanted to do it again, and how adamant she was.

"Even after all your seasickness?"

"Yes."

"What about you, Pip?"

"I agree with Alice," she said conclusively.

I felt a dull ache of pride. I smiled and held my own doubts deep inside. We had five months to enjoy the Caribbean, before we had to confront an ocean again.

Glossary of Terms

Abeam: At a right angle to the length of the boat.

Anchor windlass: A mechanism that is used in yachts to raise an anchor, through the chain or warp being wound around a drum.

Autohelm: A device used to steer a boat automatically, usually electrical, hydraulic or mechanical.

Backstay: Wiring that supports the mast. It leads from the top of the mast down to the stern of the boat, and can be used to tension the forestay.

Beam reach: Sailing so that the wind is hitting the boat at about a 90° angle. A beam reach is usually the fastest point of sail.

Bearing away: To turn a vessel away from the wind.

Beat or Beating: To sail as close to the wind as possible

Bilge: The parts of the hull that curve inwards to form the bottom of the boat, inside.

Bilge pump: A pump to remove water from the inside of the hull.

Bimini: A cover used to shelter the cockpit from the sun.

Binnacle: Pillar holding the steering wheel and compass, with a small platform useful for mugs and glasses.

Block: One or more wheels with grooves in them (pulleys) designed to carry a line and change the direction of its travel, to attach the line to a spar, and to enable lighter handling of the line.

Boat hook: Metal device with a fitting (usually hook-shaped) often mounted to a stick that is used for the grabbing of buoys, ropes etc.

Boom: The pole to which the foot of the mainsail is attached.

Bosun's chair: A harness used to hoist a person up the mast (when attached to a halyard), to enable inspection or maintenance of the rigging.

Bow: Front edge of a boat.

Broad reach: The point of sail between a beam reach and running.

Bulkhead: Panel that divides the interior of the hull and is often constructed in such a way as to stabilise/strengthen the structure of the boat.

Cabin: A room on a boat for passengers and crew.

Cabin sole: The floor of a cabin.

Camcleat: A cleat (see below) that is opened by lifting a handle, a little like opening a stapler.

Chain plate: A fitting that is used to attach stays to the structure of the boat, connecting the mast to the keel.

Chart: A map that is used in navigation.

Chart plotter: Charts on an electronic screen.

Class: A group of boats of the same (or similar) design, relevant for races and regattas.

Cleat: Fitting that is used to fix and secure lines that are in frequent use.

Clew: The lower aft corner of a sail.

Clew Outhaul: A rope that pulls the clew towards the aft end of the boom.

Close reach: Steering off a close-hauled course by approximately 20 degrees.

Close-hauled: To sail a boat as close to the wind as possible.

Coaming: A barrier extending above the deck to protect the cockpit from wind and water.

Cockpit: The place on the deck from where the boat is handled or commanded; varies in size and importance from boat to boat.

Companionway: Stairway, ladder or entrance to the cabin.

Crosstrees: See spreaders below.

Cruising shute: A sail halfway between a spinnaker and a genoa.

Cunningham: Device to pull the mainsail tighter, in order to control and flatten it.

Davit: A metal arm that projects beyond the side of the boat to raise objects from the water. Often there are two pointing aft, which are used to lift a dinghy.

Deck: Solid covering over the hull.

Depth sounder: An instrument that uses sound waves to measure the distance to the seabed.

Dodger: A screen that protects the cockpit from wind and water.

Downhaul: Rope that is used to pull a pole or sail down.

Downwind: All courses further away from the wind than a beam reach.

Draft: The depth of water that a boat draws.

EPIRB: Emergency Position Indication Radio Beacon. Radio signalling aid that allows the transmission of emergency position calls.

Fairlead: A fitting designed to control the direction of a line with minimal friction.

Fender: A cushion-like object that is placed along the hull to protect it from collision with other boats, pontoons or other structures, to prevent damage, normally when mooring or rafting up.

Forestay: The wiring that supports the mast and keeps it from falling backwards. Leads from masthead to bow.

Galley: The boat's kitchen area.

Genoa: A large headsail, which overlaps the mast and often meets the deck with its foot.

Gooseneck: A universal joint fitting that links the boom with the mast.

Guy: A rope controlling the spinnaker pole.

Gybe: To change direction when sailing in a manner such that the stern of the boat passes through the eye of the wind and the boom changes sides.

Halyards: Ropes or wires for lifting or lowering sails and associated spars.

Hanks: The metal or plastic clips that attach a sail to a forestay or mast.

Hatch: An opening in the deck to enter the space below it.

Head: The top-corner of a sail.

Heads: Toilet facility on a boat.

Headsails: All sails that are used forward of the foremast.

Heel: The tilting of a boat into an angle whilst it sails.

Helm: The wheel or tiller through which you control the rudder and consequently the boat's course.

Inner Forestay: As forestay, but leading from three quarters of the way up the mast down to a strong point in the centre of the foredeck. Can be detached.

Jackstays: Ropes or wires that run along the sidedecks to allow the crew to attach harnesses for self-protection in case of foul weather.

Jib sheets: Ropes that allow you to pull in the genoa or loosen it.

Kicking strap: A hydraulic ram or block and tackle used to hold the boom down, also called vang.

Lazyjacks: Lines or wires that are rigged from high up on the mast, down to the boom, to retain the mainsail when it is lowered, making the sail easier to pack away.

Leech: Aft edge of a sail.

Leech line: The rope or wire that runs through the leech of the sail and controls its tightness.

Leecloth: Cloths raised along the side of a berth to keep the occupant from falling out when the boat is healing over.

Leeward: The direction facing away from the wind.

Luff or luffing or to luff up: The forward edge of a sail; the verbs describe the action that brings the boat's bow closer to the wind.

Mainsail: The large sail.

Mainsheet: The rope used to control the mainsail, attached to the boom.

Manrail: A fence-like structure around the perimeter of the deck designed to prevent man overboard.

Mayday: An internationally valid distress signal that has highest priority of all signals.

Mooring: Action that secures a boat to a pontoon, anchorage or buoy.

Painter: Mooring line attached to the bow of a dinghy.

Planing: A boat travelling so fast, that hardly any part of the hull is under water; gliding.

Pulpit: Metal railing or frame around the bow of a boat, mostly for safety reasons.

Pushpit: A pulpit around the stern of a boat.

Reaching: Holding a course with the wind roughly abeam.

Reef: To reduce the size of a sail during periods of strong wind.

Rig: The sum of all sails, spars and masts on a boat.

Rigging: The sum of all ropes, lines and wires that hold and control sails and mast on a boat.

Rudder: Underwater board that enables the steering of a boat.

Running: A point of sail where the boat has the wind coming from aft of the boat.

Running Backstays: A wire or rope, one on the port side, one on starboard, that helps to bend the mast backwards and to windward, which improves the trim of the mainsail when sailing upwind. It leads from roughly three-quarters of the way up the mast, aft to a block at the stern.

Saloon: Central living space below decks.

Scupper: Drains in the decks or inner parts of boats (cabins, cockpit and alike) that lead water overboard.

Sea cock: A valve in the hull that protects the plumbing pipes of a yacht against ingress of water from outside the vessel.

Sheets: Ropes that are applied to a sail in order to control and adjust it.

Shrouds: Part of the rigging that helps to support the mast by running from the top of the mast to the side of the boat.

Spinnaker: A lightweight, triangular sail that is used in front of all other sails for sailing downwind.

Spinnaker pole: A pole standing at a right angle to the mast, the other end attached to the spinnaker, to hold the windward clew of the spinnaker at a fixed position (controlled by the guy).

Spray dodger: see Dodger above.

Spreaders: Synonym for crosstrees, horizontal structures that branch off the mast towards the sides of a vessel to control the angle of the shrouds.

Stay: A line or wire that supports the mast, leading in a direct line from near the top of the mast down to the hull.

Staysail: A triangular sail similar to the genoa set on a stay forward of the mast but aft of the forestay.

Stern: The back end of the boat.

Tack/tacking: Forward lower corner of a sail/ steering the bow of a vessel through the wind.

Tender: Small boat that is used to transport passengers to or from bigger vessels.

Topping lift: A rope or wire that holds up the boom when a vessel has no mainsail up.

Topsides: The part of the hull between the water surface and the edge of the deck.

Transom: At the stern, the aft edge of the boat's hull.

Traveller: A track holding a block, through which the mainsheet is threaded, the other end of the mainsheet being attached to the boom. This enables the angle of the mainsheet to be altered for different points of sail .

Uphaul: A rope used to control the height of a spinnaker pole.

Upwind: Any course closer to the wind than a beam reach.

Warp: Anchor line or mooring line.

Winch: A mechanical device that is used to pull in ropes; stronger than several people.

Windlass: See anchor windlass above.